THE ANSWER IS GOD

The answer

New York   Toronto   Lond

is God

The inspiring personal story

of Dale Evans and Roy Rogers

Y ELISE MILLER DAVIS

McGraw-Hill Book Company, Inc.

Library of Congress Catalog Card Number: 55-9539

Published by the McGraw-Hill Book Company, Inc.
Printed in the United States of America

To Robin,

without whose brief visit this story of
her parents' lives could not have been

ACKNOWLEDGMENTS

My deep gratitude goes to Dale and Roy Rogers, who generously and openly shared their lives with me during the countless weeks I spent with them, both in their home and on tours. And to their children and the many members of their personal and business families—especially Art and Mary Jo Rush—who treated my repeated visits with sympathetic understanding, opening for me both their hearts and their files, patiently answering questions, steadfastly searching their busy brains. My appreciation goes also to the host of others whose memories contributed to this record of the Rogerses' lives—their friends, business associates, and fans. My special thanks for help on this book goes to my dearest friend and wisest counselor—my husband—who shared this project with me as he shares all things. And to our daughter, eleven-year-old Rayna, who always has served as my firmest critic, but who this time took particular interest in my subjects because she, like millions of her counterparts, is a dedicated fan of Roy Rogers and Dale Evans.

Elise Miller Davis

[*Publisher's Note:* Ten per cent of the author's royalties from *The Answer Is God* is being donated to the National Association for Retarded Children.]

When Elise Miller Davis first came to us with the idea of putting down the story of our lives, we thought that it just wouldn't work. It couldn't be possible for anyone outside to understand all that was behind the tremendous change that had taken place in our lives. Elise lived with us and shared our home and our life for many weeks. She became over that long period an intimate friend. But it was not until we actually sat down and read *The Answer is God* that we realized how deeply Elise understood what had truly happened to us both. She saw, almost in a way that we ourselves hadn't even seen, the whole pattern way back in our lives that seemed to lead inevitably to our conversion. We hope that what Elise has written here will help others to see the Way as we have, will help others to find out that the answer for all of us really is God.

Roy Rogers and Dale Evans Rogers

CHAPTER ONE

It was typical of the way Roy and Dale do things

—to have met the situation head on by calling a meeting of the whole gang and candidly explaining their decision. The organization had been making last-minute preparations for the team's appearance at New York's Madison Square Garden. And business troubles were suddenly threatening. Roy and Dale Evans Rogers had decided to add a religious number to their program. The decision had met with strong disapproval from many quarters. Their whole future might well be in the balance.

It was nearly three o'clock before everybody had gathered in the living room of the Rogerses' suite at the Sherry-Netherland Hotel, because of the traditional parade always held to mark the opening of a Madison Square Garden World Championship Rodeo. The parade had left the Garden at half past ten and reached City Hall about noon. After a short show on the steps for the mayor, the troupe had made the slow journey back through the crowded streets to the Garden. That meant Roy and Dale had jogged about twelve miles on pavement, over three hours on their horses, constantly waving their arms, constantly smiling.

Dale's make-up, on since early morning, was faded and smeared. She looked weary and a little forlorn in her slipper socks and old cotton quilted peignoir. In one hand she was holding a partially consumed corned beef on rye. In the other, half a glass of milk. Nobody, as usual, had had a decent lunch. Small, overly proper Jim Osborne, the Rogerses' business manager, sat near Dale, his owllike eyes sweeping the room. Pat Brady, Roy's comic side-kick, was chewing gum. His flaming red hair clashed with his maroon corduroy jacket. He looked ill at ease and restless. He didn't usually attend such meetings.

Roy had walked into the room last, dropping down in an easy chair. His boots, as usual, had been kicked off and his feet, in wool socks, were propped on the low coffee table. His skin glistened with traces of oil used after the hard scrubbing it had taken to remove his parade make-up. His upper lids were even puffier than usual, his eyes mere slits. Every now and then he reached down to pat the big dog, Bullet, panting happily on the floor beside him.

Larry Kent, manager of the merchandising end of Roy Rogers Enterprises, his close-cropped hair splotched with gray, puffed anxiously at his pipe. With his wife Dorothy, he sat on the sofa opposite Jim Osborne. Al Rackin sat in a corner alone reading a carbon copy of Dale's book manuscript. "I'd been in the East since early July, laying groundwork for the Garden appearance and our tour which was to follow," he comments, "and so much had happened in my absence, so swiftly, I was finding it difficult to catch up."

Helen Young, secretary to Art Rush, Roy and Dale's personal manager, had arranged for all telephone calls for an hour to be routed to another room, where two secretaries were stationed to take them. She was at the desk beside her boss, shuffling through letters and telegrams and piles of typewritten notes. Every minute of every hour of this trip was to be filled tenfold. And requests for appearances were of necessity being turned down by the dozen. The Rogerses' penetration into the hearts of the American public was incredible, the pleas and demands becoming increasingly impossible to fill. The switchboards at the hotel and at the Garden had been swamped for days with an endless stream of awed little voices, "May I speak to Roy and Dale, please?"

"I thought of the sponsors as I sat there," Jim Osborne says. "The network people, the advertising agencies, the comic-book publishers,

2

the newspapers that carry our strips, the records, the fan clubs, Roy's ten years as number one western star at the box office, his eighty-sixth movie playing currently and pulling them in at the Paramount, the licensees whose annual gross on our products was nearing thirty million. I thought of the hospital visits that had been set up, the ice-cream party for underprivileged children, the lad from England who—competing with 82,000 classmates had won a visit with Roy and Dale—was waiting to join us. I thought of the ever-increasing pleas concerning sick children, the fatally stricken ones whose parents were trying to arrange a call or a visit with the Rogerses, hoping to fulfill a dying child's only request—to see or hear his idols. And the calls from other parents, even doctors, seeking help when seriously ill youngsters refused medicine or therapy or food. And I could only wonder why—at a time in their lives when most parents would have taken to their beds with grief, with the death of their little daughter, Robin—this crazy, wonderful pair were wanting to increase their load. There were those people who were very dubious about the future of Dale's new and yet unpublished book, *Angel Unaware,* and their desire to adopt a little Indian child. And from the objections we were receiving about the religious portion they were adding to their show, I could not help but fear that our King and Queen might be on the verge of ending up with crowns of thorns. I simply felt that the public was going to find it difficult to understand all this, and I saw clearly that truth *was* stranger than fiction."

At last Art Rush called the meeting to order. And it was obvious that he had never found it more difficult to be a good manager. He is a deeply religious man. And in his heart he agreed with Roy and Dale. Yet a manager, like a parent, is in times of stress expected to use his head, not his heart. And the doubts and fears of others had been rubbing off on Art like soot. Finally he reached the subject, the real reason for the meeting. But Roy quickly interrupted.

"Buckaroos," Roy Rogers spoke calmly, more sure of himself than anyone in the room had ever seen him, "Mama and I asked you all to come up here so we could explain our decision that's been kicking up so much dust." His eyes went across the room to Dale and his face crinkled into a fleeting smile. Then it smoothed and was solemn again. "As you all know, for years I've kept wondering why I landed in the spot I'm in. I've said it and said it: I'm not really good-looking, I can't act, and there are dozens of people who can sing better. Still, millions of little children all over the world love me enough to pray for me every night. *Why?* I've asked that question over and over. Then a little girl came to our house to live. And she taught our family a lot of lessons and brought us a lot of answers." He paused. "It's just that—that Mama and I think we found a message on the cross we've had to bear. And we feel if we carry that message while we work, we can help a lot of parents and children everywhere. We think we know now why God gave us success, what He means for us to do with our lives, and . . . *and we're going to do it.*"

Art Rush's basset-hound eyes went over the room, pleading for comments. *"We* understand the way you feel," Jim Osborne spoke up, "but we're just afraid the public won't. Many of our business associates feel that people will think it's bad taste to mix your personal life with your professional one. The most generous in the Garden tonight may recognize the loftiness of your aims, but they may feel you're out of place. The less generous may think it's . . . well, pure corn. And there may even be those who. . . ."

"We just hate to see you in for a bunch of trouble, kids," Larry Kent broke in to say.

"If God be for us, then who can be against us?" Dale cried, her green eyes blazing.

Jim Osborne's glance lit on Pat Brady. "And for a moment I felt better," Jim says. "Against all warnings, Roy and Dale had stuck to their guns about giving Pat a break in TV, and it had worked out well." Jim Osborne cleared his throat and spoke blandly. "Pat," he asked, "you've been in show business all your life. What do you think?"

Pat Brady pursed his lips and blinked hard in his usual exaggerated

4

fashion. "Me? I'm just a wrangler around here," he said shyly. "Whatever Roy says goes. He's the ramrod."

"No." Roy rose with finality, ending the meeting. "Mama and I have decided. The Lord is our ramrod from now on."

A few hours later, out front at Madison Square Garden, the lighted marquee proclaimed that at 8:30 P.M. on September 24, 1952, the "King of the Cowboys" and the "Queen of the West" were appearing IN PERSON. The Garden's heavy doors were opened wide. Hundreds were still trying to get in. Placards stated plainly that this performance was sold out. S.R.O. signs had long been removed. Yet pushing, persistent hopefuls stood by for possible last-minute cancellations.

Inside the Garden over fifteen thousand excited people filled the arena seats, the mezzanine, and the balconies. Many of them were squealing children garbed in cowboy suits, hats, and boots, loaded down with toy six-shooters and other reasonable facsimiles of Western trappings. The arena floor was transformed into a turf, covered thick with 600 tons of rented dirt and tanbark. Over all hung the smells and sounds of 700 untamed beasts—buckin' broncos, Brahma bulls, Longhorn steers, calves. Around the entrance chutes could be seen many of the 200 cowpokes—bull riders, broncobusters, steer wrestlers, calf ropers—who were waiting to risk limb and neck for a chance at six world titles and a prize kitty of $130,000. Soon cowboy clowns, their every antic a flirt with death, would be fighting bulls. There would be trick riders, fancy ropers, and a bevy of beautiful cowgirls. And a horseback quadrille. And a wild horse race—the first since 1945, when one rider was killed.

A heavy wire netting screened the arena seats against possible flying bodies and runaway animals. Flags and balloons waved from many levels. Red, white, and blue bunting was draped everywhere. The crowd began to grow quiet, the cries of venders and the munching sounds of popcorn and peanuts began to fade. The forty-piece cowboy band was warming up for the grand entry.

Standing near the press box, Al Rackin, the Rogerses' publicity

5

director, wearing his inevitable sport jacket, cap, and overshoulder camera, surveyed the colorful, noisy, smelly scene. For months he had called and now the people had come. Columnists all over the nation had been dropping bits about the coming show. Art Rush and the Garden's Ned Irish had worked six months on the contract. Roy Rogers was receiving the highest guarantee and greatest percentage ever given by Madison Square Garden for any act—an average of $3,000-plus a day; a deal that should net him about $100,000. The show, with forty-three performances in twenty-six days, was expected to play to 750,000 and gross $1,000,000. New York newspapers had carried items for weeks: Dale Evans, making her debut appearance at the Garden, would be the first woman in the twenty-seven-year history of Championship Rodeos to receive star billing. Along with King Roy and Queen Dale, of course, would be their famous mounts, Trigger and Buttermilk. Pat Brady would ride his ornery jeep, Nellybelle. Bullet, the educated German shepherd dog of the Rogers TV series, would be at last making his first personal appearance. Roy was slated to put his eight Liberty Horses through a precision drill. And he would perform his incredible shooting act. Everybody would sing, accompanied by "The Whipporwills," a five-member Western musical group.

"I thought about all the preparations for the show as I stood there," Al Rackin comments, "and the thousands of people and millions of dollars that comprise the industry that *is* Roy Rogers and Dale Evans. I looked at the men in the press box and at the crowds in the audience. And I wondered what they'd think if they knew about the scene that had taken place a few minutes before in the Rogerses' dressing room."

In a last attempt to persuade them to remove the religious number from their show, a committee had called on Roy and Dale Rogers. Roy had heard them out and then he walked across the room and put his arm around the shoulders of his wife. "If we can't do our religious number," he said firmly, "we won't go on at all. Mama and I have talked it over. We'll pack our trunks this very night and head back for California."

6

"You are making a mistake, Roy," a man in the group spoke up. "If you insist on getting mixed up in this faith business, we for one won't buy your products."

Roy Rogers stared at the man in disbelief. He snatched up his large white Stetson and flung it to the floor as his voice rose to a shout, *"Then don't buy 'em!"*

"When I returned from escorting out the irate committee," Art Rush says, "Trigger and Buttermilk were being led to their entrance posts. Perfectly groomed, the horses were wearing their identical lightweight plastic show saddles and were a breath-taking sight of animal beauty even in the dimness. Roy was standing nearby, talking with a little boy about nine. A man, who I presumed was the child's father, was with them, and it was obvious that he was trying hard to hold back tears."

"I'm real gussied up tonight, buckaroo," Roy said, smiling at the youngster. "My trousers are brown with white stripes. And my wool shirt is turquoise—a sort of blue-green with a rose yoke. It's covered with rhinestones. Leather fringe is my trade-mark, you know, and old Nudie, our tailor, has really got me hung with it." Roy leaned down and picked up the boy, placing the small hands on the tiered fringe. "Now feel my kerchief," he said, "rose and turquoise print." He put the child down, removing his uniquely shaped ten-gallon Stetson with the finely chased silver band. He placed it in the boy's hands. "Pretty heavy, huh?" As the child's fingers went lovingly over his gun belt, Roy described the famous gold bullets and guns in detail.

"Still, it wasn't until he'd set the boy on Trigger and was leading the little hands over the horse that I realized the youngster was blind," Art says. "And suddenly I remembered something Roy had told me right before we left California. 'Maybe that lady is right, Buck,' he'd mused. 'Maybe I didn't get to be a doctor for a reason, after all. Maybe the Lord does mean for me to do my best toward healing broken hearts.' And then," Art Rush goes on, "the words my wife Mary Jo had said two years before, the night Robin had been born, came echoing back, 'To have Roy and Dale go through so much, God must have in mind for them a great destiny.'"

How did such a change come about in Roy and Dale Rogers that they were willing to risk their whole careers for the sake of adding a religious number to their program? What was the pattern that brought these two people together and then led them to make this move that might easily have jeopardized their whole future? This is the story of the miracle that came into their lives, a miracle that has brought help and restored faith to thousands of other Americans. It's a story that begins in an old red-brick tenement building at 412 Second Street in Cincinnati on November 5, 1911.

CHAPTER TWO

The first piece of property Roy Rogers had ever bought was a chicken ranch for his parents in the heart of California's San Fernando Valley. Roy's mother, Mattie Slye, sat on the porch of its little white bungalow one afternoon talking with her husband. She was rubbing her right knee. "Leonard opens at the Garden tonight, Andy," she said.

"Yeah, he sure does," and Andrew Slye grinned proudly.

"Leonard looks so much like you I never know whether to laugh or cry," she commented. "When you two smile, your whole face just corrugates. Andy," she went on in her crisp voice, "I don't think I have but one regret in my whole life."

"What's that, Mammy?" he asked. He knew what was coming. He had heard it dozens, no, hundreds, of times.

"When Leonard was born, if I had to cry because he was so ugly, why did I ever have to tell anybody?"

"Oh, it doesn't make any difference, honey. Leonard's handsome enough now to make up for anything."

"I don't care. It was wrong. I never should have done it. Maybe that's one reason our boy always was so shy." She settled deeper in her chair, letting her mind wander back forty-one years to the two-room tenement flat in Cincinnati, where on November 5, 1911, the

9

ugly baby, someday to be known as Roy Rogers, "King of the Cowboys," was born.

Roy Rogers was born as Leonard Franklin Slye. Andrew and Mattie Slye already had two pretty little girls, Mary and Cleda. The scrawny, homely boy was a shock. "But he's a man-child just the same," Andy Slye said, with a grin.

At seventy-two Andy Slye is still a small, easygoing, twinkling man with a flair for spinning tales and a knack for using tools. Much of his early life was spent on the wharves of Portsmouth, Ohio, watching hour after wonderful hour as ships from romantic, distant lands unloaded and loaded their mysterious cargoes. To satisfy his wanderlust, teen-age Andy joined a traveling carnival as a laborer. Later he worked as an acrobat. Strumming the mandolin or guitar by ear, he was in demand to play at square dances. And for a time he entertained on a showboat.

Brown-eyed Mattie Womack was working in a laundry when she met and fell in love with Andy Slye. Raised in Kentucky, she too played stringed instruments with native talent and ease. Two years older than Andy and crippled in babyhood by infantile paralysis, she proved a settling influence. He took a steady job and soon they were married.

When Leonard was born, his father was working in a Cincinnati shoe factory. A few months later Andy decided the confinement of such a job was no longer bearable. Enlisting the aid of his blind brother, Will, he set to building a houseboat. And on July 12, 1912, the Slye family boarded their new home and floated off down the Ohio River.

The little cotton-haired boy was not to remember those happy, carefree days, napping in a basket on the deck of the houseboat while his parents lolled in the sunshine, strumming their guitars, singing their beloved folk tunes. For when he was barely four, Kathleen, the fourth and last child, was born to Mattie and Andy Slye, and her coming forced the wanderers back to land. By that time, Mary, the eldest, was nearing school age. And, Mattie told her husband, they might as well face it—it simply took money to eat.

For almost four years the boy's home was aboard the anchored houseboat, living, as he later was to put it, "half on the bank, half in the Ohio River." Andy had found a job at Portsmouth. But often it was up to the young son to bring home fish and rabbits to augment the family's scanty fare.

With all this, it is no wonder that the little boy early developed skills which were to serve him later. Nonetheless, the river folk said, they had never before seen such swimming and fishing; this tiny, skinny fellow was an expert. Family friends were amazed at the perfection he achieved in whittling slingshots. And—they were equally emphatic—he used them with the steady hand and dead eye of a marksman. Relatives admitted that the lad sang with a truer note than any of them, strummed a sweeter tune. Why then, everybody asked everybody else, should a child of such talents be so shy?

"He always seemed fine with other children," Mattie Slye says of those days. "But just let an ordinary grown person come near him and he scurried away like a mouse."

But if these were the things that were seen in the little boy whose photograph of the time shows his blond hair cut Buster Brown fashion, his cap turned sideways—much like Jackie Coogan—what no one yet saw, what no one yet guessed, was the fact that a secret, burning passion had taken hold in his small heart. He hugged it, he lived it, he dreamed it. Leonard Slye wanted to be a doctor!

How it began, when it began, nobody really knows. As far as memory serves, there was no shining moment, no ringing of bells. The Slye family was a healthy lot and they were very poor. They seldom needed or could afford the attentions of a doctor. But somewhere, at some time, the child discovered—as many children have done—that in the depths of a black leather bag, behind the folds of a starched white coat, lay a strange and wondrous power—the power to heal. The important thing was that this child never forgot that discovery. It was to plague him and drive him and frustrate him for years. And finally, it was to influence his life and those of millions of people.

In small Leonard's case, the relentless yearning to heal possibly stemmed from love for his crippled mother—a deep compassion for her and his blind Uncle Will. For if the Slye family was often too poor to set a bountiful table, they were enviably rich in shared interests, close companionship, and boundless love. In fact, they were so demonstrative, so openly frank in their affection for each other, that friends termed them downright sentimental.

Andy Slye was such a doting father that he was completely unable to lay a hand on his children. "Pour enough love in and some of it will stick" was his excuse to explain what Mattie called plain weakness. Thus on occasions such as the day small Leonard threw all the silverware over the side of the houseboat, just to hear the "plunking noise" as piece by piece hit the water, Mattie realized any punishment was up to her. "The little girls often took advantage of my inability to catch them," she admits. "But not Leonard. By the time he was six he'd become so acutely aware of my lameness that he just stood and waited. Pale and trembling, maybe, but without a sound." And how, Mattie Slye smiles at the question, could you spank such a child? To tell the truth, she usually didn't. She hugged him instead. "You wait until I'm big like a doctor," he whispered into her neck one day, "I'll fix your leg so it will walk good. And I'll fix Uncle Will's eyes so they'll see, too."

As time passed, *fix* became the most important word in the boy's vocabulary. And it became increasingly obvious to his parents that his deep compassion was spreading to all of God's creatures. Almost daily he would bring some kind of broken stray to the houseboat for Mattie to help him *fix*. One time it was an abandoned waif, cold and pitifully frightened. Another time a gentle, trembling old man who was found to be suffering amnesia. And there were hungry animals by the dozen. "But I don't think it was until he found the mongrel puppy with the broken leg," Andy Slye said, "that we realized just how far the doctor idea had gone." Leonard was playing on the riverbank one Sunday morning with his sisters when he came upon the small furry mound crouched behind a large rock, licking its paw and crying mournfully. Gently the boy gathered up the puppy and hurried to the houseboat. There his father agreed the dog's leg was broken. Quickly Leonard set to work whittling a splint. For almost an hour he wrapped and rewrapped the strips of cloth Mattie had found for a bandage. He fed the pup warm milk and settled her on an old quilt, patting and crooning until she slept.

For days the boy nursed and fretted over his small patient. At long last the great moment came when his parents agreed he could free the dog's leg. With shining eyes he began slowly unwrapping the bandage. Suddenly the puppy jumped from his arms and scampered across the deck of the houseboat. But the boy's face froze in horror. The dog trotted on only three legs. The fourth was helplessly crippled. The bone had knitted improperly. The job was a failure.

"The boy's grief was an awful thing to see," his father says. "He ran from the houseboat to the riverbank and fell face down to the sand, sobbing almost hysterically. I followed him and tried to explain that he'd done his best, that perhaps he'd saved the dog's life, that at least he'd done the leg up better than it was." But the disappointed, heartbroken child wept on. "I don't want to just do things up better," he cried. "I want to *fix* them."

By 1919, Andrew Slye was able to buy a small farm 11 miles up the hollow from Portsmouth in the hilly brush country known as Duck Run. Eight-year-old Leonard, with his father's knack for tools, contributed much toward the building of the six-room farmhouse to which the family moved from the houseboat. There was no refrigerator in the little boxlike house, no plumbing. But a photograph shows that somehow Mattie managed lace curtains at the parlor window.

Much has been told of the hardships suffered by poor people trying to eke out a living from poor land, and the Slye family seemed destined to suffer them all. Finally when the sugar bowl on the pantry shelf became empty not only of cash but of sugar too, Andy returned to his city job. Mattie and the four children remained on the farm to run it as best they could.

Left as the man of the family, most of the dawn-till-dusk chores of farm life fell on Leonard's small shoulders. "I simply had to learn," he was to say later, "that no matter if the sun was scorching hot or rain was falling in sheets or snow was up to my knees, a cow was still a cow. She had to be fed and milked. Eggs had to be gathered. Chicken houses had to be cleaned. And hogs had to be slopped."

By the time he was barely tall enough to reach the handles, the boy was behind a plow almost every day. But the thing the neighbors talked about most was his ability to handle the large, ornery mule. "Leonard just seemed born being good with and good to animals," his sister Mary says. "We kids finally decided he knew a secret magic. Several times I saw him capture a queen bee in a box and quietly bring the whole swarm back to our farm. Never once was he stung. When I tried it one day, I was bitten so badly I developed a high fever. He had four pet skunks that he named and taught to answer his call. For him they showed complete self-control. One day Pop spoke to one of them and Mom had to burn his overalls."

Today Andy and Mattie Slye sit by the hour reliving the unbelievable feats their son performed with animals. He had a trained rooster that he carried around on his shoulder. And in high school he taught a ground hog to sit patiently while he practiced playing the clarinet. "One day the boy smuggled the ground hog to school," his mother says. "And when it came time for assembly, Leonard put the animal in his desk. Soon, however, the pet heard Leonard's clarinet tooting in the auditorium. She crawled out and followed the sound until she found her master. When the ground hog interrupted the program by climbing into Leonard's lap, he expected a scolding. But the band leader was so impressed that instead he tried to buy the animal. The few dollars would have meant a lot to us then, but Leonard wouldn't sell."

Mixed with the endless hard hours of plowing and felling trees and splitting logs—to keep the wood box full—were the good times. Spring and summer brought picnics and hikes over the Ohio hills, swimming and fishing in the two creeks near the farm, every outing increasing the boy's knowledge and love of nature. There were singsongs around summer campfires and the square dancing his parents loved. "Leonard called a square dance well by the time he

14

was ten," Andy Slye remarks. "And if folks are amazed today at the way he hits clay targets with his fancy guns, they should have seen him with a homemade slingshot and beans for ammunition. He was so crazy about hunting, and so good at it with his bow and arrow and slingshots, I got him a rifle for his twelfth birthday."

Andy received his pay every two weeks in those days, and they provided occasions for him to visit his family, loaded down with gifts for all. The time he brought home Babe, a black mare that had seen better days as a sulky racer, was a memorable event in the boy's life. "All he'd ever had to ride was the old mule," Mattie recalls. "And although we were never able to buy him a saddle for Babe, he soon was learning to sit and ride with grace. Many a time I saw him working away, trying to teach that mare some of the very tricks that Trigger performs today."

Occasionally Leonard was allowed to ride Babe into Portsmouth to visit his father, and on rare Saturday afternoons he attended a motion picture. The youth fell head over heels in love with cowboy star Hoot Gibson. Many years later when he met and became close friends with Hoot, he told him about the small darkened theater where, to the twangy whine of the player piano, midst the smell of popcorn, damp feet, and cheap deodorant, a little wide-eyed boy had sat spellbound for wonderful hours in the world of cowboys and Indians.

A reporter once pounced on this story with the idea that from the moment the lad set eyes on a western movie he set his heart on someday being "King of the Cowboys." "That was no more true," he says today, "than reports that I was born and raised on a ranch in Wyoming. Except for the deep-down dream of being a doctor, I don't think I thought of anything at that time except just once getting to sit down to a table to eat all I could hold and just once going to bed to sleep as long as I wanted to."

As time passed, difficulties of balancing the family budget increased with the needs of four growing children. Finally the day came when there simply was no money to buy even school supplies.

Leonard took over the job of plowing a neighbor's rocky hillside farm. When he was able to work all day every day, from sunup to sundown, he received his highest wages—a dollar a week.

"I didn't wear shoes regularly until I was nearly grown," he says. "To toughen my feet I ran barefoot over a course of tough weed stubbles. I finally grew skin an eighth of an inch thick on the bottom of my feet. They were just like elephant's hide."

Many a night the lad was to fall asleep at the kitchen table as he studied his lessons by the light of a kerosene lamp. In the mornings he had put in several hours of farm work before he walked the 3 miles to the little one-room Duck Run schoolhouse. And finally weariness and hunger began taking their toll. His school marks fell alarmingly.

The young would-be doctor, who so wanted to be a good scholar, was frantically frightened. The champion of all games and sports from marbles to wrestling, who had been born with the coordination of a cat, was ashamed and embarrassed. And almost overnight quiet, bashful Leonard Slye turned into a show-off. "Not knowing just what to do, I did what I know now most frustrated kids do. I became a smart aleck. I began taking ridiculous risks while riding Babe. I gathered audiences to watch me fearlessly kill snakes with sticks. And one day I tried to jump from one tree to another and nearly broke my neck." Later his mother, relieved to know he wasn't badly hurt, quipped, "Well, son, I'm glad to have it proved that you aren't a monkey because here lately I've been having suspicions."

Inevitably the boy's resentment turned toward his teachers. Those who came to Duck Run usually weren't exactly the pick of the profession and few stayed longer than one term. Leonard chose to welcome a new one by placing a frog in the teacher's desk drawer. "But first you should know," his sister Mary says, telling the story, "that at home we'd been taught that the greatest sins were the dishonest ones, that lying was absolutely the worst thing a human being could do. But no matter what mischief we kids got into, Mom and Pop taught us we'd escape severe punishment if we told the truth."

16

Accordingly, when the new teacher faced the giggling students and demanded that the guilty one rise, Leonard Slye got up. His reward for confessing was a severe lashing. Stunned, the boy took his punishment in silence. But his confusion in the ways of the world increased. And rebellion smoldered.

One day soon it flared openly. When a classmate was receiving what Leonard felt was an unjust beating, he suddenly jumped from his seat and tried to intervene. Following his example, other boys jumped up too. The resulting bedlam amounted to mutiny in the little schoolhouse. Leonard Slye was whipped unmercifully. When he arrived home that afternoon, Mattie wept at the sight of his bruises and welts. "But she was to cry a lot more that day," he says. "It was about the worst one in our lives. Somewhere I'd picked up the idea that by splitting a crow's tongue you could teach it to talk. I picked that afternoon to see for myself. Luckily Mom found me out in the barn with a kitchen knife poised over the bird, ready to operate. She arrived just in time. After a stern lecture she sent me to bring in the mule. My sister Kathleen went with me. Just as we neared the barn, leading the mule by the reins, he went berserk and tried to run away. For the first time he wouldn't listen to me. Realizing we couldn't hold him back, I hollered for my sister to follow me. We went round and round a big tree. I was hoping the winding reins would stop him. About that time my dad ran out of the house, and just as he passed the mule the ornery animal reared and kicked. When I heard my dad scream, I looked up and saw his whole knee split wide open. I remembered that because of the ice and snow we'd sharpened the mule's shoes to a knife's edge. I simply went crazy. All I could think of was that now my dad was crippled too. I picked up the pitchfork by the barn door and started ramming it into the side of the mule. It took the whole family to pull me away. I really had murder in my heart."

Still at fever pitch the next day, Leonard called all the boys together and suggested they cause as much trouble for the teacher as possible. They soon proved themselves adept. By the end of the term, the teacher was happy to resign. "I hadn't heard of a juvenile

17

delinquent then," Roy Rogers says. "But I still quiver when I think of the symptoms I was showing." At this crucial time, just as if the Lord had intervened, Roy now feels, Guy Baumgartner came to teach at Duck Run school. Leonard was in the seventh grade when he met the man who he feels immeasurably influenced his life. They are still close friends.

The instant the children set eyes on the new teacher they sensed a difference. Guy Baumgartner smiled a lot. And his eyes twinkled. Conducting no lessons that first day, he suggested that the children play games while he took them one by one for quiet, casual chats. The students soon realized that instead of punishing them for playing baseball on the school grounds, this new man wanted to play with them. He loved the game and knew a lot of rules and tricks used by *real* professionals. Guy Baumgartner liked basketball too. And picnicking and hiking and exploring caves. He even told the children to call him "Guy" instead of "Mr. Baumgartner."

"We've let him join our gang," Leonard happily reported to Mattie. "He's our friend—not an old teacher." And so the storm calmed at Duck Run school. And the course of Leonard Slye's life was changed.

At Christmas time Guy helped the children put on a play. He chose Leonard to be Santa Claus. "It was my first role," he says, "and if I live to be a hundred, I'll never forget the misery I suffered reciting lines before an audience. I know now I would never have done it for anybody in the world but Guy. He not only helped me bring my grades back up, he taught me some of the most valuable things I ever learned about handling groups of children."

Besides presenting knowledge as if it were a game, Guy Baumgartner found new targets for his students' energies. Among them was a 4-H club. Solemnly Leonard and seven other boys pledged their heads, hands, hearts, and health to becoming good farmers, homemakers, and citizens. And so it came about that Leonard Slye got his first real glimpse of the outside world.

Encouraged and aided by Baumgartner, Leonard raised a little pig named Martha Washington. For months he carefully fed her at six in the morning, at noon, and in the evening at six again.

Patiently and regularly he combed her bristles and manicured her nails. And for his pains he was justly rewarded. Martha Washington took the blue ribbon at the Scioto County Fair. Her master's prize was a week's visit, expenses paid, to the state capital.

Proud, but often wiping her eyes with her apron, Mattie trimmed her son's hair, washed and ironed and mended his few clothes. Andy brought him a spanking-new pair of shoes and took his son to the woodshed, away from the womenfolk, for a private talk. At long last Leonard was ready for the trip. His cap freshly brushed, his tie hanging almost as long as his heavy coat-sweater, he struck out for the city of Columbus, Ohio—the whole family gathered on the porch to bid him farewell, weeping and throwing kisses until he faded from sight. "We always were the kissingest and cryingest family you every saw," his sister Cleda explains.

Leonard Slye spent a whole week in the capital city of Columbus, wearing shoes every day and sleeping in an honest-to-goodness hotel. "My eyes nearly bugged out of my head when I saw an elevator going up through the middle of a building," he says. "I spent my entire first day riding up and down, up and down." Puzzled, the elevator operator finally talked to the hotel manager.

"Is this your first time in Columbus, boy?" the manager questioned Leonard. "Yes, sir, and it's the first time I ever stayed in a hotel and the first time I ever saw an elevator," he replied with the candor that's typical of him to this day. Smiling, the hotel manager made a list of things around the city he thought the visitor should see.

The stores and theaters and restaurants were fascinating, all right. But mainly the youth was stirred by the sight of the big university. He roamed the campus and toured the library. Toward dusk he found a stone bench and rested, drinking in the sight of the buildings. Inside those beautiful stone structures, he knew, a fellow could learn to be a real doctor. Maybe, he figured, if he couldn't ever be a doctor, he might be a dentist. "It dawned on me as I sat there," he says, "that it might be cheaper and easier to be a dentist than a doctor. I happened to remember that Mom had once paid a dentist

19

two dollars to pull a tooth and she'd had to pay a doctor three dollars just to look her over. For a while then I settled on hoping to at least being a dentist."

But Leonard Slye was destined to be neither. As the days and months slipped by, family finances seemed to go from bad to worse. Finally the terrible day came when Andy had to tell his son that they must give up all the animals, including Leonard's pets and his herd of mongrel dogs. The simple truth was that the Slye family had scarcely enough food to feed themselves.

Martha Washington, the prize pig, had so far produced only one small litter. Andy and Mattie agreed that the only sensible thing to do was to slaughter her for eating. Leonard cried like a baby. Unable to watch the rites of slaughtering and smoking the meat, the boy hid all day in the hayloft.

"But as winter set in, and even the last of the vegetables were gone," he says, "I became so hungry I finally joined in the eating of Martha. I'm still ashamed to admit it, and every bite I swallowed almost choked me. But the important thing was that I ate. It was the first time I realized that a really hungry person will do just about anything to get food."

Somehow Leonard managed to attend McDermott High School, near Portsmouth, for two years. At seventeen, however, he knew he had to help out with family finances. Instead of returning to school for his junior year, he took a job beside his father at the U.S. Shoe Company in Cincinnati. By this time his two older sisters had married. Mary lived in California. Cleda and her husband took over the farm at Duck Run. Mattie, Kathleen, and Leonard moved into Andy's small duplex in Cincinnati.

For a time Leonard tried to set aside some of his small weekly earnings, still secretly hoping for a medical education. For months, after working hard all day at the shoe factory, he attended night school from eight until half past eleven. The routine was grueling. He was too weary to work well at his job and too tired in the evening to learn. And there seemed no time to prepare assignments. One dreadful night he fell asleep in class. When he awoke to laughter, the shy, awkward boy was miserably embarrassed. "Maybe I just wasn't a scholar," he says. "Anyway, that night I gave up. I never went back to school."

Leonard celebrated his bittersweet decision by splurging twenty dollars of his savings at a pawnshop for a secondhand guitar. Evening after evening he played for his family and friends, pouring his heartache into the most mournful of his folk tunes.

To Leonard Slye, a creature of the open spaces, the walls of the shoe factory were those of a prison. For the first time he really understood his father's hatred of such work. One Monday morning, after a glorious weekend visit to the farm, Leonard awoke with the feeling that going back to the factory would be a fate worse than death. Gloomily he dressed and went to breakfast. His parents were nowhere in sight. The kitchen was deserted. Going to their bedroom, he found Mattie gently wiping Andy's forehead with a wet cloth.

"Pop never had such a headache, son," Mattie said, worriedly. For an instant Leonard was frightened. Then he had a hunch.

"I've got ninety-one bucks saved up, Pop," he said. "And you ought to have close to a hundred. What do you say we quit our jobs and all go out to California to visit Mary? She says it's beautiful country."

Leonard's hunch had been right. The too-ill-to-go-to-work Andy sat upright. His blue eyes suddenly blazed with excitement. As her menfolk jabbered away, Mattie sighed and slipped from the room. There was much packing to be done.

It was June, 1930. A great depression was hovering over the land. But the family laughed merrily as they loaded their old jalopy with luggage and lunch pails and canned goods and camping paraphernalia. As they pulled out of Cincinnati, Andy was at the wheel of the 1923 Dodge, Leonard was strumming his guitar, and everybody was singing at the top of their lungs.

The trip over mountains and desert was to take almost two weeks. In New Mexico the jalopy broke down. In Arizona it just gave up. It took almost their entire supply of cash to buy the necessary parts. When he finally had the motor humming again, Leonard borrowed

21

a paint brush and painted a sign on the back of the Dodge: DON'T HIT ME, BIG BOY, I'M GETTING OLD!

The sign was still there twenty-three years later when the car was displayed for millions of TV viewers the evening Roy Rogers was the honored guest on Ralph Edwards's famous television program, *This Is Your Life.*

In 1954, the Dodge division of the Chrysler Corporation, sponsors of the Roy Rogers radio show, took over the car for museum purposes.

CHAPTER THREE

When the family finally arrived at Mary's home in Lawndale, California, they were a travel-weary, penniless group. Leonard and his father got jobs driving dump trucks. Shoveling and hauling gravel and sand in the scorching sun was not exactly the vacation they had dreamed of. "But we were outdoors," says Andy, "and not in a danged shoe factory."

The relatives "visited" almost four months. Back in Ohio, Leonard was completely miserable. California, with its romance and beauty and great open spaces, had got in his blood. A short time later, when Mary's father-in-law decided to visit the West Coast, nobody was surprised that Leonard went along "just to help with the driving."

In the spring of 1931, Leonard Slye was working with a highway gang, building a road near Castiac, California, when his parents, having disposed of their Ohio property, returned to the West Coast. Soon he was back driving a truck with his father. Things went along well until the morning they reported to work just in time to see their employer's trucks being towed away. He had gone bankrupt.

Leonard and his father looked around for other jobs. Soon they were seriously pounding the pavements. But like millions of other Americans at that time, they began to realize the depression wasn't just talk. It was real. There simply were no jobs to be had.

To keep body and soul together, Leonard and his father and a cousin, Stanley Slye, went out near Tulare to become migratory fruit pickers. In the old Dodge truck they traveled from orchard to orchard, picking peaches and grapes by day, pitching camp by the roadside at night. On their uncertain pay, food was a little hard to come by. When they had eaten all the food they had brought along and had reached the point where they no longer could look a peach or a grape in the face, Leonard whittled a slingshot and set out to hunt rabbits.

"I'll never forget that first night we fried a cottontail," he says. "Pop was boiling some coffee, too, and things were smelling mighty good. Suddenly, as from nowhere, I noticed that pinched-face kids, quiet as Indians, were surrounding us. Some of them had bony, mangy dogs that looked as pitiful as their little masters. I've carried that scene in my mind to this very day. If you ever see a really hungry child, it's a sight you'll never forget."

The Slyes fed the children and their dogs, of course. And later the whole world was to see such scenes in John Steinbeck's *Grapes of Wrath*.

One particularly depressing evening Leonard turned to his music. He and Andy and Stanley dug out their guitars and mandolins from the back of the truck and began to harmonize. Strangers from camps nearby soon gathered around, a few shyly joining in with harmonicas, violins, and musical saws. From then on the Slyes conducted nightly singsongs around their campfires. Occasionally Leonard called a square dance. As he watched the faces of the singers, pouring their frustrations into the melancholy folk ballads, or listened to the laughter of the dancers as they swung their partners, he began to see, for the first time, a real purpose in his music.

In the fall, Andy gave in once more. A job opened up at a Los Angeles shoe factory and he took it. But this time his son was adamant. "Music is the only thing I really know, Pop, and I love it," he explained. "It makes me feel happy to play and it seems to make other folks feel happy to listen. I'll never get to be a doctor or a dentist, so I'm going to try my hand at being a musician." Andrew Slye would have been the last person in the world to object.

Noticing that most Western entertainers worked in groups, Leonard talked his cousin Stanley into joining him. Calling themselves "The Slye Brothers," the wiry, hollow-cheeked youths played at beach parties, square dances, and lodge socials. "The pay was never set. We just passed the hat." Before long an "agent" spotted the boys and proposed some theater dates. The dates were few and the theaters everything but first-rate. "Our financial agreement was pretty sketchy, too, and somehow no money ever appeared." One day the agent failed to appear also. Stanley Slye threw in his cowboy hat. But Leonard refused to give up so easily. He played briefly, for free, with a group called "Uncle Tom Murray's Hollywood Hillbillies," and then decided to try his luck in an amateur contest that was being broadcast weekly over a small station at Inglewood. To settle the problem of a Western outfit to match his tunes, his sister Mary decorated one of his work shirts with bright-colored cloth squares, patchwork fashion. His mother carefully pressed his only pair of cowboy pants. And, dressed to the teeth, the whole Slye clan attended the audition. "But when the announcer called for the contestants to come to the stage," Mary says with a laugh, "my brother froze to his chair. I nudged him a couple of times. And finally I just stood up and pulled. I ended up by practically dragging him the entire length of the aisle."

Once on the stage, however, strumming his beloved guitar, Leonard relaxed and lost himself in song. The family was very proud, and when he had finished they clapped with gusto. "But the applause seemed confined to our row," Mary says. "He didn't even place, much less win."

The next day, however, Leonard Slye learned his efforts hadn't been entirely in vain. He received a call from a man who had admired his renditions, the manager of a Western musical group called "The Rocky Mountaineers." Playing a weekly program over a Long Beach radio station, they received no pay, the caller explained, but they

25

were allowed the privilege of plugging over the air their services for local shindigs. Leonard jumped at the chance.

"Our name was pretty fitting," he says. "We were a bunch of underfed hillbillies, just like cartoon mountaineers. And, to put it mildly, our careers were rocky."

One of the musicmakers was married, and the rest of the gang bunked and boarded in his small cottage. Every night the single fellows drew for places to sleep in the tiny living room. Their choice: straight chairs or the floor.

The group's theme song was "Rock Me to Sleep in My Rocky Mountain Home," written by a fellow named George Brown. Brown later became Billy Hill and composed the famous "The Last Roundup," a tune that was to prove important in the career of Leonard Slye.

Soon after tenor Slye joined "The Rocky Mountaineers," the group added a baritone named Bob Nolan. Canadian-born Nolan and Leonard became friends and later were to work together in many motion pictures. Among the scores of popular Western songs to be composed by Nolan was the hit "Tumblin' Tumbleweeds," another number important in the career of the future Roy Rogers.

As time went on, the group continued to use their mouths more often for singing than for eating. Bob Nolan quit to take a steady job, caddying at the Bel-Air Country Club. Gritting his teeth, Leonard talked the fellows into finding a replacement. They inserted an advertisement in *Variety*. "Wanted," it read, "a good baritone and yodeler to join Western musical group."

The advertisement was answered by a would-be showman who had just arrived in California from Oklahoma in search of such a golden opportunity. He was Missouri-born Tim Spencer. In the years that followed, Spencer was to have over a hundred Western tunes to his credit. In 1938 he was to write "Pioneer Mother of Mine," sung by Roy Rogers in his first starring role. Later, Spencer's "Roomful of Roses" made the *Hit Parade* and stayed for thirteen weeks.

Through the years Tim Spencer has known success and much heartache. Today, a reformed alcoholic, he is in full-time Christian work. He and his wife Velma are close friends of the Roy Rogers family. "I love the guy," Tim says of his pal, "mainly, I think, because as Leonard Slye or as Roy Rogers, I've never once heard him ask, 'How deep the valley?' He just always said, 'Let's get across it.'"

There were many valleys to be crossed after the "Mountaineers" disintegrated. Tim, Leonard, and a friend, "Slumber" Nichols, joined another bunch of hopefuls who called themselves "The International Cowboys." They were hardly international or cowboys, and Leonard found himself again playing on a radio program without pay. At this juncture, a "booking agent" presented himself. "I suggest a barnstorming trip through the Southwest," he said grandly. "Those folks will appreciate fine Western music."

With the hazy idea that bookings were arranged, Leonard, Tim, and "Slumber," with two "International Cowboys" known merely as "Cactus Mac" and "Cyclone," set out in a jalopy owned by "Cyclone." "Our tour was destined for the doubtful honor of being the most unsuccessful of its kind in history," Roy Rogers says. "As we jogged across the country, we spent half our time yodeling to high heaven and half voting on a new name for ourselves. We finally agreed on 'The O-Bar-O Cowboys.' We'd had a wire to open in Yuma, Arizona. But when we arrived, loudly announcing the fact through megaphones as we rode down the streets, we couldn't seem to find anybody who was expecting us."

In Phoenix, Arizona, the "O-Bar-O's" learned they had arrived sooner than they were scheduled. They practically starved during the week's layover, and when their opening date arrived, the show flopped with a thud.

"We drove on to Miami, Arizona," Roy says. "It turned out to be a ghost town. The mines had been closed for months and there weren't a dozen people left. One of the boys left his watch so we could get out of the tourist court. I told the boys," Roy says, "that Phoenix was better than Miami. In Phoenix, at least we had people even if they wouldn't have us."

It was at Miami, however, that Leonard Slye met his first ardent fan. Watching the boys rehearse, a young woman took a real shine to the tenor-guitarist. When the group departed, she impulsively jumped into a parked car—definitely not her own—and struck out after them. A few miles later, the boys gave up the run. Stopping their car, they got out and grimly faced the pursuer. "It took some tall tales on our part about what a sheriff would do to a young lady in a stolen automobile to get her to turn around and go home," Roy recounts.

It wasn't until they reached the village of Safford, Arizona, that the group enjoyed success: a net of four dollars apiece. "Cactus Mac's" home town, Wilcox, was the next stop. As the weary bunch drove into Wilcox, they were surprised to find large signs decorating the main street: HOME-TOWN BOY MAKES GOOD! WELCOME, CACTUS MAC AND FRIENDS!

"I thought we should take advantage of such hospitality by throwing in a little extra," Roy recalls. "The theater had folding chairs, and I hit upon the idea of removing them between evening performances and staging a square dance. We drew a crowd all right, but we forgot to watch expenses. Floor wax and printed circulars ate up our profits." As the boys prepared to pull out of Wilcox, "Cactus Mac" decided home was simply too good to leave. He quit. "Cyclone," the owner of their ancient vehicle, declared he was returning to California. Leonard finally was able to talk him into going on to Roswell, New Mexico, instead. Such powers of persuasion changed the course of Leonard Slye's life.

In Roswell, with less than two dollars between them, the boys learned they still were off schedule. They managed to talk a tourist court manager into extending them credit and a radio station manager into letting them go on the air to plug their coming show. Because "Cactus Mac" seemed known in the vicinity, they had decided to retain the handle "Cactus Mac and His O-Bar-O Cowboys." On their second day in Roswell, a husky stranger appeared at their door. "Where's 'Cactus Mac'?" he asked. "I'm him," Leonard said with a gulp. The stranger stared, puzzled. "Well, goldarn, cousin," he said, shifting a huge wad of tobacco from one jaw to the other, "you shore have changed since the last time I seen ya." Bashful Leonard

Slye tried to explain. For a while he called himself "Mesquite." Finally he settled for plain Len Slye.

Dead broke, the boys borrowed a rifle from the radio station manager and went hunting for cottontails. They boiled water in their room on a hot plate and tried some indoor cooking. But the pickings were mighty lean. Hunting again, Leonard saw a hawk on a telephone wire nearly two hundred yards away. "I had one bullet left," he said. "I allowed two feet for the drop and drilled it. When we cleaned and cooked the hawk, it was so tough we could hardly get our forks through the gravy."

If the fellows now recount their experiences in a light vein, they failed at the time to be laughing matters. "People make fun of me sometimes because I still read menus down the right side," Roy says, "but I can't help it. I was broke so long and hunger tore and gnawed so deep into my stomach walls I've never forgot the feel."

In Roswell, hunger finally crept its way into their radio program. Talking about food between musical numbers one day on the air, Leonard commented, "What I wouldn't give for a piece of one of my mom's lemon pies." After the program Leonard was called to the telephone. "If you'll sing 'The Swiss Yodel' for me tomorrow on your program, I'll bring you a *whole* lemon pie," a feminine voice said. All day and half the night Leonard practiced "The Swiss Yodel." The next day he sang it at the top of his lungs and from the depths of his heart. He waited at the radio station but no girl appeared and no pie.

When the boys pulled up at their tourist court, however, their spirits rose. In front of their door stood a woman and a young girl. Both were holding lemon pies. "I'm Mrs. Wilkins from across the street," the woman said. "And this is my daughter Arlene. She fairly loves yodeling."

As empty as it was, Leonard's stomach suddenly seemed full of butterflies. The giver was more important than the gift. Arlene Wilkins was the prettiest girl he had ever seen. "Enjoy your pies, boys," Mrs. Wilkins was saying. "But don't forget to return the plates."

29

The next day Leonard, sleek and shining, appeared at the Wilkinses' door with the empty plates. His visit resulted in an invitation for the boys to attend a fried chicken dinner. More important, it was to result a few years later in gaining him a wife.

Finally opening in Roswell, the boys' show failed as miserably as their others had done. Desperate, Leonard talked the Lions Club into putting on a square dance. The group netted ninety-seven dollars. They couldn't quite believe there was that much money in the world. Giddy with success, they set out for Lubbock, Texas. Car trouble left them broke once more. But Leonard seemed beyond caring. Dazed by love, he spent most of his time writing letters to Arlene Wilkins.

Lubbock, Texas, was unimpressed with the entertainers, and slated to go on to Del Rio, the group agreed to return to California instead. Home again, the starving, penniless musicians bade each other farewell. Tim Spencer went to work for Safeway Grocery Company. "Cyclone" headed for his home in Kansas. "Slumber" went to Fort Worth to a radio job with a flour concern. Only Len Slye continued on the same path.

Going from one minor radio stint to another, Len finally joined "The Texas Outlaws" at station KFWB, singing for little more than his supper.

One day in 1934, talking with his friend Tim Spencer, Len said, "Come on, try just once more with me, Tim. We're pretty good. And so is Bob Nolan. Let's find Bob and try a trio." Finally Tim and Bob agreed. So "The Pioneer Trio" went to work in earnest, rehearsing eight and ten hours a day. They worked out unusual arrangements which they played, without pay, on an early morning program over Los Angeles station KFWB. Without warning, "The Pioneer Trio" hit pay dirt!

When Bernie Milligan happened to hear the program, he was so impressed he selected the group for his prophetic column "Best Bets of the Day" in the Los Angeles *Examiner*. The radio station decided that if they were that good, they were worth a salary. And as staff musicians, their popularity steadily increasing, they began to eat regularly at long last. They added a fiddle player, Hugh Farr, and changed their name to "The Sons of the Pioneers."

By 1935, "The Sons of the Pioneers" had a radio sponsor. "A lot of exciting things began happening to us," Roy says. "We had a few guest shots on big radio programs and even appeared in a movie. But the thing I'll never forget was the chance to appear with Will Rogers."

Len Slye had been an adoring fan of Will Rogers for years. And he and his co-workers were surprised and pleased one day in 1935 when they received word that Will was a fan of "The Sons of the Pioneers" and hoped they could appear with him at a Salvation Army benefit at San Bernardino. When the evening arrived and the program was over, Will shook hands all around, thanking the boys warmly. "I won't be seeing you for a while, fellows," Will Rogers said. "I'm taking off tomorrow with Wiley Post for Alaska."

"We had no way of knowing," Roy says sadly, "that we'd just worked with Will in his last public performance. And we didn't dream that we'd never see him again." Nor did the entertainer then called Len Slye dream that someday his own name would be Rogers, and that because of the name and his own homespun qualities and his own grass-roots language, he would often be mistaken in the future for the great American humorist's son.

In 1936, "The Sons of the Pioneers," as well known for their plaintive, haunting melodies of unrequited love as for their dashing cowboy songs that echoed the hoofbeats of galloping ponies, were booked for the Texas Centennial at Dallas. On his way to Texas, Len Slye stopped off at Roswell, New Mexico. And on June 14, 1936, wearing a navy-blue windowpane-plaid jacket and white duck trousers, he stood in the Wilkinses' living room beside his beloved Arlene, in her white, filmy bride's dress, to repeat the vows that made them husband and wife.

"The Sons of the Pioneers" returned from their highly successful Dallas engagement to join Peter Potter's radio show *Hollywood Barn Dance*. Bits of screen work, alone and with the group, began coming Len's way. On radio programs and in western movies,

31

comedies, and short subjects he appeared with such names as Bing Crosby, Gene Autry, Dick Foran, Phil Regan, Charlie Starrett, El Brendel, Joan Davis, Mary Carlisle, Larry Gray, Jo Stafford, and others. In early 1937, he succeeded in getting a screen test at Universal Studios. The only other contender for the role was a fellow named Bob Baker. Baker got the contract.

Len Slye was heartsick for months. He had seemed able to go so far and that was all. One fall afternoon when he stopped by a hat store in Glendale to see about getting his one and only cowboy hat cleaned and blocked, he was feeling particularly gloomy. As he talked with a clerk about what might be done with the tired Stetson, the door of the shop opened with a bang and an excited young man ran in, exclaiming loudly that he needed a cowboy hat right away. "I hear Republic Studios is testing tomorrow morning for singing cowboys," he explained.

Uninvited, Len Slye was at Republic's gate bright and early the next morning. He had no studio pass and made the grave error of admitting to the policeman at the gate that he had no appointment either. Desperate and determined, Len hung around outside the gate for hours. At noon his chance came. He slipped in with a large group of employees returning from lunch. Just as a policeman spied him, Sol Siegel, the producer, walked by. Familiar with "The Sons of the Pioneers," Siegel recognized him.

"Hello there, Slye," Siegel greeted him. "Did you want to see us about something?"

Stricken with the shyness he suffers to this day, Len went through his lifelong ritual. He ducked his head, pawed the ground with the toe of his boot, licked his lips, wiped them with the back of his left hand, and licked again. "Yes, sir," he finally managed to say. Smiling, the executive took Len's arm and led him to a fancy office.

Len Slye sat mute while Siegel lighted a cigar and gazed thoughtfully. "You know, Len," he said, "I've tested more than a dozen cowboys. I don't know why I didn't think about you." Then, quickly getting down to brass tacks, Siegel added, "Well, where's your guitar? I'm looking for a singing cowboy."

32

For the first time Len remembered that he had left his all-important prop in his old jalopy, parked two blocks away. Siegel said to hurry and fetch it. And hurry Len did. He ran all the way to the car and all the way back. When he returned to Siegel's office, he was panting heavily. He tried to sing but he was so out of breath he couldn't even talk. Siegel smiled. "Rest a few minutes, son," he said kindly, "till you get your wind back."

Ten minutes later Leonard Franklin Slye was sitting on the corner of producer Sol Siegel's desk, strumming and singing with all his heart and might. The song was Bob Nolan's "Tumblin' Tumbleweeds," the popular theme song of "The Sons of the Pioneers." After two more numbers, Siegel rose. "I think you're just about what we're looking for, Len. We'll test you tomorrow morning." Then came an afterthought. "You aren't tied up, are you?"

Len's heart lurched. He *was* tied up. With "The Sons of the Pioneers" he was under contract to Columbia Studios to provide background music for Charlie Starrett's pictures. Len talked with his buddies and then with Columbia's brass. Everybody agreed it was too good a chance to miss. And Columbia said that they would release him if he could find a satisfactory replacement for "The Pioneers." Len struck out in his jalopy for Sunset Beach on the Coast Highway to talk to his friend Pat Brady.

Pat Brady was a member of a string quartet that was currently playing at an eatery called Sam's Place. Many a night, after a performance, "The Sons of the Pioneers" had dropped by Sam's for coffee and stayed on to join the host musicians in a jam session. Len had taken a liking to Pat. "Mainly, I think," he says, "because he was the only guy I'd ever met who seemed as miserably shy as I was." When Len learned that Pat also had come from Ohio, their kinship strengthened. And as time went on, other links were revealed. Len noticed that although the redhead insisted on being the buffoon type, he grew mighty serious when he talked about kids or animals. One night he showed Len a poster he had drawn that had taken a prize in a community chest contest. It pictured a forlorn little boy —his cap too large, his coat tattered, his pants baggy and patched.

33

With an apologetic expression on his thin face, the child stood beside his puppy gazing hungrily into a butcher's window. The caption read: BUT THE DOG LOVES HIM, ANYWAY. DO YOU?

Pat told Len, as they looked at the picture, that although he had practically been born in the proverbial theatrical trunk, and had spent most of his life traveling and working with his parents, who were smalltime tent-show performers, he had had no ambitions for show business. "I lost my first juicy role," he added wryly, "for interrupting rehearsals of a school play with tunes on a duck call that I had rigged up to sound like a muted trumpet." The truth was, he confided, that he yearned to be a commercial artist.

Len remembered all this as he drove the 50 miles from the studio to Sam's Place. When he found Brady and told him about the hearing with Sol Siegel, his pal was excited. "I've come to ask you to do me a favor, Pat," Len said with his usual frankness. Then he told him about his contract with Columbia. "I can't promise that you'll work out with 'The Pioneers,'" Len went on. "I can only say you'll be doing me a big favor if you'll try so I'll be free to test for Republic." Pat Brady agreed. He has never been sorry. And his friend, who soon began establishing a reputation in the world of show business for his honesty and deep loyalties, has never forgotten.

On October 13, 1937, Republic Studios signed a contract with the almost unknown Len Slye. The reason they had been anxious to sign anyone at all was not generally known. The truth was that their star in the field, Gene Autry, was threatening to strike for more salary. And they believed in being prepared.

For several months an unhappy Len, his name changed by the studio to Dick Weston, sat around, idle and neglected. Finally he was allowed to sing a solo in a picture "The Three Mesquiteers." Then one day Autry suddenly took his threatened walk. Republic pulled another name out of the air for their new star—this time Roy Rogers—and handed him a role intended for Autry—the lead in "Under Western Stars."

"I was a nervous wreck all through the shooting," Roy says. "I

34

muffed lines, I ruined make-up, and if I'd ever really known how to ride and grab a gun from a holster, I couldn't remember at the right times. The studio decided my shoulders were too narrow and put me to doing a hundred handstands a day to develop them. Meanwhile the tailors started padding my shirts."

The shooting over, the star went, with fear and trembling, on a personal appearance tour with his picture. Off screen and on, he was a sensation. Young girls swooned over the assorted dangers he overcame. Women went for the boyish appeal that belied such feats. Old ladies marked him for the son they had always wanted. Men agreed that as handsome as he was, he was no sissy. The critics liked his music. And the children loved him for the mysterious reasons that children have but can never explain.

If the studio had set out to make just another potboiler, they must have been happily surprised. "Under Western Stars" was a smash hit at the box office and was voted the best western of the year.

While Arlene wrote glowing letters to her parents, Andy and Mattie drove from town to town, following their son's picture. After seven such trips, somebody thought to give them a print.

The new Roy Rogers was simply stunned. When a studio employee called him in to see the first roomful of fan mail that had arrived, he asked, "Well, Roy, how do you feel?"

The farm boy from Duck Run shyly hung his head. "Like a shooting star, I reckon." With a half-smile he quietly walked away.

CHAPTER FOUR

Almost from the day the first batch of mail arrived, Roy Rogers has insisted on bypassing studio and sponsor facilities to handle it himself. Through the years he has received some fifteen million letters. And to assure himself that all are properly answered, he has always seen to it that at least one member of his family worked carefully with his fan mail department. In the early days when a reporter once asked Roy why he was so finicky about this, the cowboy was quoted as saying, "Well, the way I figure it, if folks are nice enough to write to you, the only per-lite thing to do is answer."

For two years the costs of maintaining his fan mail department exceeded Roy's studio salary. And he had to depend on income from outside activities to get by. He was searching for one such source of income when he opened the Hitching Post in Studio City in 1939, a store that carried Western apparel and equipment for the horse-loving set. But it, and a similar place later opened on South Los Angeles Street, were to serve as grim proof that whatever his talents in those early days of his career, business acumen wasn't one of them.

By the end of 1939, Roy Rogers had completed his thirteenth successful picture. He was barnstorming in their behalf as few stars have done—before or since. On one such personal appearance tour he played fifty-five theaters in fifty-two days. By this time Roy was riding and roping and pulling a gun from a holster with the kind of skill a cowboy hero needed to spend his time galloping through mountain passes and over deserts to rescue heroines, widows, and children from the assorted bad men of such places as old Caliente, old Cheyenne, and old Carson City. And although he disliked doing so, he was making his employers happy by attracting attention with the loud, fancy cowboy regalia he wore at all times. He was making them equally unhappy—because they were ever concerned with his safety—by zooming back and forth from his home to the studio on a shiny motorcycle he had purchased to satisfy his boyish love of adventure and speed.

Home was a five-room frame house and his wages were a hundred dollars a week when Roy received a telephone call one day in March, 1940, from a man named Art Rush. Vaguely he knew Rush was an agent. And because of unhappy experiences with such men, Roy was wanting no more of them. But when Art suggested that at least they lunch together, Roy suffered the malady that has shadowed him through the years: he simply couldn't say no. And he has never got over being thankful that that particular time he couldn't.

It might be said that if the whole world were combed, it wouldn't be an easy task to find two people who appear to be as different as folksy cowboy-to-the-core Roy Rogers and the man who has been his closest friend and personal manager for fifteen years—urbane, well-dressed W. Arthur Rush. But, as usually proves true, there are more ties that bind than meet the eye.

Although he was actually born in Graysville, Pennsylvania—on April 2, 1907—Art Rush has always considered Ohio his home. For when he was just a baby, his parents moved to the hamlet of Hanoverton, Ohio, and he grew up in the Buckeye State. The Rush children were reared in a home where love for the church and for music pervaded. Their mother was the church organist.

An outstanding scholar, Art Rush always was torn between his thirst for knowledge and his flair for dramatics and athletics. But at the ripe old age of ten, he had firmly made up his mind to be a

37

doctor and had set to work in earnest to prepare for that aim. Art had regular jobs before and after school, on weekends and during vacations. By the time he was thirteen he had saved enough money to build a chicken house and stock it with 100 chickens. Egg money from it, plus jobs sweeping out classrooms, waiting tables, and cutting hair—a skill he picked up when he was the handy man at Hanoverton's barbershop—put him through college.

A prominent alumnus and trustee today, Art Rush first attracted attention at Bethany College in West Virginia with the radio plays he wrote, directed, and chose to broadcast atop the college tower, 250 feet in the air. He became intrigued with the medium, and from then on worked around radio stations whenever possible.

At Bethany College, Art concentrated on his pre-med work. By then his dream had crystallized. He yearned to attend the Rush School of Medicine at Chicago, named for his famous forebear, Benjamin Rush, whose signature appears on the Declaration of Independence. By the time Art graduated from college, however, the depression was casting its shadow. So with heavy heart he gave up his dream of being a doctor and went to work to help out his family.

In late 1929, Art boarded a bus for California to seek his fortune in the field of radio. At first he was turned down everywhere. Finally he had to take a job as a shipping clerk.

By 1931, Rush ran a switchboard at night for a burglar alarm company and worked days in the prop department at M-G-M Studios. Meanwhile he pioneered in the writing and selling of package radio shows. After a few minor business successes, Art landed a job with RCA Victor, working without pay for two months to prove himself, and he rose rapidly. Before he was twenty-five, he was their youngest executive.

For RCA Victor, Art handled musicians for symphonies and operas, spotting new talent and directing recordings. In his swank office he had test machines for the artists to okay their records, and over its threshold streamed such famous artists as Nelson Eddy, Lily Pons, Leopold Stokowski, John Charles Thomas, José Iturbi, etc.

One day after working with Nelson Eddy, who was recording numbers from *Naughty Marietta,* Art Rush happened to notice a newspaper folded in Eddy's pocket. Art removed the paper and studied the picture that had caught his eye. "Hey, look, Nelson," he said excitedly, "here's a girl who's been haunting me for years. She was Apple Blossom Queen at Winchester Festival in Virginia in 1929. And I saw a life-size picture of her every day for a year in a photographer's window at Wheeling. I've been dying to meet her ever since."

"Hmmm," mused Eddy. "Mary Jo Matthews. She's that new starlet who won't go out with anyone."

"Nelson," Art Rush implored, "I've *got* to meet her."

"Say," the famous singer said, "you sound serious."

"I am," Art admitted.

"Okay, pal, let's see what we can do." Nelson Eddy picked up the phone and dialed a number. "Hello, Mary Jo, this is Nelson Eddy," he said. "I would like very much to . . . er . . . give a party for you so that you may meet . . . er . . . some of the people in the industry. How about next Saturday evening?"

As lovely as she was, and as used to being sought after as she was, Mary Jo Matthews was still just a starlet. She was completely taken aback by such hospitality from the upper echelons. True, her parents had talked long and hard before she left home about the dangers of taking up with people she didn't know well. But, she quickly argued with herself, everybody in the world knew Nelson Eddy!

"How nice of you, Mr. Eddy," she gathered her wits and finally answered. "Saturday evening is fine, and thank you so much."

The next morning Mary Jo checked with her studio. They found that Nelson Eddy *was* entertaining the following Saturday evening in her honor. So, charging it all up to the strange things she had heard about Hollywood, Mary Jo Matthews donned her best bib and tucker and went to the affair.

As soon as Mary Jo arrived, Art Rush hovered near. With elaborate casualness Nelson Eddy introduced the pair. "Nobody got in another word with either of them the rest of the evening," Nelson Eddy remarked afterward. "And five months later they were married in Yuma, Arizona."

In 1939, when he was managing director for Columbia Management of California—with 300 artists under contract and 22 of them simultaneously on the air—Art Rush came near to suffering a complete collapse. When he was well again, Mary Jo persuaded him to take things easier. And he opened a small artists' management office of his own. The first clients of Art Rush, Inc., were the members of the "Sportsmen Quartet"—still with Jack Benny. Nelson Eddy, whose friendship and help Art feels had always contributed greatly toward his success, became the second client. To round out his list, Art Rush felt he needed one more artist, with nonconflicting talent. And so it came about that he called Roy Rogers.

At lunch that day, Roy squirmed. "I like the way you talk, Mr. Rush," he said finally. "But with you handling Stacey . . . er . . . Staceywaskey [he meant Leopold Stokowski] and all those other classy folks, I just don't think I'd fit in. Me, I'm just a hillbilly."

Art Rush went right on talking smoothly. He liked the West, he said. And although he loved classical music and had many friends among its stars, he was fond of others too. "When I was a kid, I had a pony and played cowboys and Indians," Art added. "I loved Hoot Gibson. And Will Rogers was one of my favorite people of all times."

The blue eyes of Roy Rogers—whose ruddy, open countenance could never be called a poker face—widened as far as their heavy lids ever allow. "When you were a little boy, what did you dream of growing up to be, Mr. Rush?"

Art looked puzzled. "A doctor," he said. "Why?"

But this time Roy Rogers was the one to go right on talking smoothly. "Where'd you come from, Mr. Rush?"

"Ohio. But why?"

Roy's face crinkled into a grin. He rose, hitched up his silver-buckled cowboy belt and extended his hand. "Okay, Buckeye," he said, "it's a deal."

Completely in the dark as to just what had clinched the deal, Art clasped Roy's proffered hand.

That handshake is the only contract they've ever had.

With Art Rush at the reins, Roy Rogers began to accumulate a little money as well as fame. One of the first things Art did was to call in E. James Osborne—of the then existing firm of Osborne and Harvey—an investment counselor who handled his own and Nelson Eddy's affairs. Jim Osborne soon was at work salvaging the remains of Roy's Hitching Post. And Art booked Roy for some personal appearance tours, over and above those he was making with his pictures. They were highly successful, and the returns from them seemed to the cowboy a real bonanza.

Ambitious for his client, Art Rush managed a talk with him as soon as it was feasible. "I think you can afford to move out of that small house now, Roy," he mentioned tactfully.

"How much can I spend for a home, Buck?"

"Jim says you can go as high as ten thousand."

When Roy Rogers searched the San Fernando Valley and finally found the small ranch he wanted, he stocked it with 3,500 chickens. He was realizing a long-standing dream. But the place was not for himself.

There was a small white bungalow on the property, and the day he handed its keys to a surprised Andy and Mattie, their son said, "Now, Pop, you can putter around in the sunshine all you want." Leading Mattie into the house, he showed her a large bolt of material. "And now, Mom, you can make all the lace curtains a house will hold."

On the pantry shelf in the kitchen Mattie and Andy found a dozen large sugar bowls. Each one was stuffed to the brim with greenbacks.

The year 1940 continued to be a happy, eventful one for Roy Rogers. He added seven more pictures to his flourishing crop. And he succeeded in getting his former musical group, "The Sons of the

41

Pioneers"—by then headed by Bob Nolan and composed of Tim Spencer, Pat Brady, Lloyd Perriman, and Hugh and Karl Farr—signed to a seven-year contract to appear with him in pictures.

That settled, Roy called in Art and Jim. "I've got a problem," he announced. "I'm in love." His advisers were aghast. Didn't he know that a cowboy hero was the protagonist in the American morality play? That he not only had to be fair, honest, and brave, but above scandal too? And what about his wife, they sputtered. He and Arlene had always seemed so devoted. What on earth had happened?

Roy Rogers grinned. "But Arlene is a girl," he said. "I'm a cowboy. I'm in love with a *horse*." And as Roy grew serious, it was generally agreed that a cowpoke without his own horse was only half a man. So Roy set out to buy Trigger, the golden-hued Palomino he had been renting since the first days he chased villains down the Western street on Republic's lot.

Trigger was among a string of horses owned by Hudkins Stables. Roy had been smitten by Trigger's beauty and brains the first time he had seen the stallion. Glenn Randall, a wrangler with Hudkins, had been drawn to Trigger too. And he had always made it his business to handle the horse and to work closely with Roy during training sessions. Roy talked over the matter with Randall and he too agreed that Roy should own Trigger. And he promised to join the Rogers forces if Trigger did.

"I sure don't have twenty-five hundred to pay you," Roy frankly told the Hudkins people when he inquired about Trigger's price. "But if you'll just let me take him over, I'll pay you in installments as fast as I can." And, he added, he would do everything possible to see that Hudkins horses were always used in his pictures. The Hudkins men agreed. And to this day their horses are still used whenever Roy Rogers works in motion pictures and TV.

The following summer while on tour, Roy lunched one day at the Variety Club in Dallas. He told his friends there about all the wonderful things that had been happening and climaxed his report with the news that he now owned Trigger. "Trigger shares top billing with me," he said. "And he has a contract that calls for three close-ups and a direct part in motivating the plot in each picture. He gets his own fan mail and his own salary. I'm afraid that pretty soon he's going to be so rich he'll be wanting to buy a string of *people!*" The laughter increased as Roy went on talking enthusiastically about Trigger's tricks. "He learns so fast he already knows dozens," Roy declared. "He can count up to twenty-five and he can add, subtract, and multiply. He can untie knots, open doors, cover himself with a blanket, shoot a gun by pulling a handkerchief tied to it, and I don't know what all. But he sure gave me a scare a few days after I'd bought him." Then Rogers told the following story.

Glenn was grooming Trigger on the studio lot one morning when he suddenly saw a demibuilding on wheels coming toward them. He screamed, "Watch out for Trigger!" Then he realized that nobody was pushing the demibuilding. Because of a high wind, it was rolling on its own.

Roy was in the make-up department when he heard Glenn's cry. Apron flying, he got outside just in time to see Glenn jump back as the demibuilding crashed into Trigger. The wonder horse was knocked down and almost buried by the wreckage. "All I could see were bits of that beautiful mane and tail," Roy said. "People came running from everywhere. It took four of us to lift off the debris. When we had freed Trigger, I saw that he was breathing, but he didn't move. I nearly fainted. I fell to my knees and began talking to him while Glenn ran for a vet. Then slowly Trigger opened his eyes. And suddenly he smiled that impish smile I'd taught him." Roy laughed merrily. "It dawned on me then that the old boy had merely been showing me he'd mastered our latest trick. He was playing dead!"

"You know, Roy," one of the fellows spoke up, "you've talked more today than we've ever heard you. You seem so happy that now you must have everything on earth you want."

"No," Roy said, suddenly serious. "Arlene and I want a child more than anything in the whole world, and it looks like we're not going to have one."

43

"Why, we ought to be able to help out there," put in another member of the Variety Club—an organization made up of men in show business who do philanthropic work for children. And after lunch Roy was taken to visit an adoption home.

On returning to his hotel, Roy Rogers hurriedly called California. "Arlene, guess what. I've just found a blonde we can't live without!" And he went on to tell his wife about the baby girl at the adoption home who already had charmed his heart. Arlene was beside herself with joy. And when the baby was four months old, the Rogerses returned together to Dallas to proudly drive her home. Tim Spencer's wife, Velma, was back in Lubbock, Texas, visiting her family at the time. The happy couple stopped by to see her and show off Cheryl Darlene. "I've never in my life seen anything to equal the look on Roy's face when he showed me that baby," Velma says.

In those days not only was the western formula—which allows a cowboy hero no romance except kisses from his faithful steed—strictly adhered to, but marriage itself was considered taboo for movie stars. Ardent fans preferred to believe that their idols loved only them. So when diapers began to flap on the Rogerses' clothes-lines, they provided a juicy bit for a columnist to whisper to her readers. In effect, she said that Roy Rogers, the handsome cowboy who had millions of feminine hearts beating faster, not only had been happily married behind their backs for several years, but now he was a proud papa too. For a time letters of protest flooded in from Roy's fans. But he soon settled the matter as simply as he does most things.

"Aw, shucks," he said, "Arlene and I were married long before I ever had a screen test, much less became a star. And if it hadn't been for her love and encouragement, I might never have made it." He began including his wife and baby in all interviews and publicity pictures. And before long the fans took Arlene and Cheryl to their hearts too.

Roy took advantage of the situation by telling endless stories, just as all proud fathers do, about his wonderful daughter. His favorite concerned the time Arlene was visiting her parents in Roswell and

44

took Cheryl to see her first movie. It was a Roy Rogers one, of course. And the baby sat spellbound all through the picture. When it had ended, however, Cheryl hadn't had enough. "More Daddy," she cried. "More Daddy, more Daddy, more Daddy." Finally Arlene had to bundle up the child and leave. "Taking her to the show wasn't such a good idea," she laughingly told a friend later. "Cheryl was so fretful after that I had to cut our visit short and take her back to California to Roy."

Just as he had fought hiding the fact that he was married, Roy fought other things he termed "plain silly phoniness." "I simply raised Cain when the studio started using stunt men to double for me in dangerous scenes. But they explained that they had too much money invested in my career to take unnecessary chances with my safety." Roy objected too when Glenn began using a double for Trigger in chase scenes. "Trigger can do anything. He doesn't need a double," Roy insisted.

"But I soon settled that," Glenn Randall says. "I pointed out that as smart as he was and as much as Roy loved him, Trigger was still just a horse. And if he wore him out running, he would only shorten Trigger's life span."

If Roy hadn't before realized what valuable property he had become, he should have got an inkling when "Roy Rogers Day" was celebrated at the World's Fair in New York. The event amounted to his first national splash in personal appearances. "And it was a great day at Flushing Meadows," Art Rush says. "My kid caused more commotion than the water fountains!"

Roy had twenty-six starring roles to his credit when 1941 drew to a close. One December afternoon—Sunday, the seventh, to be exact—he was returning from a hunting trip with his close friend Mel Williams of Marysville, California. As the pair emerged from a wooded area, Roy asked, "Do you hear voices?"

Mel stopped and listened. "I sure hear something, Buck. Sounds almost like bees humming."

As they neared the highway, the hunters realized that every automobile in the heavy traffic seemed to have a radio going full blast.

45

When they reached their station wagon, Roy turned the radio on immediately.

"When we heard the dreadful news about Japan's surprise attack on Pearl Harbor," Mel Williams says, "Roy's ruddy face turned white."

"Looks like we're in for it for a long time," Roy Rogers said. "Come on, let's get home. We've got a lot of work to do."

CHAPTER FIVE

On April 18, 1945, Roy Rogers received a citation from the United States Department of the Treasury for distinguished services rendered in behalf of the War Savings Program. On presenting the citation at Uline Arena, Washington, D.C., E. C. Harloff said:

It seems to us of the District of Columbia War Finance Committee that any decoration we can bestow upon your already embellished record is akin to gilding the lily.

Your War Bond record of having been responsible for the sale of over a million dollars of Bonds is notable in itself; but it gains added significance when appraised in the light of your untiring effort in Red Cross and Community War Fund Drives and above all the many hours you have spent in bolstering the morale of our fighting men and women in many hospitals throughout the land.

Your cooperation has been effective, spontaneous and gallant and so on behalf of myself and the United States Treasury, it gives me great pleasure to present to you this citation.

At the time he received this honor, Roy was finishing what he thought was the last of his countless wartime hospital tours. He had been classified as 1-A, and in Hollywood, Art Rush was busy closing Roy's affairs, canceling all plans and bookings. But it worked out that Roy was never to enter active service. His tour completed, he was on a plane flying homeward when he opened a newspaper that

47

headlined the fact that the age limit for servicemen had been lowered. So Roy's picture schedule went back into effect and he continued the morale work which had earned citations from the Army and the Navy too.

Roy Rogers had begun his celebrated war work soon after Pearl Harbor. He took advantage of his personal appearance travels to appear at benefits, to sell war bonds, and to inspire his fans to help with scrap-metal drives and other activities necessitated by a country at war.

Trigger, with an increasing bag of tricks, always went along to help lure the crowds. And people alternately gaped and howled as the wonder horse did everything from dancing the *rumba* to drinking milk from a bottle, unaided. On one tour of Texas for the Eighth Service Command, Roy and Trigger made 136 appearances in 20 days. Roy came down with a strep throat in Amarillo and returned from that trip with a deep bronchitis that left him forever susceptible to colds.

It was during the war years that Roy steadily rose to international fame. People who had never seen his pictures saw him in person and were smitten. His movie fans declared that the screen had failed to do him and Trigger justice. And as time went on, letters addressed merely "Roy and Trigger, U.S.A." had no trouble reaching his door.

Roy became concerned, however, by the phone calls that were coming from children all over the country. He loved talking to the children but he worried about the expense. When a little boy called him for the third time from Kentucky, Roy said, "Pardner, what does your mother have to say about all these long-distance calls?" "Oh, it's okay, Roy," the child assured him. "I always call when she's not home."

In 1942, the year his name was legally changed to Roy Rogers, the cowboy finally got around to buying a fitting home. Located in the San Fernando Valley, the place had formerly been occupied by W. C. Fields, Don Ameche, and Martha Raye. Rumor had it that upon purchasing the property Roy promptly emptied the swimming pool of water and filled it with hay for his horse. He actually did use his tennis court for square dances. But as un-Hollywoodish as his tastes were, Roy Rogers still loved swimming, fashionable or not. And he used the pool often for his own strokes as well as for dips with his adored little daughter, Cheryl. For safety's sake he built a high wire fence around the pool.

In the late summer of 1942, the Rogers family could hardly believe their good fortune when they learned they were going to have a baby. Roy talked endlessly about his coming man-child, always speaking of the unborn baby as "our little buckaroo." When the baby arrived on April 18, 1943, however, Roy had to quickly coin a word. "Our buckaroo was a buckarina," he said, with a laugh. "We've named her Linda Lou." And Roy was so excited over Linda Lou that he was completely unable to work. Production on a new picture had to be delayed a whole week.

On his newly acquired 6 acres Roy began gathering a variety of dogs. They ranged from those with pedigrees to those with just empty stomachs who had strayed into the yard. And he bought 300 homing pigeons, many of which were later used by the Signal Corps. "That fellow is so good at training them," one officer remarked, "that any day now we're expecting him to cross a pigeon with a parrot and come up with a bird that can carry verbal messages!"

Except for a brief visit for the *première* of his first picture on Broadway at the Criterion Theater, Roy made his initial appearance in New York in May, 1942, when he participated in the ten-hour Victory Parade. Grover Whalen set aside a no-horse ruling to invite Roy and Trigger and stationed them between the automobiles of the governor and the mayor. The following October the amiable cowpoke seriously invaded the sophisticated metropolis when, dressed in an all-white outfit with red boots, he came tearing into the arena on Trigger at Madison Square Garden for the first time. "When we showed Roy his name on the marquee," a Garden official says, "he blushed a deep scarlet and ran back into the building." Before his performance on opening night, Roy hid in the animal quarters with Trigger. "I was scared stiff," he admits. "I simply couldn't face anyone."

If Roy Rogers was impressed by New York, the city was equally impressed by him. In his nineteen-day stay he broke all attendance records at the Garden. And his studio and managers saw to it that his behavior in public was that of no shrinking violet. With a battery of cameras in attendance, Roy and Trigger registered at the Dixie Hotel upon their arrival. In special rubber shoes, Trigger pranced into the lobby and signed in for himself by making an X with a pencil held between his teeth. Then with more aplomb than the elevator operator displayed, Trigger rode upstairs beside his master, entered their suite, backed himself into a chair, and waited to be interviewed. When dinner was served the horse, a napkin was tied around his neck and he daintily munched a carrot. Finally he lay down on the floor beside Roy for a nap and carefully covered them both with a blanket. The reporters were beside themselves. But what astounded them more than anything was Trigger's well-mannered restraint. Who ever heard of a horse that was completely housebroken? they asked. And just how Trigger was trained in the matter still remains one of Roy's most carefully guarded trade secrets. "Spending as much time as he does in hotels, theaters, and hospitals, this ability comes in mighty handy," Glenn Randall says. "And it's conceded by most trainers to be Trigger's greatest accomplishment."

To put it bluntly, Roy's handsome horse with the four white stockings and the perfect blazed face is vain. "And with all that fanfare in New York," Roy recounts, "he began to show what a ham he really was." Trigger soon became so fond of applause that he allowed his vanity to ruin his tricks. "For instance," Roy says, "Trigger can walk nearly a hundred feet on his hind legs. And for a 1,100-pound animal that's no easy task. Yet after a few feet the audience would become excited and start clapping. And the minute he heard applause he'd stop walking and go to bowing."

During one number Roy always got off Trigger and performed in front of the microphone with his guitar. Trigger finally got to the point where he didn't like waiting on the sidelines out of the spotlight. One evening he began inching up to his master. The next evening he became bold enough to nudge. And the next, when

50

Roy continued to ignore him, Trigger took a quick nip at the rear of Roy's handsome cowboy pants. "I was so furious, I simply stopped the show," Roy says. "Trigger was behaving like a naughty child. During workouts he was wonderful. But in front of audiences he'd act up. He thought, I guess, that in front of people I wouldn't punish him. Well, that night I was so mad I fooled him. I lectured him good, right there before thousands of people. And then I sent him out of the arena without allowing him to finish our number. I was a little shaky for a minute. But, thank goodness, the audience cheered my discipline. And believe me, the old boy began behaving better after that."

If Trigger was jealous of his master, it might be said that sometimes his master was jealous too. One evening Roy received a note backstage at the Garden. "Dear Mr. Rogers," he read, "I've seen all your movies several times each, and I've seen your performance here five times. The reason I follow you so closely, however, is to watch your horse Trigger. As far as I'm concerned, he's the finest performer in the world today, the handsomest, and the most talented. And the only one that I'll ever have any real interest in seeing."

"I really did a slow burn," Roy said, with a laugh, "until I finished the letter and realized the writer was a veterinarian."

During the war years much of Roy's fan mail contained sugar for Trigger. But when people could get their hands on the famed, beloved horse, all was not sweetness and light. They delighted in pulling hairs from his beautiful tail for souvenirs. "When we returned from that first trip to New York," Glenn Randall says, "the poor thing was practically bald. And for a while in pictures Trigger had to wear a sort of hanging toupee."

And often all was not sweetness and light for Roy either. As every professional entertainer knows, there are bugs in the business, called hecklers. And Roy usually managed to ignore them until their load of beer or their nearby neighbors shushed them. But one night at the Garden a sailor in the balcony refused to give up. Finally Roy stopped the show and said, "Is there a jockey in the house?" Several voices hollered "Yes!" and Roy drawled, "Will one of you please ride that jackass in the balcony out of here." The sailor was not heard from again.

One evening toward the end of their Garden engagement, when Roy entered the arena on Trigger at a dead gallop, the horse's foot penetrated the too-wet turf, struck concrete, and slipped. Roy was thrown through the air and he struck a concrete wall with a sickening thud. "We could tell by his glazed eyes that he was knocked punchy," Art Rush says. "But he followed his instinct, I guess. He got up, ran and mounted Trigger, rode out and reentered at his usual pace. The crowd cheered like crazy but we were worried to death until intermission when a doctor could thoroughly examine Roy." Another time his escape from serious injury was even more narrow. Trigger slipped as they were circling the arena, and as Roy fell from the saddle, his spur caught in the stirrup. "The crowd was furious when Trigger didn't stop running," Glenn says. "They became almost hysterical watching him drag Roy by one leg. But the truth was that Roy's heel accidentally was giving the horse a cue to run. And poor Trigger was just caught between the devil and the deep sea. Several wranglers and I ran into the arena and stopped Trigger. Luckily Roy wasn't hurt except for scratches and bruises. I remember that time the doctor laughed after he examined Roy. 'The good Lord must really be saving you for a purpose, Roy,' he said."

In those days "The Sons of the Pioneers" and his comic sidekick, Gabby Hayes, appeared with Roy on most tours. The gay cowboys gave Art Rush and Jim Osborne many a fit. "We named Art 'Old Mother Rush,'" one of "The Pioneers" says. "He was simply a pain in the neck. He was always quoting the Bible and telling everybody to go to church and save their money and get plenty of sleep and eat properly. To send him into a real tizzy we used to pile empty beer bottles in our wastebaskets."

"Jim Osborne was no better," another member of the troupe adds. "We called him 'Old Moneybags.' He allowed Roy fifteen dollars a week in spending money and had to okay every purchase Roy made

52

—from a jackknife to a new pair of boots. If anybody ever wants anything from Roy Rogers, they're wasting their time asking him. Jim Osborne is the man to see. And he's as tough as they come."

There were times when Roy was tempted to join the cowboys in their colorful escapades. "But I'd take one look at that sorrowful manager of mine and I knew I couldn't do anything to hurt 'old sad eyes,'" Roy says. "I'd take off my regalia and turn in to get plenty of sleep like a good boy should. Art would all but tuck me in. Then he'd sigh and go to his room to read his Bible till the wee hours."

In 1943, the year he won the title of "King of the Cowboys," Roy toured Canada. It then could be said that Trigger was one horse who had traveled in de luxe fashion over land, sea, and air. "We'd come a long way from the days when Trigger rode in an open trailer, hitched to an old flivver," Glenn Randall says. "I usually drove while Roy strummed his guitar. We bumped and yodeled over many a hill and dale."

Roy Rogers went on the air with his own big-time radio program in November, 1944, for the Goodyear Tire and Rubber Company. His six to eight pictures a year began to include a new brand of Western musicals with leading lady Dale Evans. By then his records were selling like wildfire; millions were reading the *Roy Rogers Comic Book,* and after a few false starts, Art Rush was setting up a large-scale organization to lease the Rogers name to licensees for the manufacture, on a royalty basis, of Western regalia and trappings for small fry.

With Roy becoming the hero of children all over the world, with fan clubs in most major American cities and many foreign countries, and with the studio claiming that his mail had long surpassed the record count once set by Clara Bow, everybody except Roy Rogers himself seemed to realize the scope of his penetration. Once, when asked to appear at a benefit, he was quoted as saying, "Well, I sure would like to. But the cause is so important I'd rather see you folks get a *big* star." And when a group of boyhood friends from Duck Run visited him, they reported that Roy Rogers was still the country

53

boy they'd grown up with as Leonard Slye. "His shirt might be fancier," one commented, "but underneath is still the same heart that would give you the shirt if you needed it."

In January, 1943, Roy was invited to the White House, along with a list of such impressive persons as Lawrence Tibbett, Sir Cedric Hardwicke, Edgar Bergen, Loretta Young, James Cagney, and Fred Waring, to celebrate the President's birthday. "On the *Super-Chief* he was as quiet as a bashful child," one star said later. "He just sat there, solemnly clutching a handsome new guitar he'd bought especially for the March of Dimes ball and a pair of silver spurs marked 'To F.D.R. from Roy Rogers.' "

Roy's lack of interest in socializing and gaining culture provides many a headache for Art Rush. In 1945, one evening in New York, Art and Arlene prevailed upon the cowboy to spend his first evening at the legitimate theater. The show was *Oklahoma!* It so happened that Roy had once been asked to read for a part in *Green Grow the Lilacs,* from which *Oklahoma!* was adapted. But because of other commitments, Roy had been unable to oblige. During the performance, Roy Rogers began to squirm. "I'm certainly glad I didn't get mixed up in this sissy thing," he whispered to Art. "Who ever heard of cowboys dancing like that and using such flimsy belts and cap pistols?" By intermission Roy had had enough. He vowed he was leaving. "You can't do it, Buck," Art insisted. "The whole audience is agog because you're in here tonight. Can't you picture the headlines tomorrow: ROY ROGERS, KING OF THE COWBOYS, WALKS OUT ON OKLAHOMA! It would be a mess—for you and the show too."

"Well, all right," Roy said, as he gave in. "But if I stay, I'm going to take a good nap for myself." And back in his seat again, Roy kicked off his boots and curled up to sleep through the rest of the performance. The correct, ambitious W. Arthur Rush could not have been more miserable.

"But no matter how much he embarrasses me," Art Rush says, wryly, "he seems to have a knack for always coming out on top. We both love baseball, and I'll never forget the day we went to see the St. Louis Cardinals play the New York Yankees. It was 1945, the day

54

Johnny Lindell made his famous slide." The occasion began as a successful one for Art Rush. On entering the stadium, his kid, as he calls Roy, received an ovation equal to that of the teams. Then Roy was taken to visit both dugouts to be photographed with the players. And then he was posed with Judge Kenesaw Mountain Landis, Governor Dewey, James Farley, Babe Ruth, and Connie Mack. Finally the star was ushered to his box. "When we sat down," Art says, "I noticed that four gentlemen were already seated in the second row. And Roy, Steve Edwards, Ned Irish, and I settled on the front row. Just as we sat down, the nightmare happened. Droves of children came from everywhere, descending on our box to get Roy's autograph. The police were trying to calm matters when suddenly Roy was pushed back and the kids descended on the man behind him. When I turned around and saw that the man's cigar had been smashed and ashes were spilled all over his vest, I nearly fainted. Because by then I saw too that the man was Herbert Hoover."

"Oh, we're so sorry, Mr. Hoover," Art sputtered. "Please forgive us, sir. It was an accident."

Herbert Hoover smiled broadly. "It's quite all right," he said, warmly. "I'm a Roy Rogers fan too."

By the time Roy finished his fourth engagement at Madison Square Garden in 1945, the show had grossed over a million dollars in thirty-three days. Art Rush was so proud and happy that he decided he'd indulge in a little humor too. At the time Roy was using "Home on the Range" in his show and often called upon the audience to sing it with him. So for days Art Rush secretly rehearsed "Home on the Range." He was so afraid he'd forget the lyrics that he sang everywhere, in taxis and in bed. "I kept telling him he'd have to sing only a few bars and then the audience would carry him," Mary Jo says.

Finally Art's great moment at Madison Square Garden arrived. Dressed in cowboy regalia, he entered the arena with a group of performers who had solo bits scheduled to precede "Home on the Range." It wasn't until all the regular cowboys had done their bits and he was preparing to sing "Home on the Range" that Roy realized he had failed to call on one member of the group. He looked at the "stranger" and then did a double take. Art smiled and cleared his throat to take over. But Roy switched numbers. "Folks," he said into the mike, "we have a guest star with us this evening—none other than the famous Mr. Bull's-eye Rush. He will now do my shooting act for me."

Roy removed his guns from his holsters and handed them to Art Rush. The confused stagehands began readying the clay targets. "I missed every single target," Art Rush admits. "And those forty-fives nearly kicked my arms off. Needless to add, I've never since bothered Roy while he was on stage."

Much to the consternation of his business associates, Roy Rogers had graduated from a motorcycle to an airplane by the fall of 1946, when he organized and went on tour with his own rodeo. Literally and figuratively, he was riding high. He had everything on earth he wanted except a son. And on October 28, Arlene gave birth to a boy. When he learned the baby was a boy, Roy yipped as loud as only a cowboy-father could. "And if a simple, swell guy like Roy Rogers could ever become cocky, I'd say that at that time he was," a friend comments.

But as Roy Rogers himself was often to say later, the Lord didn't allow him to stay cocky for long. Early on Sunday morning, November 3, when the baby was six days old, the telephone rang at the Rogers home. Would Mr. Rogers come to the hospital at once? Roy and Mrs. Wilkins, Arlene's mother, got to the hospital in record time.

When they reached Arlene's room, they saw doctors and nurses crowded around her bed. A short time earlier, while chatting with her nurse, Arlene had suddenly gasped and fallen into unconsciousness. Artificial respiration, injections, and oxygen did no good. Arlene Rogers was never to rally. She had suffered a fatal embolism.

The night before, Art Rush had worked late in his study. Mary Jo was guarding the telephone downstairs, determined not to wake him. But when one call came, she ran upstairs. "I don't know who's on the phone, Art," she said, rousing her husband. "But it must be urgent. It sounds like a child crying."

Sleepily, Art Rush reached for his bedside phone. "Buck," he heard Roy's sobbing voice, "Arlene's dead."

"Where are you?" Art cried.

"At the hospital."

Art Rush doesn't remember whether or not he pulled on trousers over his pajamas. He grabbed a topcoat and flew down the stairs. "Something's happened to Arlene at the hospital," he cried over his shoulder to Mary Jo. "Call Jim Osborne."

When Art reached the hospital, he saw a sight that engraved itself on his heart. Sitting on the bumper of the station wagon, Roy Rogers was surrounded by dozens of excited children. Tears rolling down his cheeks, he was trying to answer the kids' pleas for autographs. "My heart cracked when I saw my dazed, grief-stricken kid trying to be what for years he'd been groomed to be—Roy Rogers, 'King of the Cowboys.' It came to me then that Roy had reached the point where parents all over the world were turning to him with their problems of child care. What Roy Rogers said to eat, the kids ate. What Roy Rogers said to do, the kids did. I wondered achingly how he'd be able to settle his own problems as a parent now. What would he tell two little girls waiting at home for news of their mother? What would he tell a little boy who was never to know her?"

Art Rush knew that his kid was up against something that neither he nor Jim nor any human being could solve. "I knew we needed help," Art says. "And I asked for it. I bowed my head and prayed."

"Come on, Art, pull yourself together," came the crisp voice of Jim Osborne. "The thing to do now is to get Roy home."

CHAPTER SIX

The position of Dale Evans in the entertainment field is unique. Since the presound, serial days of Pearl White, Dale is the only woman star who has made a name for herself in westerns. And it is said that since Calamity Jane, there hasn't been a girl like her in the action arena. Yet Dale Evans didn't go West with dreams of someday being "Queen of the West." In fact, she tried her level best not to land in such a spot. And, seemingly, nobody could have been less prepared for a job.

"Now that I know what God had in mind for me," Dale comments, "I can look back and understand so many things. But for years I fought tooth and nail. At times the force I was battling was so strong I could almost feel it. Yet never once did it dawn on me Who that force might be."

Dale Evans was born as Frances Octavia Smith on October 31, 1912, in Uvalde, Texas. She has one brother, Walter Hillman Smith, Jr., to whom she is very devoted. The Smith family was neither rich nor poor. They were solid, middle-class citizens whose female relatives usually took to teaching. And the many musicians among them reserved their talents for the church.

Walter and Betty Sue Smith expected their daughter to grow up to be a lady too. And ladies, they were certain, did not perform on the stage. "But Frances came into the world wanting to be a professional singer," her mother says. "For years we prayed that she'd outgrow it. We simply couldn't understand how a child from our household could have such ideas." Frances also came into the world with something besides ideas: a real talent. She has always had a voice that could pour out and run over your heart.

Dale says that her childhood as Frances Octavia Smith was uneventful. "I had the same mumps, birthday parties, music lessons, and Easter dresses that most little girls have." But there was one difference worth noting. She spent most of her time at the piano playing tunes out of her head or before a mirror "selling" the lyrics she made up to go with them.

One Sunday when she was three years old, Frances toddled away from her parents at church and interrupted services to sing a solo for the congregation. "Everybody but her father and I thought it was cute," Mrs. Smith says. "But we were embarrassed and shocked," she adds.

Walter and Betty Sue Smith were in for a serious shock when, at fourteen, their daughter disappeared. They were living in Osceola, Arkansas, at the time. Elopement fever swept the high-school crowd and Frances and a youthful sweetheart joined several other couples in a mass wedding. After involving herself in such a silly, kid stunt, Frances was scared. It took her three days to gather enough courage to call her parents and confess that she had gone to Blytheville, 18 miles from Osceola, to be married. At the moment the couple were with the groom's mother in Tennessee.

A short time later, the Smiths moved to Memphis. And it was there, less than a year after her marriage, that Frances gave birth to a son. She was fifteen years old.

By the time Tommy Fox arrived on November 28, 1927, his father had deserted his mother twice. And when the baby was just a few months old, they were left for the last time. The young couple had moved to Blytheville. And at Easter, Frances had taken the baby to visit her family in Memphis. One day relatives notified the Smiths that Frances' things and the baby's had been found dumped in their garage. Then soon came the inevitable letter. The bridegroom felt he was too young to be tied down to a wife and child. He wanted his freedom.

Frances suffered a near breakdown. Despite everything, she still loved her young husband. She was heartbroken, bewildered, frantic. And she was appalled by the word divorce.

Frances waited a whole year before she could bring herself to start divorce proceedings. Then she attended a business school in Memphis and took a job with an insurance company. At this juncture the girl was beginning a long, hungry search. A search for success that she thought would mean security for her baby. She had developed what amounted almost to a complex about her rash marriage. And she had made up her young mind that her son would never suffer because of it. If he had no father, she would be both mother and father.

Frances' bitter regrets, her fears for her son, and her secret pledges to him were someday even to threaten her health. About this period she has only this to say: "I just didn't give anybody or anything a real chance. I went around with a chip on my shoulder that had a spring attached. It was just as if I were silently daring anybody to slight or hurt or reprimand Tommy. And I was grimly determined to let nothing stand in my way of making good for him."

One day at noon, alone in the insurance office where she worked, Frances was munching a sandwich from her lunch sack when she began humming a tune. Soon she was lost in composing a song about Tommy. And by the time her boss returned from lunch, she was singing at the top of her lungs. "When I looked up and realized he'd been listening," she says, "my heart sank. He was a stern man and I figured I was automatically fired." But the boss surprised her. "Say, that's some voice you have there, child," he said. "How about singing for us sometimes on the company's radio program?"

Soon Frances was singing regularly on the local radio program. Officials of the company, co-workers, and friends were full of praise. She even received a few fan letters. And overwhelmed by such success, Frances quit her job and went to Chicago, ready to crash big-time radio. It wasn't long, however, before she realized she had pressed her luck a bit fast. The depression was on. Established performers were doing well to find work. And thousands of unemployed men and women were searching for any kind of job.

Finally Frances came to her senses and decided to return to a typewriter. At that, it was weeks before she found work. "And I was paid fifteen dollars a week," she says. "On that kind of salary anybody should have known you couldn't pay rent, nursery-school tuition, and wages for a woman to watch your child after school hours, and eat too. But I was stubborn. I vowed I'd make good if it killed me."

And it nearly did. As the days and weeks went into months, Frances wrestled doggedly with her problems for survival. All day long, away from Tommy, she worried about his safety. And at night she slept fitfully, dreading morning when they'd have to set out in opposite directions—she for work and Tommy to walk alone to his nursery school.

One snowy, gray morning Frances awoke feeling unusually tired and depressed. After she had given her son his breakfast, packed his lunch, and with effort and grease had conquered his little cowlick, she buttoned him up in a blue snowsuit and went outside to stand at the foot of their apartment house steps until the departing child became a tiny blue dot in the snow. With a sickening pang it came to her how terribly alone they were—how terribly alone Tommy would be if anything happened to her.

"I know now how very unfair I was being to my parents," she says. "They wanted to help but I wouldn't let them. I was so ashamed of hurting them. And I was trying to make it up somehow by proving that I could take care of myself and Tommy."

On her way to work that morning, Frances stopped by an office in her building to see about buying some life insurance. During her lunch hour she went to a doctor for the necessary examination. Soon she realized that the doctor was giving her more than routine attention. And finally he faced her gravely. "You are quite ill, young lady," he said. "How long has it been since you've had a decent meal?"

Before she left the doctor's office, Frances had poured out her whole story. Since she had come to Chicago she had been spending every available penny on food and milk and cod-liver oil for her son. "If you really love your child, you will go home to your family at once," the doctor said, not unkindly. So for the first time since she had earned her first dollar, Frances turned to her parents for money. She wired for a ticket home.

By this time the Smiths were living on a cotton farm at Italy, Texas, near Dallas. Frances' parents and brother welcomed her and Tommy with tears of relief. Frances was found to be suffering a severe type of anemia. She was hospitalized immediately, and the recovery was difficult and slow.

In 1934, physically well at long last, Frances gave in once more to her nagging dreams of being a successful singer. She managed a radio job at Louisville, Kentucky. And, again resisting her parents' offers, she took Tommy along. "I didn't make much of a dent in radio history in Louisville," she agrees, "but I did get a new name."

Joe Eaton, the program director at the radio station, felt that Frances Smith was no name for a singer. And briefly, she changed to Marion Lee. Then one day Eaton said, "Let's select one for you that's easy to spell, pronounce, and remember." He thought a minute. "How about Dale Evans?" And with no further ado, Dale Evans she became.

One evening in Louisville, after feeding and bathing Tommy and tucking him in bed, Dale settled down to read the evening paper. Her eyes fastened on the smiling face of a little girl with raven curls. "I was so excited to see her picture in the paper," Dale says. "She was the daughter of a friend of mine, and I was simply wild about her." Then suddenly Dale's heart began to pound. The paper stated the child was dead. She had been fatally burned in her Halloween costume while her mother was at work.

Dale Evans paced the floor most of the night. "I was so grief-

62

stricken and sorry for my friend," she says. "And the tragedy awakened all my old fears for Tommy." But there was more too. Dale began to face some truths. Tommy loved farm life, his grandparents adored him, and with Hillman away at college, they were lonely. Before morning, Dale Evans had made her decision. By the time Tommy awoke she was all packed. And after visiting the mother of the little accident victim, Dale and her son left immediately for Texas.

"It would be nice to be able to say that everything went smoothly after that," Betty Sue Smith comments. "But it didn't. Everybody was happy but our daughter. She had given in but she hadn't given up. Hour after hour, day after day, she sat at the piano, playing and singing endlessly. And her voice seemed more lovely than ever."

Mr. and Mrs. Smith began having secret talks. Perhaps it was wrong to refuse such talent and ambition. At any rate, they simply couldn't bear to see their daughter so miserable. "Why don't you try to get a radio job in Dallas?" Dale's mother suggested one day. "Perhaps that's a way to have your cake and eat it too." So Dale dressed herself up and boarded the interurban for the city. She auditioned for Jimmie Jeffries, whose popular *Early Birds* program still broadcasts over station WFAA. Dale Evans clicked. She worked in Dallas and spent her weekends at the farm with Tommy.

They were wonderful weekends. Tommy, by this time, was a husky little fellow of eight, with solemn brown eyes and a crooked front tooth. He had a bird dog named Kate and a bicycle and skates and plenty of space to enjoy them all. From the time he had stood in his crib, wiggling his fat little body to the rhythm of his mother's songs, he had shown a great love for music. He was taking piano lessons and doing well in school.

Ironically, when the success that Dale had long dreamed of began to show signs of coming, it was only to threaten her peaceful setup. Firmly she refused all offers so she could stay on in Dallas. But in 1937, when she got a chance to sing with Jay Mills's Orchestra at the Edgewater Beach Hotel in Chicago, she realized it was a matter of now or never.

"Go right ahead and don't worry about Tommy," Betty Sue Smith told her daughter. "He's happy with us and he can visit you any time you wish. After all, he's not a baby any more." So Dale took a last look at the beloved cowlick and the crooked tooth, and left for Chicago.

"But Mother had hardly unpacked before she called for me," Tom Fox says. "And I was so excited when she consented to let me ride the train all by myself. I was just ten at the time, and I had some trip. I was to change in St. Louis, but our train was late so I missed my connection. When finally I got to Chicago, Mother was fit to be tied. I couldn't understand why. I had a perfectly swell four hours in St. Louis, reading comic books and downing chocolate sodas!"

A few months later Dale was offered a job with Anson Weeks, and she toured the country with his band for almost a year. "It was the best deal I'd ever had," she says, "and I should have been happy. But I wasn't. I'd taken Tommy back to my folks and I simply wanted him with me."

The tour over, Dale returned to Chicago, determined to set up a home for her son. And she did. She took a job as staff singer with WBBM, a CBS station. And for nearly three years she worked there with Caesar Petrillo and his orchestra. Tommy was enrolled at Lane Technical High School and was playing the flute with gusto. They could not have been happier.

Dale had plenty of time in those days for extra jobs, and for a while she was on the *Sister Emmy and Cousin Myrtle* show with Fran Allison, now of *Kukla, Fran, and Ollie* fame. One day in 1940, Dale was asked to make a recording for a commercial audition with a Western musical group, "The Sons of the Pioneers." While they were waiting around the studio, Dale taught the gaily garbed cowboys the lyrics to a song she had written, "My Heart Is Down Texas Way."

"Wow, would Roy cotton to this one!" commented Pat Brady, one of "The Pioneers."

"Who's Roy?" Dale asked.

"Now, don't tell us you haven't heard of Roy Rogers," put in

64

Wally Jordan of the William Morris Agency. Dale admitted that she hadn't.

"He's a singing cowboy out in Hollywood," Jordan went on, "and five will get you ten that he'll soon be the hottest thing in America. He's not only talented and good-looking, but he's a fine boy."

Dale Evans shrugged. "Come on, fellows, let's get down to business. I'm worried about this transcription." And she had cause to be. When the unknown sponsor heard it, he turned thumbs down. But it was just as well. "The Sons of the Pioneers" were soon signed by Republic to play in Roy Rogers's pictures and Dale Evans got an opportunity to appear at Chicago's Chez Paree, one of the most famous night clubs in the world.

When Dale opened at the Chez Paree, Ethel Shutta and Ray Bolger were headlining the show. The stars brought down the house but Dale Evans went over with a dull thud. "I didn't even get enough applause for one encore," she says. "I flew back to my dressing room and bawled."

Pretty soon Dale heard a knock, and gulping back her tears, she opened the door. "I could hardly believe my eyes when I saw Miss Shutta and Mr. Bolger standing there," she says, "and I could hardly believe my ears when they said they wanted to help me."

Ray Bolger didn't waste time mincing words. "Your voice is good, kid, but your material is lousy," he told Dale frankly. "Don't you have any *good* numbers?" Dale mentioned a few she had worked up but the pair shook their heads. "You need original stuff to compete with the noise in a night club," the rubber-legged comedian went on. "Have you ever thought about hiring a writer?"

"I've written some songs myself," Dale said shyly, "but I've never had enough nerve to do them in public." Urged, Dale brought out a number she had jotted down to the rhythm of a train's wheels, when a short time before she had gone to Texas to see her family. "This is leap year, you know," she explained. "So I called it 'Will You Marry Me, Mr. Laramie?'"

Ethel Shutta and Ray Bolger pulled up their chairs and set to work in earnest, helping Dale revise her song. When finally they all

65

were satisfied, Bolger suggested that he stooge for Dale during the number. And, as is now minor show-business history, Dale Evans and her "Will You Marry Me, Mr. Laramie?" went over with a bang.

Out of a clear sky, one day in 1941, Dale received a telegram from Hollywood. It was signed by an agent named Joe Rivkin, who said that he and his friend Danny Winkler, who was then casting director at RKO, had heard about her success at the Chez Paree and had been listening to her regular Sunday morning program over station WBBM. PLEASE SEND PHOTOGRAPHS RIGHT AWAY, the message read. PARAMOUNT IS LOOKING FOR A NEW FACE TO STAR IN "HOLIDAY INN" WITH BING CROSBY AND FRED ASTAIRE.

"I was flabbergasted," Dale relates. "The movies were the last thing on earth I would have dreamed of trying. I didn't think I was pretty enough, and I certainly didn't pretend to be an actress. So I ignored the wire."

In a few days Dale heard from Rivkin again. This time his message was more urgent and Dale sent some pictures. "I figured that would hush him," she said, with a chuckle. But to the contrary, Joe Rivkin wired, COME AT ONCE.

Dale talked the matter over with Tommy, with friends, with herself. The consensus was that she had nothing to lose. So Dale arranged a short leave from her radio job, splurged her savings on two elaborate outfits, and grabbed a plane. The flight was rough and she suffered assorted miseries, including a severe earache.

"I didn't sleep a wink all the way from Chicago to Los Angeles," she says. "Finally I quieted myself by reading a story about a typical Hollywood agent. I didn't know it, of course, but I could not have selected better background material. As I stepped off the plane, I saw a little guy pacing and puffing and chewing at his nails. I said to myself, 'That *has* to be Joe Rivkin!'"

When Dale walked up to him, Rivkin stepped back. He grimaced, horrified. "*You* are not Dale Evans!" Meekly an exhausted Dale said that she was. "Well, you certainly don't look like your pictures," he commented curtly. Then with no further preamble Rivkin asked, "Say, how old are you, anyway?"

66

Dale Evans was twenty-eight, but her Chicago friends had already briefed her on what Hollywood considered a delicate subject. She studied the ground. "I'm twenty-two."

At that moment Rivkin spied her wedding ring. Without a word, he removed it from her finger. "Well, kid, from now on you're twenty-one and single. Let's go."

In the car, all the way from the airport, Joe Rivkin studied his new client with open distaste. "The color of your lipstick is awful," he said. "And you've got your mouth painted all wrong." When they reached the Hollywood Plaza Hotel, Rivkin steered his charge straight to the beauty shop. Addressing the operator as if Dale were thin air, he ordered, "Slap some blood into this face and then see what you can do with it! We're due at the studio for lunch in an hour." As Rivkin marched out, he called back over his shoulder, "And comb that hair!"

Dismissed from the beauty shop, Dale quickly went to her room to change her clothes. She donned the expensive black dress she had bought in Chicago, a large, droopy black hat, silver fox furs, and long white gloves. "I was pretty gussied-up for the likes of me," Dale says. "And I was so proud when I stepped off the elevator."

But when Joe Rivkin saw her, he did a double take. He almost choked. "My God, what now! Do you think maybe your agent just died?"

Dale Evans had had just about enough. "In the East," she said coldly, "this is considered a very proper outfit."

Rivkin snorted. "Well, kid, you aren't in the East now. You're in Hollywood!"

Joe Rivkin groused all the way to Paramount Studios, but when finally they reached the offices of William Meiklejohn, the casting director, Dale's agent turned to peaches and cream. And Bill Meiklejohn endeared himself to Dale forever by giving her the first warm smile she had seen since leaving Chicago. "By golly, young lady," he remarked, "you look exactly like my wife did when she first came to Hollywood."

When the trio entered the commissary for lunch, everybody in the place turned to stare at the new face. "And," Dale, remembering her session at the beauty shop, says, "they didn't know just *how* new it was!"

During the luncheon Bill Meiklejohn watched every move Dale Evans made. Rivkin's nervousness was on the increase. "Now, Bill, isn't she beautiful?" he asked over and over. "Isn't she everything I said?"

Ignoring Rivkin, Meiklejohn addressed Dale, "How old are you, Miss Evans?"

Rivkin piped up, "Twenty-one."

Meiklejohn addressed Dale, "Can you dance?"

Rivkin piped up, "Dance! Why, she can give Eleanor Powell a run for her money!"

Dale Evans pushed back her chair, her green eyes blazing. "Now look, fellows, this has gone far enough! I can't even do a time-step, and Joe Rivkin, you know it!"

Dale says that she had always heard about people turning the color of an eggplant but that time Joe Rivkin really did. And Bill Meiklejohn laughed, but his laugh had a hollow ring. "Well, you're here, so we'll go on and make the test anyway," he said. "We'll put you under the care of Bill Russell, the talent coach."

Dale Evans was rehearsed for a scene from "Blue Angel," a Marlene Dietrich picture. She was told that MacDonald Carey would play opposite her in the test. And she was fitted in a dress that had been created for Barbara Stanwyck. All seemed to be going well until the day before the test was scheduled. Suddenly Dale decided she could wrestle with her conscience no longer, and she called Rivkin aside. Taking a deep breath, she blurted, "I'm not twenty-two; I'm twenty-eight! And I have a son half as old as I am!"

Joe Rivkin stared at her, wordless for the first time. His hands went to his temples. "Wait!" he moaned finally. "Don't say another word. Quiet! Let me think!" He paced and puffed. Then suddenly he snapped his fingers. "I've got it! We'll put him away in a school!"

Poor Rivkin didn't know it but he had said the worst.

"He won't be put anywhere but at home with me!" Dale Evans snapped.

68

Joe Rivkin waved his hand for silence. There was more puffing, more pacing. Then a triumphant smile. "Why, he can be your kid brother!"

Dale cocked her head as she always does when she is thinking. It was one way, she knew, if not the best way. And most important, Tommy could be with her and she'd be sure of making enough money to send him to college. "I'll have to talk it over with my son before I decide," she said. "If he objects, I can't do it."

When they had finished rehearsing at the studio, Rivkin took Dale back to the Hollywood Plaza. "Now, don't worry about anything tonight," he cautioned. "Be asleep by eight o'clock so your voice will be rested and clear for tomorrow." As he walked away, Dale heard him mutter, "And maybe that'll get rid of some of the lines under her eyes."

The next day Dale's test went off without mishap. Besides the "Blue Angel" scene, she sang two numbers—"I Don't Know Why I Love You Like I Do," and her own "Will You Marry Me, Mr. Laramie?" The wait for a decision was three weeks long. But finally Rivkin phoned.

"I can laugh now," Dale says, "but I was so furious and frustrated at the time that I burst into tears." Paramount's verdict had been: Her voice is good. She needs to lose weight. But we couldn't use her under any circumstances because the role calls for dancing and we already have too many singers.

When Rivkin had relayed the message, Dale hung up the phone, outraged. A few seconds later Joe called again. "But Dale," he shouted, "you didn't let me finish. Twentieth Century–Fox has seen the test and want to sign you to a one-year contract."

"I've already had enough of Hollywood's ways," Dale said, in tears.

"They'll pay you three times what you're making in Chicago," Rivkin told her.

So Dale returned to Chicago to talk the matter over with her thirteen-year-old son. Tommy Fox was a devout, serious lad. Two years before, in Texas, he had joined the church, and he spent much

69

of his time reading the Bible. Dale knew in her heart that her child yearned to be a minister, but he always spoke of becoming a musician, and her heart ached over the reason. For years Tommy had struggled with stammering. And his mother secretly blamed his unsettled childhood for the condition.

"I have a chance for a contract in Hollywood," Dale told her son. "If I take it, I can be pretty sure of your going to college to continue your music. But," and Dale paused, "until I'm established, I'll have to say you are my brother."

Tommy Fox stared at his mother. "They're funny out there, honey," Dale went on. "If they know I'm already twenty-eight years old, they won't feel I'm worth the necessary investments."

"It sounds sort of silly," Tommy commented. "But you can do anything you want, Mother, as long as I myself don't have to lie."

So Dale called Joe Rivkin and it wasn't long before he found them an apartment. Betty Sue Smith met her daughter and grandson in California and stayed until they were settled to her satisfaction. "Now, Dad says you are not to kiss anybody on the screen," Mrs. Smith told her daughter on leaving. "And you are not to show your legs. We just don't trust acting people."

Although Dale Evans already was signed, Twentieth Century-Fox ordered a new test to be made. Afterward Tom Moore, the talent director, asked Dale to read a poem for him, "The Hound of Heaven" by Francis Thompson.

"For goodness' sake, why?" Dale asked Tom Moore.

"Because I sense some kind of spiritual quality in you, Miss Evans."

"How he saw anything in me but bleached hair and heavy make-up at the time, I don't know," Dale says. "At any rate, I read the poem—or at least I spoke the words. And when I'd finished, I could see he was very disappointed."

There were many others in Hollywood who were critical of Dale Evans. She was put on a diet, her lower teeth were filed and fitted with temporary caps, she was given dancing lessons, and sent to dramatic school. Flossie Friedman, the drama coach, asked Dale to read Kipling's "If." When Dale had finished, Miss Friedman shuddered. "Tell me, dahling," she said, with a frown, "are you kidding? Or do you really talk that way?"

Years later Dale was to meet Flossie Friedman at a party. "I'd already been in westerns a long time," Dale says. "I went up to her and said, 'Hi, Flossie, how're things?'" Miss Friedman recoiled with horror. Then looking over her shoulder as if she were preparing to impart an international secret, she whispered with exaggerated lip movements, "*Theengs,* dahling, *theengs*—not *thangs!*"

During her year with Twentieth Century–Fox, Dale Evans was given only two bit parts. "The salary was nice and I needed it," she says, "but I worried constantly about not making any progress." Dale kept busy, however, entertaining at training camps around the country, an activity she maintained throughout the war years. It was reported that she recorded more "Personal Albums" for overseas broadcasts to servicemen than did any other Hollywood personality. And she appeared regularly on *Command Performance* and *Mail Call* broadcasts for the armed forces, besides her many benefit and hospital shows.

Dale usually did her "Will You Marry Me, Mr. Laramie?" for the boys, and they loved it, especially when she asked one of them to stooge for her as Ray Bolger had done. But one day she got hold of a captain who evidently had left his sense of humor at home. All through the song he stared at Dale, puzzled. When she had finished, he leaned over and whispered, righteously, "I'm sorry, lady, I guess you think I'm single, but I'm not. I've got a wife and five kids back in Georgia."

Dale Evans feels that she learned a lot of what she knows about show business from working with experienced stars during the war. "I'll never forget the time I went to northern California with Pat O'Brien and Marlene Dietrich," she recounts. "We could not have performed under worse conditions, but I noticed that Miss Dietrich prepared herself as carefully as if we'd been going on at the Palace. She put on everything from her false eyelashes to her long black sequin dress, and when she and Pat went out there, they gave those soldiers all they had. It was the first time I realized the obligation real entertainers feel toward their audience. And it was a lesson I've never forgot."

For a while Dale Evans had hopes for a test she had been asked to make for a Kay Kyser picture for M-G-M. But nothing came of it, and time was running out fast on her contract with Twentieth Century–Fox. Desperate, Dale finally contacted Joe Rivkin, who by that time was in the service, stationed at Sheppard Field, Wichita Falls, Texas. "I'm going to be dropped by Twentieth. I just feel it," Dale said. "And I need an agent pronto."

"Joe wrote back that there was one and only one he'd trust," Dale says. "He told me to see a man named Art Rush."

"The day Dale Evans walked into my office," Art Rush picks up the story, "she looked for all the world like a little doll in some kind of bonnet-type hat. She was so pretty and cute I doubted seriously that she had a real voice. And I had never taken any women clients." But it just so happened that Rush had heard that Edgar Bergen's radio program needed a girl singer. And he told Dale that he would come to her home that evening to hear her sing.

Driving to Dale's home in Westwood that night, Art told his wife Mary Jo to prepare herself for a disappointing and wasted evening. But after Dale's first number, the Rushes rose to their feet, delighted. And they worked late preparing Art's new client for the radio audition.

Bergen's program was sponsored by Chase and Sanborn, and Dale walked in for her audition to face three stern men—Edgar Bergen, Tony Stanford, and Ray Noble. "Charlie McCarthy was there too, of course," Dale says. "And I remember thinking to myself how bored he looked, lying limp across Bergen's lap."

But even the discerning Charlie McCarthy couldn't stay bored long. Edgar Bergen soon grabbed him up to give Dale Evans a long, low whistle of approval. For after she had sung "Will You Marry Me, Mr. Laramie?" "Blue Skies," "On the Sunny Side of the Street," and a Spanish medley, the stern group was all smiles. And after

Art Rush had effected Dale's release from Twentieth Century–Fox, she was immediately signed for her first big radio show.

Relatively speaking, things were going well for Dale Evans, and she told herself she should be happy. But she was miserable. She deeply regretted her decision to have Tommy pose as her brother, and she cried herself to sleep many nights because of it. "I felt that if he didn't have a real father, the least I could do was let him acknowledge his mother," she says. "And everywhere I looked, I seemed to see happy parents proudly carrying little children. One time at Christmas there was a party, and everybody brought their sons and daughters. I took Tommy all right, but I had to say he was my brother. It simply made me sick for weeks. Once at a football game somebody turned to me and said, 'My that's a good band for high-school kids.' I wanted to yell, 'My son plays the flute in that band. He's a fine musician.' But I couldn't. I was living a lie, and I hated every minute of it."

Thinking Dale was brooding about her career, Art Rush encouraged her to spend more and more time in war work. One evening after a performance at Victorville Air Base, Art brought over Roy Rogers to meet Dale Evans. "Well, here's my boy," Art said, beaming. "What do you think of him?"

Dale Evans looked the cowboy up and down and silently decided that she couldn't think less. "I guess I was jealous of Art's attentions to another client," she says today. "And because Roy just stood there, saying nothing, I figured he was stuck-up."

But whether she liked him or not, Dale Evans was destined to see a lot more of America's "King of the Cowboys"—and soon. One day, while playing golf at Lakeside Country Club, Art Rush learned from Republic Studios executive Armand Schaeffer that they were planning a musical picture and needed a new face. Hurriedly Art dug up the test Dale Evans had made for Kay Kyser's picture and showed it to Schaeffer. Impressed, Schaeffer called in another Republic official, Moe Siegel. Siegel took an immediate liking to Dale Evans and she was signed up.

"So it might be said that I really made my movie debut in 'Swing

Your Partner' in 1943," Dale says. "It was a sort of hayseed musical, but at least my role was better than the bits I'd drawn previously."

After the picture was finished, Dale was told to report to the studio for the rehearsal of another. If she had objected to appearing in a hayseed musical, it is easy to imagine the shock she felt upon learning that her next venture would be a Roy Rogers western. "I know I held my mouth open a full five minutes when I walked onto the set and saw all those cowboys."

Up until that time Republic had been borrowing Roy Rogers's movie heroines from other studios. But since they had an idle girl on their hands, they had decided to use her. "And she's from Texas," one official pointed out. "She's bound to know about horses."

What Dale Evans knew about horses wasn't much. She hadn't been on one since she was seven years old. "My father once bought Tommy a little pony," she says. "But the first time Tommy tried to ride, the pony threw him. I ran and gathered up my howling but unhurt child and howled as loud as he did. We both agreed then and there to stick to music. Horses just weren't for us."

A few minutes after Dale had arrived on the set, Roy Rogers walked over and solemnly shook hands. Rubbing his chin, he looked her over and his doubt was plain to see. "You sure don't look like a filly who could handle a horse," he drawled.

Dale Evans simply didn't like this clairvoyant cowboy. Putting her hands on her hips, she looked him straight in the eye. "I'm from Texas!" she snapped.

At that crucial moment came the sound of reprieve. Moe Siegel had arrived and he was objecting. Miss Evans's voice was not suited for westerns. They were saving her for musicals.

"Dale practically danced off the set when they dismissed her," Pat Brady recalls. "But she'd already made a big impression on us 'Pioneers.' We hadn't seen her since that day years before in Chicago. Yet she walked up to every one of us and called us by name. We thought she was some gal."

Busy months were ahead for Dale Evans. She completed several pictures in rapid succession. Her records were selling well. And she still was on the Chase and Sanborn radio show every Sunday afternoon at five. The show was rehearsed on Sunday morning and every Sunday at noon Dale and Art Rush lunched at the Hollywood Brown Derby. Art didn't know it, but he was swiftly losing favor with his client.

"He sounded exactly like a broken record," Dale says. "We'd sit down, and except for his order to the waiter, all I'd ever hear was Roy Rogers, Roy Rogers. I got so tired of the name Roy Rogers I thought I'd scream." And one Sunday Dale did just that. She jumped from her chair, threw her napkin on the table, and shouted at her manager, "I'll be dad-burned if I'm going to sit here one more minute of one more Sunday and listen to Roy Rogers, Roy Rogers! What about me? I'm your client too, remember? And while you're running all over the country putting on rodeos, just what am I supposed to be doing? Staying in Class B musicals all my life? This is it, Mr. W. Arthur Rush. I've had enough of you *and* your Roy Rogers. I'm finding me another agent!" And with that, Dale Evans stalked out of the Brown Derby.

Dale not only got herself another agent; she got two agents. She hired a fellow named Al Rackin to handle her publicity, such as it was at the time. And she signed with Danny Winkler, whom Joe Rivkin had mentioned in the telegrams that brought her to Hollywood, to manage her affairs. "Things would have been a lot easier for me," Dale recalls, "if I'd only realized I've had a real Manager since the day I was born."

A short time after she changed agents, Dale visited her family in Texas. And from Italy, Texas, she went to Abilene to put on a show at Camp Barkley. Returning to California, Dale checked with the studio and was told to report for the rehearsal of a new musical the following Monday morning.

But when Dale arrived at the studio, she learned the rehearsal had been canceled. Moreover, the picture had been canceled. Moe Siegel was leaving Republic.

The news left Dale Evans panic-stricken. And at that confused moment, Herbert Yates, Republic's big boss, walked up. "I'm starting a new brand of western musicals for Roy Rogers," he said crisply. "I'd like to see what you can do with them. The first will be titled 'The Cowboy and the Señorita.' "

Dale Evans froze in the middle of a breath. It was 1944, Tommy's graduation year. Plans already had been made for him to enter the University of Southern California. Her contract with Chase and Sanborn was expiring, and she had no immediate prospects for another radio show.

Dale faced Herbert Yates, opened her mouth to answer but no words came. She took a deep breath and tried again. "Whatever you wish, Mr. Yates," she managed finally to say.

CHAPTER SEVEN

As bad luck would have it for Dale Evans, a riding scene was scheduled for the first day's shooting of "The Cowboy and the Señorita." When, with the aid of two wranglers, Dale finally had mounted a horse, he proceeded to buck with great enthusiasm. "I bounced so hard," Dale says, with a laugh, "that the temporary caps on my lower teeth flew out of my mouth. As the horse stepped on them I heard a crunching sound that told me I'd just lost my three-hundred-dollar Hollywood smile. I already had arranged for riding lessons and I certainly couldn't pay for them and more teeth too. So I was forced to enter a new era of naturalness!"

Dale tried to keep two jumps ahead of the script with her secret evening riding lessons. But the ornery horse she rode in the picture insisted on keeping two jumps ahead of her. And it was all poor Dale could do to limp through the final scenes. She had high hopes, however, that nobody had discovered how green she had started out or how black and blue she was ending up. But her hopes collapsed the day Roy Rogers smilingly whispered in passing, "I think you're breaking some kind of record, Miss Evans. I've never seen so much sky between a horse and a rider in my life!"

For her role of Señorita Ysobel Martínez in the picture, Dale had to wear a black wig and assume a Spanish accent. "Mixed with my drawl, I guess it did sound pretty awful," Dale tells. "But I simply could have conked Roy the day he commented teasingly, 'You know,

77

Miss Evans, I think you are the discoverer of a new brand of Texas-Spanish. It sounds sort of like *sí, sí, you all!*"

When "The Cowboy and the Señorita" was finished, Dale Evans went to Texas for a short vacation with her family. One evening a group of friends entertained at dinner for her at the Century Room in Dallas's Hotel Adolphus. After the ice show there, the orchestra leader announced the presence of Dale Evans and invited her to take a bow. The spotlight swung to Dale's table and, dripping in orchids, she smilingly rose on her four-inch heels and began walking toward the bandstand. Completely forgetting about the ice, she slipped and fell flat on her face. News of the incident soon reached Hollywood and Dale promptly received a telegram from Roy Rogers: OH, WELL, IT COULD HAVE BEEN WORSE. AT LEAST THIS TIME YOU DIDN'T DROP YOUR TEETH.

But there were no two ways about it; when their first picture was released, a team had been born. And Republic Studios quickly put Dale in three more pictures with their "King of the Cowboys" that year.

Heretofore, leading ladies in westerns had usually been pale, fragile creatures, seemingly able to muster only enough strength to point their finger and say, "They went thataway." But Dale Evans was bringing new talents to the westerns. With her way of wrapping a lariat around the words of a song, her short fringed leather skirts and dainty cowboy boots, she was marking the introduction of glamour into the celluloid sagebrush. And even Roy Rogers had to admit that she was becoming a mighty accomplished equestrienne along the way.

As time passed, and Dale made picture after picture and tour after tour with Roy and "The Sons of the Pioneers," she began to realize that no human being in his right mind could help liking Roy Rogers. "He's just so plain and humble," she once commented to Tim Spencer. "He reminds me a lot of my brother Hillman."

About this time Dale wrote in a letter to her parents: "I have never once seen Roy Rogers fall prey to the Hollywood malady known as upstaging. And as far as he's concerned, scene-stealing

78

doesn't exist." On another occasion she wrote: "No matter what comes up, I notice that Roy is always for the underdog. And he does so many wonderful things for everyone he works with. No, you'll never have to worry about me as long as I'm a member of his troupe. He's a fine person and a good friend. The best way to describe Roy Rogers, I guess, is to say he *rings true.*"

Dale Evans also admired and respected Roy Rogers because he was so obviously a devoted family man. He often brought Arlene and their little girls to the studio. And Dale, like "The Pioneers," soon became almost a member of the Rogers family. Cheryl and Linda loved playing in Dale's studio dressing room, trying on her Western regalia, dabbling in her make-up kit. And when the group was on tour, Roy talked incessantly about his family, always bemoaning his losing battle for more time to be with them.

Later, when he was to lose his wife so tragically, Roy's problems were to become much graver. He was to go through a desolate period of shock and loneliness. Dale Evans was to listen to it all, offering sympathy and whatever help and advice she could, aching for this crushed man whose heart was breaking for two little girls and a motherless infant son while his life belonged to millions.

There had been many, many times that Dale had so yearned to talk to Roy about her own son and her own heartaches that she had been forced to clench her lips to keep from doing so. But she had heard and later seen for herself that the one thing Roy Rogers hated most in all the world was a lie. "There is only one thing worse than a lie and that is the person who tells it," Dale had heard him say often.

"I kept remembering those words all the way to the auditorium the night of Tommy's high-school graduation," Dale says. "I left off all make-up that evening, wore dark glasses, put my blond hair up in a snood, and dressed in an old suit. Nobody in the place noticed me and wouldn't have recognized me if they had." Dale took a seat in the back row of the auditorium and battled with a lump in her throat through most of the exercises. Tommy Fox had composed and conducted a concert arrangement for the high-school orchestra.

79

Now Tommy was playing with the orchestra, playing his flute, and Dale gazed at her child adoringly, her heart wrenched with love and pride. It was a night she had worked hard for and long dreamed of. But she felt a void too, an emptiness that gnawed like a physical pain. For she was learning what most of us learn sooner or later—sorrow can be borne alone, joy must be shared.

After Tommy had attended U.S.C. for a year and a half, he turned eighteen and enlisted in the Army for an eighteen-month term. A near crisis occurred when he was inducted at Fort MacArthur, because just as he had done at school and at his church—in those cases Dale refused to lie—he listed his parent's name and occupation. The name of Dale Evans caused quite a stir among army newsmen. But finally Dale, still living with the fear that her career would be ruined, was able to talk them out of breaking a story.

"By the time I got in, the war was over," Tom Fox says. "But I thought I'd get to do occupational duty. I was really wrong. At Fort MacArthur I contracted pneumonia. While taking basic training in the state of Washington, I picked up the mumps. And while on duty in Washington, D.C., I came down with pneumonia again. About all I saw were the walls of U.S. Army hospitals!"

Dale Evans drove alone many hours of many nights, after hard days on location, to visit her son as often as possible. After she had kissed him good-by and left one evening, a buddy of Tom's remarked, "Gee, fellow, you not only have the most devoted sister I ever saw—but the best-looking!"

If, after the period of "The Cowboy and the Señorita," Dale Evans had learned to like Roy Rogers, she still was unable to say the same for his horse Trigger. Dale resented more and more having to take second billing to a horse, and rumblings of her dissatisfaction were heard as early as August, 1945, when a young woman named Maxine Garrison interviewed Dale for the Pittsburgh *Press*. "The Queen of the West has a 'to be or not to be' that could make Hamlet sit up and take notice," Miss Garrison wrote. "As she explained it to me, the heroine in a western is always second-string. The cowboy and his horse must come first." Later in the article came the dilemma: "Dale Evans really wants to do straight musicals. Can she do them and westerns at the same time? Or would she be smarter to stick to westerns, in which she's already attained a stature accorded no other girl in the field?" Prophetically, the author ended her long piece: "Watching Dale on the set, doing her scenes with tireless sparkle, I decided she's likely to find the right answer to her question. Remembering the down-to-earthness which marks her conversation, I think she's a gal who'll be able to face whatever life has to offer."

Today Maxine Garrison is a member of the Rogers business family. She had no way of knowing that seven years later she would meet Dale Evans again on entirely different ground. "I did the article in the light vein," Maxine comments. "But in my heart I knew Dale was seriously perplexed. She seemed to be wanting to go one way while something was constantly pulling her another."

As a result of Maxine Garrison's piece, and the publicity that followed it, Republic Studios got floods of mail. One petition from a Roy Rogers fan club was signed by 3,000 names. "Please don't leave Roy," the youngsters begged Dale. "We love you together." So together Roy Rogers and Dale Evans stayed, making ten more pictures in rapid succession.

The following August, when the Rogers troupe returned from a personal appearance tour, Dale Evans and Roy Rogers were signed for radio by Miles Laboratories.

While on the tour, one morning in Dallas, the gang had just left the Baker Hotel when an explosion rocked the building. A short time before, Dale Evans had barely escaped serious injury in Las Vegas when she walked away from under a balcony seconds before it collapsed. And just before that, a horse she was riding had gone berserk and raced madly four times around the arena before wranglers could stop him and rescue Dale. The unknowing crowd had gone wild, applauding what they thought was an extra bit of incredible horsemanship. And the cowboys all had congratulated Dale, feeling it was almost a miracle that even she had managed to hang on during such a ride. But when finally she reached her dressing room, Dale suffered near hysteria.

Roy and Pat Brady talked it over when the usually plucky woman member of their group began to show increasing nervousness over her repeated brushes with death.

"She needs cheering up, Buck," commented Brady.

"I'll buy her a present," Roy decided. "All girls like presents."

The day Roy handed Dale a small box, he said, "I've a hunch that the good Lord has decided you're a mighty fine partner for me and is saving you for that purpose. We've made seventeen pictures together and no telling how many tours, and our only scars have been narrow escapes. So I've bought you this friendship ring, and I want you to always wear it because I've asked it to guard you wherever you go."

Nobody dreamed that someday the ring would be fashioned into a wedding band.

In early 1947, Dale's family and friends decided that she was displaying some very strange symptoms. She dyed her bleached hair a reddish brown. She bought and furnished a new home. She wrote song after song and took to retrimming hats like mad. Saying she was lonely and homesick, she wrote her mother to come to California for a while. And finally she reached a decision. "Playing in westerns is strictly a second-fiddle job for a woman," the announcement stated. "And I feel I've served my apprenticeship. I thought I might work my way out through radio. I was with Bergen, Carson, Durante and Moore. But where did it lead to? A regular singing spot on Roy Rogers's radio show *Weekly Round-up*." And there were other releases: "I simply can't compete with that horse Trigger. The only chance I have to be billed as a top-liner is to get out of westerns. So I've decided to change my riding pants for an evening gown. I think it might be nice to be kissed by a hero for a change. And I look forward to singing songs with somebody besides a cowboy who only has eyes for his horse."

When Dale finished "The Bells of San Angelo," she firmly believed it would be her last picture with Roy Rogers. And Republic Studios soon formally announced that Dale Evans was slowing her pace from a gallop to a drawing-room glide in a new-type role in a picture titled "The Trespasser." On March 21, 1947, the Hollywood *Reporter* had this to add: "The reason that Dale Evans is no longer leading lady in those Roy Rogers westerns is because of the widespread and false rumors that the two were altar-bound. Too bad."

In May, Dale went on a personal appearance tour as a singer. She was highly successful everywhere and stopped off in Chicago to be on a program that was part of the city's I Am an American Day celebration and enjoyed a reunion with her old friend Fran Allison. In June, Dale went to Atlantic City for an engagement at the Steel Pier.

It so happened that Roy Rogers was in New York at the time, appearing with his thrill circus. One day Roy said to Art Rush, "Say, Buck, I hear Dale Evans is in Atlantic City. Let's run down and see her."

"Why?" Art asked, with much innocence.

"Oh, I don't know," Roy replied, with a shrug. "The fans want her back. And I just thought maybe we might try talking some sense into her head."

Art Rush smiled to himself. And to keep the same knowing smile off the faces of reporters, he suggested that Roy leave his telltale regalia at the hotel during the trip. So the pair headed for Brooks Brothers and carefully selected the cowboy's first "civilian" outfit in years, which Roy calls his store-bought suit. But they need not have bothered. That evening when they were ready to go to Atlantic City, crowds swarmed from everywhere the minute they stepped off the elevator at their hotel. "I do believe that Roy might be the one person in the world who's completely unable to disguise himself," Art Rush says, jokingly.

Recognized again in the audience at the Steel Pier, Roy Rogers was asked to take a bow. After the show, Art and Roy invited Dale to supper. When Roy brought up the subject of movies, Dale cut him off short. "I'm doing okay as a singer, thank you."

When Dale Evans returned from her personal appearance tour, she began another picture, "Slippy McGee." It was destined to be as mediocre as her first effort out of westerns had been. The exhibitors and fans besieged the studio. Have you people in Hollywood lost your minds? Roy Rogers and Dale Evans were a successful team. For heaven's sake, put them back together!

On August 30, Republic Studios announced that Dale Evans was going back into westerns. And on September 2, *Variety* commented: "Could it be love? Roy Rogers and Dale Evans are having dinner together frequently and rumors of a romance are circulating again."

The dinner conversation would have been a disappointment to a lot of people had they been able to tune in. Roy Rogers has what some people might consider old-fashioned ideas about the rearing of children. And he talked to Dale by the hour about his motherless brood, his hopes for them, his disappointments and frustrations, his worries over having to be gone from home so much. Previously, Roy had concluded that he could no longer bear to live in a house that held so many memories, and he had purchased a ranch called Sky Haven at Lake Hughes and had moved his children and their nurses there. Jim Osborne and Art Rush had gone into a tail spin over what they termed another of Roy's ridiculous buys, and although years later Roy was to make his advisers eat crow by selling the isolated property at a nice profit, at the time their argument did have its logical points. Having to drive 55 miles of hairpin curves at all hours in all kinds of weather to go back and forth from home was simply no route for a speed demon like Roy, especially in his disturbed state. Yet Dale Evans understood what Roy was trying to do in choosing to live what everyone called "nine miles from nowhere." He was running away from life, from the world, from grief. And her heart ached anew for the man she increasingly adored.

At this time Roy was preparing to leave California on a rodeo tour. And when Dale decided to go back to westerns, the studio began hurrying the finish of the picture she was making so she could accompany the troupe. The rodeo opened in Philadelphia. From there they went to Detroit, St. Louis, and Chicago.

One night in Chicago, when they already were on their horses awaiting entrance cues, Roy pulled up beside Dale and with no preamble whatsoever said, "Every king needs a queen." Then he drew a tiny jeweler's box from his shirt pocket, took out a small star ruby in a plain gold Tiffany setting, and slipped it on Dale's finger. It so happened that Dale's birthday was near. "What's this for, my birthday?" she said with a laugh, somewhat taken aback. At that moment Roy's entrance cue came and he dashed off on Trigger, waving a hand to Dale, using his fingers like a mute.

"I realized that he was making with a sign language," Dale remarks. "And it came to me that he'd been doing the same thing for weeks, waving in the oddest places, using his fingers in a goofy sort of way." Dale was to get no explanation for all the mysteries until after the rodeo that night, when Roy invited her to go out for a bite to eat. The gang usually went together for a late supper to what they call a ham-and-eggery, but that evening Roy took Dale alone. Shy Roy Rogers ordered a second platter of ham and eggs and a third glass of milk before he could bring himself to pop the question. "I simply couldn't hold any more food," he confesses, "so there was nothing left to do but say that speech."

Ducking his head close to his empty plate, Roy began. "That ring isn't exactly for your birthday, Dale," he said. And his face was solemn with deep emotion. "I know now how much I need you for a partner." Dale tried to say something, but Roy was determined to finish. "And Cheryl and Linda and Dusty could sure use a mother." Then his face crinkled into a grin. "Even Trigger is off his feed."

Dale Evans's heart was pounding. "Just what are you trying to say, Roy?"

The cowboy had what Dale calls the nerve to be surprised. "Why, I'm asking you to marry me, New Year's Eve. . . ."

"Look, Roy," Dale said, "I want to help you all I can. But it takes

85

an awful lot to make a good marriage. And, besides, there are a lot of things you don't know about me."

"I've known more for a long time than you think I know," Roy replied. "And the most important thing that I know right now is that I love you."

Dale's eyes opened wide, filled, and brimmed over. "But you've never said *that* before!"

"Aw, I have, too," Roy argued. "I've been telling you for weeks with my finger signals. It was a code we used back in Duck Run. Look." Then Roy held up one finger, four fingers, three fingers.

When Dale had got it, she laughed through her tears. No wonder children loved this glorious, wonderful man. He was so like a child himself.

Roy and Dale sat in the restaurant until the place closed. When she reached her hotel room, she called California and talked with her son. Then, still in her rodeo regalia, she lay across the bed, staring at the ceiling. "For the first time since I'd been a little girl I felt like I wanted to pray," Dale says. "I just wanted to say thank you to Somebody for all the happiness I was feeling."

To Dale such happiness just seemed too much, too good to be true. But it *was* true, and at last, at long last, she could admit it to herself —she was helplessly, completely, eternally in love with Roy Rogers.

To this day every gift, every letter, every card, every telegram exchanged by Roy and Dale Rogers bears the code numerals 1-4-3. Perhaps Scotland Yard would never find the code baffling, nor would many children past the age of seven. But a lot of Western Union employees over the country have been seen to shake their heads, completely stumped. For their benefit, the Rogerses explain that 1-4-3 means "I love you."

When the eight-week tour was over and the Rogers troupe returned to Hollywood, everybody was all smiles. But there were some words of caution. Western fans would never put up with such foolishness as a romance, they warned. Children would call Roy a sissy. His career might be ruined. Roy Rogers's original contract with

Republic was nearing its end. And there was much speculation in many circles about whether or not a new one would be signed. Nonetheless, on November 19, 1947, *Variety* carried this announcement: "Roy Rogers and Dale Evans will be married December 31."

The columnists never had it so good. Dale Evans—who today has seventeen registered songs to her credit—had a new one out. Ironically, her recording of it was released almost simultaneously with the wedding announcement. Its title: "Don't Ever Fall in Love With a Cowboy (He'll Love His Horse the Best)."

Inevitably the blow fell. One evening in their living room while half listening to the radio, Dale and Tommy heard the voice of Louella Parsons tell the world that Dale Evans had a twenty-year-old son. Dale sat white-faced, almost paralyzed from shock. Then she rose from her chair and went over to put her arms around her son. "It's the best thing that could have happened, Tom. Don't you see? Now I'm really free."

"I'll be grateful to Louella Parsons the rest of my days," Dale says, "for forcing me out of that ridiculous lie."

Later, talking with Roy Rogers, Tommy mentioned that his mother seemed deeply troubled over the effect the marriage might have on Roy's career. "I think she has it in the back of her mind just to bow out and retire from public life," Tommy added.

"No, she mustn't do that," Roy said quietly. "I need her beside me wherever I go. We'll have a lot of jobs but we'll do them together. And from now on we're partners in everything."

Later, in a long letter to his grandparents, Tommy wrote: "Roy Rogers is an exceptional person and I think I love him almost as much as Mother does, and I've asked permission to call him Dad. Everyone remarks that this surely is a marriage that was made in heaven. I pray that is so, for I can't quite forget the years of hell my wonderful mother lived through to earn it."

CHAPTER EIGHT

Roy and Dale Rogers look back and are certain
that no performance they've ever seen or heard of in all their years
of show business has included more ingredients of an entertainer's
nightmare than did the most important one of their lives—their
own wedding.

A short time before the marriage date, it was announced that Roy
and Dale's New Year's Eve ceremony would be performed at the
Flying L Ranch, near Davis, Oklahoma, a place owned by their
long-time friends, Mr. and Mrs. Bill Likins; that only a few relatives and close friends would attend; and that the rites would be
read by the Reverend Dr. Bill Alexander of Oklahoma City, later
the national chaplain of the Republican party, whose good works
in behalf of children had resulted in a great youth foundation.

A few days before the wedding, a blizzard chose to rage through
Oklahoma and midst a mad scramble of timetables and reservations,
Roy and Dale, with Art and Mary Jo Rush, left California earlier
than planned to travel by train instead of plane. When they reached
Oklahoma City, the inevitable swarm of newsmen met them at the
station. The famous couple answered the reporters' questions as best
they could but firmly refused the photographers' requests for a
smooching pose. "We haven't kissed before a camera in nineteen
pictures," Roy said. "And we don't do it now."

Rumors concerning the wedding details had long flown thick and fast. Some had it that Trigger would be Roy's best man. And others that all principals and guests would be in Western attire. But the truth was that Roy had asked his beloved Art Rush to stand up with him. And because on this one occasion they would be not the "King of the Cowboys" and the "Queen of the West," whose lives belonged to the world, but just a couple deeply in love, whose lives belonged to each other, Roy and Dale had decided to wear conventional clothes.

But then there arose the little matter of the boots. "I haven't walked in regular shoes in over ten years," Roy moaned to his manager. "I'll fall down in 'em as sure as shootin'."

"But, Buck," Art argued, "you'll have to be fish or fowl. You can't wear boots with a conservative navy-blue suit. You'll have to wear black shoes."

Suddenly Roy's blue eyes danced with speculation. "But what if I get so nervous before my cue comes," he dropped blandly, "that I have to kick off those nice black shoes and trot down the aisle in my socks?"

Art Rush knew that his kid was up to old tricks. And it was so good to see him, after such a long period of gloom, simply giddy with happiness that Art was tempted to join in. Yet he knew that the cowboy, pushed far enough, was the proverbial "little man who can do it." So Art quickly gave in in favor of Roy's wearing boots. "And when he got all dressed up in that dark suit and white shirt," Art adds with a fond smile, "he looked so handsome and his face was shining so, I knew I wouldn't really have cared if he'd decided to go barefoot!"

Roy Rogers is always ready at least thirty minutes before any appointment. And it is commonly known that if there is anything he hates almost as much as he does a lie, it's the selfish habit some people have of being late. "Rustling the next fellow's time is as bad as rustling his cattle, and being late is nothing but a varmint's brand of meanness," Roy has been heard to say on many an occasion. At home or on tour, Roy makes it his personal business to see that everybody stays ahead of schedule. Going up and down halls, knocking on doors, he hollers his premature warning, "Come on now, gang, let's get on our horses. It's late. Let's get to moving."

But on this wedding evening nobody had to prod anybody. Everyone, including the bride, was dressed and ready far ahead of the appointed time. But as it turned out, they need not have hurried. The ceremony was two hours late!

As the set hour drew nearer and nearer, and Dr. Alexander didn't arrive, Roy became difficult even for Art Rush to handle. "I can pull a lot of strings in this world," the best man tried to reason with the groom. "But one thing I can't do is call curtain time for a wedding when there's no minister backstage, onstage, or out front to perform the ceremony!"

As everyone unhappily suspected, there was a man somewhere on a snow-covered road at that very moment, glancing at his watch even more frantically than Roy Rogers. Poor Dr. Alexander was still battling—as he'd been doing for many hours—snow, ice, and endless car troubles, trying to make his way from Oklahoma City to the Flying L Ranch.

"When it was finally decided to send out a searching party," Mary Jo says, "I left Dale in her room in the care of her parents. Knowing how Roy reacts to any delay, I could just imagine what was going on in his room. And when I opened the door and took one look, I knew I'd been right. So I settled in there to hold up my husband while my husband held up the groom!"

When even Dale began to show signs of strain, Tommy Fox—who himself had not long ago arrived with two half-frozen girls in tow, his sweetheart Barbara Miller and her sister Ethelyn—shooed everyone from his mother's room and took over the bride alone.

By the time Dr. Alexander safely reached the Flying L Ranch, everyone was in such a state and so relieved to see him that few took any notice of the clothes he was wearing. But when things calmed down, Bill Alexander—who today is one of the Rogerses' most cherished friends and in whose good works they share—had to take quite a ribbing. Obviously he had heard the wild rumors and believed them. For from old-time frock coat to string tie, Bill had arrived in the garb of a preacher of the Old West! "I guess I just fell for the adage that when one is in Rome, one should shoot Roman candles," he later commented sheepishly.

When at last the string quartet, which was to furnish the wedding music, could start tuning up in earnest, Art Rush gave his charge a final going-over. To his dismay, he found that Roy's white shirt was thoroughly soaked with perspiration, the collar wilted. Quickly rummaging through the groom's luggage, Art found only brightly embroidered cowboy shirts. Roy, inexperienced in the ways of white shirts, had brought not one spare! Desperate, Art grabbed a fresh white shirt from his own bag while Roy hastily unbuttoned his wilted one. "Perhaps those who supervise collar ads would not have okayed the fit," Rush says. "But I tied Roy's tie extra tight and hurriedly shortened the shirt sleeves with the aid of rubber bands."

Ready once more, the groom and his best man stood in their doorway, awaiting their entrance cue. Softly the musicians were playing the prenuptial number, Roy and Dale's favorite—"Home on the Range." Then the quartet went into the introduction of the "Bridal Chorus," and Dr. Alexander walked slowly down the hall, on into the living room, to take his place before the mistletoe-banked fireplace.

Art Rush heard the familiar swell of the music, the tum-tum-tee-tum getting louder, announcing the coming of the bride, and he strained to listen for the agreed cue—the opening of Dale's door that would tell them she was emerging, that the time had come for Roy and him to start down the hall. It was planned for the bride and groom to meet at the entrance to the living room so that they could take the last steps toward the fireplace-altar together.

But the bride's door remained closed.

Weakly, Roy whispered to Art, his voice a plea for reassurance, "Nothing else can go wrong, can it, Buck?"

Art Rush hoped that he could manage more strength in his voice than he felt in his knees. "No, kid, there's nothing left to happen. It's set up. The show is on. Our cue will come any second now."

But the cue *didn't* come.

"*Here comes the bride, here comes the bride. . . .*" The quartet played one chorus, two choruses, three. Still no bride came. And then through the music Art Rush was sure he was hearing the sound of running water, flushing plumbing, scurrying feet. Discreetly turning his head, he peered over his shoulder. His heart leaped! Spirals of black smoke were oozing from around the doorframe of Dale's room!

Without a word, and as slowly as possible, Art walked away from Roy's side. With years of theater discipline behind him, Roy Rogers just stood. "But sweating bullets, of course," Roy comments. "I didn't dream there was anything really wrong, though. I just figured that Mary Jo was fiddling with Dale's hair or lipstick, and I was furious." And it was not until after the ceremony that Roy or any of the guests learned what had happened.

While waiting at the door, her back to the room, straining to hear the music, Mary Jo Rush had suddenly smelled something burning. Wheeling, she saw a wastebasket—probably ignited by a guest's cigarette—crackling with flames. And before she even could move, the draperies on a nearby window were afire.

Frantic, Mary Jo pressed a buzzer that would summon help from the kitchen. Then she grabbed a carafe and dashed water on the draperies. Somehow Mary Jo got the burning wastebasket to the bathroom and dumped its contents. And leaving the smoldering shell on the tile floor there, she refilled the carafe and ran back to throw more water on the draperies. "It was not until then," she recounts, "that I remembered Dale and saw that she'd simply vanished."

Incredibly, Dale Evans was completely unaware of the commotion. "I was standing beside Mary Jo with my ear to the door while the quartet was playing 'Home on the Range,'" Dale says, "when suddenly something struck me like a bolt from the blue. I had heard and done that song countless times, but it seemed to have new meaning. And for the first time, I think, I really realized just what I was taking on. 'In a few more minutes,' I thought, 'it's going to be *my* responsibility to make a home, a real home, for Roy and those three babies.' And I felt panicky."

Almost as if mesmerized, Dale walked away from the door and found refuge in a nearby closet. For the second time in recent months she felt like praying. But this time she didn't stop with just feeling like it. "Oh, Lord," her lips moved soundlessly, "please don't let me make a mess out of *this* job. Please help me to make a go of this marriage and to be a good mother to Arlene's little children. . . ."

"Now I can look back and see that there was purpose even in that little fire," Dale says. "The delay it caused provided me with time for an unreal experience I've never forgot. And it was symbolic, I think, that I had to go in a dark clothes closet and hide my face in the hanging garments there before I could bring myself to talk with God."

As from far off, Mary Jo's cries had finally reached Dale. "Dale, for heaven's sake, where are you?" Mary Jo was almost weeping. "The house is on fire!"

Art Rush reached the scene just as several servants arrived from the kitchen. And without much further ado, the fire, having done little damage, soon was out. Taking a deep breath, Art returned to Roy's side. And as the quartet played what Roy Rogers estimates was the fortieth chorus of "Here Comes the Bride," the bride finally came.

At the sight of her, a giant sigh rippled across the living room. The group congregated there had proved themselves controlled beyond belief. In an agony of suspense, not one had moved.

It is said that all brides are beautiful. But anyone who has ever seen Dale Evans has to agree that in the matter of beauty she always has a head start. "And at her wedding she was a vision," reported Alice Likins, the hostess.

For her bridal gown Dale chose a simple Wedgwood-blue wool suit-dress. Her small off-the-face hat, fashioned from the same woolen fabric, was trimmed with veiling that ranged in shades of blue from Wedgwood to the navy of her plain calf pumps. She carried a small bouquet of pink rosebuds. And except for her engagement ring and

93

a small gold ruby-studded watch Roy had given her as a wedding present, her only jewelry was an heirloom cameo brooch, a gift from one of Roy's elderly fans.

After the groom had slipped on her finger the wedding band made from the friendship ring, and Dr. Alexander had pronounced them husband and wife, Roy Rogers took Dale Evans Rogers in his arms and kissed her. At that instant came the clicks of several smuggled cameras. And later, carried by newspapers across the nation, the pose was to awe millions of fans who had never seen their cowboy hero kiss a girl. The picture's caption: WHY, ROY!

As tradition usually has it, a reception and wedding supper followed the ceremony. But as tradition never has it, the guests stayed on and on. They were marooned by the blizzard!

About 3 A.M., after many pots of coffee had been brewed and consumed, and all conversation was wearing a little thin, Roy Rogers took the bull by the horns and rose from his chair. "I hope you folks will excuse us," he said, "but Dale and I have to turn in. We're going squirrel hunting early tomorrow morning."

The roomful of people howled. But, as usual, Roy Rogers was telling the truth. He and Dale *had* planned a squirrel hunt. And several hours later, squirrel hunting they went.

After a few more days of hunting and resting at the Flying L Ranch, Roy and Dale Rogers went to Texas for a brief visit with the Smith family. They returned to Hollywood on January 19. And on January 24, they made their first public appearance as Mr. and Mrs. on horseback when they led the Discovery Day parade at Coloma, California, which marked the opening of the centennial celebration of the discovery of gold at Sutter's Mill.

What Roy and Dale Rogers discovered for themselves, however, as they made their way through a cheering throng of 30,000 that day, was that the fans were delighted about their marriage! For the fifth consecutive year, Roy had just been named top moneymaking star in the western field. And Dale had been included in the top ten. It was the first time a woman had ever crashed the annual poll. Yet a short time later, when Roy signed a new agreement with

94

Republic, Dale was strongly warned to stay out of the cowboy's pictures lest his career be ruined.

But there were many tours and rodeos on the agenda. And it wasn't long before Roy proudly presented Dale with her own mount, Pal, a Palomino stallion, smaller than Trigger but closely resembling him. And as soon as a tailor could make it possible, Dale began appearing in regalia identical to Roy's. The team created a stir wherever they went, the "Queen" a miniature replica of her "King."

For any team to be under separate managers is bound to result in difficulties. But for two stars as much in demand as Roy Rogers and Dale Evans, it was an impossible situation. Finally Art Rush managed a talk with Dale. "With Danny Winkler handling your affairs and me handling Roy's, schedules are beginning to snarl hopelessly," Art began. "Things are simply in a mess, Dale. What do you think we should do?"

Dale Evans had long been ashamed of the way she had treated Art Rush. And she was as deeply fond of him as Roy was. "There's only one thing to do, Art," Dale said. "I'll have to leave Danny. But I know he'll understand."

"Well, I've been figuring," Art said, "and I think five thousand dollars would adequately compensate Winkler for terminating your contract." Dale agreed that the amount was more than fair. "But there's one catch," Rush went on. "Jim Osborne is the tightest business manager in the world and he would never agree to our buying the contract. He's always said I botched matters pretty badly in letting you go in the first place. So I'll have to pay Winkler out of my own pocket."

Dale Evans was plunged between the devil and the deep sea. She recognized her responsibility in the situation, and she knew a penalty, even one of $2,500, was her just deserts. But she also knew that Roy Rogers would have the laugh of his life if he learned that her early resentment and jealousy of him had ended up costing her such a wad of cold cash. Nonetheless, she said, "I insist on paying half of the five thousand." But for Dale Evans, the voice was uncertain.

Art Rush laughed, reading her mind. "Okay, but I'll tell you what.

Let's make a pact. I won't ever tell Roy if you won't ever tell Jim." And with relief and much laughter the conspirators called Danny Winkler, who agreed to the plot.

For more than seven years now, Roy Rogers and Jim Osborne have generously complimented Art and Dale on the painless handling of a problem that might have been costly or difficult. When they read this, however, the jig will be up!

Soon after they became engaged, Roy and Dale had decided that the ranch at Lake Hughes would not only be an inconvenient place for them to live but that it was also a dreary spot for the children. And just before they left for the wedding, they purchased a home built by the late Noah Beery in the Hollywood Hills.

One day, soon after they returned from their honeymoon, Dale was at the new house, readying things for everybody to move in, when she received a call from Art Rush. He was very excited. "Sit down before I tell you this news, Dale, so you won't fall down. Are you ready?"

"Ready," Dale said.

"You are wanted for the lead in the British company of 'Annie, Get Your Gun'!"

Annie, Get Your Gun was big-time musical comedy. Here was the chance Dale Evans had dreamed of and worked and hoped for all the years of her life. Art Rush expected awed silence, screams of joy, shocked tears. Any response from his client but the one he got.

"Oh, golly, Art, I'm sorry, but I couldn't possibly consider leaving now," Dale said, without hesitating. "We'll be moving into the house in a few days, and I'm in the midst of having a trophy room built for Roy's awards and stuff, and we've just learned the children were exposed to the chicken pox, and Tommy and Barbara are talking about getting married, and. . . ."

Art Rush sighed as he replaced the receiver. In life, as in show business, timing was the thing. That Man upstairs was some clock watcher.

96

CHAPTER NINE

Roy and Dale were not married long before they began to realize that it is one thing to talk about uniting two broken families—making from the ruins one happy family—and quite another thing to do it.

"Even as I unpacked boxes and barrels," Dale says, "I could see how many remnants of lives we were trying to mend together. There were all the things Tommy and I had accumulated through the years, his college and army stuff. There was the incredible amount of paraphernalia that goes with three small children. Roy's belongings from the ranch at Lake Hughes, and the overflow he'd put in storage when he moved with the children out there. And piles and piles of wedding gifts."

One morning as Dale, garbed in jeans, sneakers, and an old shirt, was working feverishly at the chores of settling, Art Rush happened to stop by. He surveyed the hodgepodge of colors and moods—a mixture a friend later dubbed "cowboy modern"—and exclaimed, "For goodness' sake, Dale, why haven't you called in a decorator to help you?"

Dale burst into laughter. "Now, can't you just imagine Roy Rogers surrounded by Dorothy Draper?" she asked.

But if Dale Evans Rogers completely understood and deeply loved the simplicity, informality, and sentimentality of her man, and knew

97

how to arrange a comfortable, livable setting for him, she soon had to face the fact that it takes more than a house to make a home. For Roy's children were open in their resentment of her.

True, the girls had long known Dale and had shown warm fondness for her the many times they had visited the studio. And even the baby had greeted her with delight on the occasions Roy had taken her to see the children at Sky Haven. Yet when the newlyweds returned from their honeymoon, Dale was met by a hostile seven-year-old Cheryl and a brooding four-year-old Linda. Roy, Jr., called Dusty, was just fifteen months old.

Dale Rogers was deeply shocked and frightened, but she tried to make light of the situation when finally she talked with Roy. "Golly, what do you think they were doing while we were gone," she said with a lame smile, "reading the Cinderella story?"

Whatever Roy Rogers felt, he tried to seem undisturbed. "Oh, you know how unpredictable children are," he said reassuringly. "And they were overtired and overexcited about our return." He patted his wife's hand. "I've been all the parents they've had for quite a while now, honey. Maybe you're going to have to put up with a little jealousy."

Actually, before his marriage to Dale, Roy Rogers had talked often and at length with his children about the new mother who was coming to live with them, and he had explained all the details that youngsters seem to need, answering all their questions. So when the children continued to show every sign of emotional upset, Roy and Dale hit upon the idea that they were fearing the unknown, worrying about the move to the Hollywood Hills. After all, they reasoned, the little girls had not forgot the sudden loss of their mother, which came without even a warning to soften the terrifying blow. And a short time later they had been uprooted from the only home they had known. And, as even Roy now realized, there had been no happiness for anybody at Sky Haven. So stop worrying, Roy and Dale kept telling each other, things will straighten out when we all get moved into the new home. But things were not to straighten out for a long, long time.

"For the rest of my days," Dale Rogers comments, "meatballs and spaghetti will smell like trouble to me. Chasing success all my life, I'd never had much time for cooking. But meatballs and spaghetti was one thing I knew how to prepare well. So, eager and ambitious, I added to the general confusion on moving day by making a large pot of the stuff." Late in the afternoon, when the children arrived with their nurse, the trio took one look at the strange surroundings and looked very unhappy and forlorn. When finally they were fed and tucked in their beds, exhausted Roy and Dale and Tommy sat down to heaping platefuls of the pungent food Dale had prepared. "Roy and Tommy at least made a pretense, winding spaghetti with their forks and spoons, but I took one whiff of that spicy, rich sauce and knew I couldn't swallow a bite." Finally everybody gave up and turned in for the night. It was a bad beginning.

The next morning, as Dale sat at the kitchen table sipping coffee, Dusty toddled in. In one hand he was clutching a toy replica of Trigger. In the other he carried one of Dale's hats. "Lady go bye-bye now," he announced hopefully, extending the hat. Tears sprang to Dale's eyes but somehow she managed to smile. "How about you and me going up to your room and getting on the floor with your blocks and making a stable for old Trigger?" she suggested, brightly. Dusty was all for the idea. And when finally the stable was completed, and Virginia, the nurse, appeared to ready the boy for his morning nap, Dusty was more than willing to hug Dale tightly when she prepared to leave his room.

Dale Rogers went downstairs, her heart lighter than it had been in many days. She went to the living room to get back to the business of arranging furniture, and was changing the position of a chair when Linda walked in. Anger quickly enveloped the small face. "Don't push that chair around," the child ordered. "That's my mommy's chair, not yours."

Dale's insides quaked. But still encouraged by her recent, if temporary, success with Dusty, she left the chair in the center of the room and managed to walk calmly toward Linda. Dropping to her knees, Dale gazed into the little girl's troubled brown eyes. "Your mommy has gone away to heaven, honey. And Tommy's daddy has gone away too. For a long time we've all been in a bad fix. But now we have a *whole* family. And we all belong to each other and everything we own belongs to each other too. That's what a family is for, Linda. To love and to share."

The child made no answer and Dale rose. Matter-of-factly she returned to the chair. "You know, Linda, I'm sure glad you came in here just now," Dale said, her voice simulating a problem. "I can't seem to get that chair in the right place, and I need help. Since you've known the chair longer than I have, maybe you can suggest the right place for it."

When the chair was at last set to Linda's satisfaction, Dale sighed. "I'm hungry, baby. Let's go out to the kitchen and see about some lunch. Emily, our new housekeeper, is a mighty nice lady. But she's new in this family too, and I'll bet she's having a time trying to find things." Linda hesitated a brief instant, searching Dale's face. Then she placed her small hand in Dale's and together they went to the kitchen to help Emily with lunch.

Unhappily, Cheryl, the eldest, and with the mind of a Philadelphia lawyer, was neither so young as Dusty nor so tractable as Linda. She gave her campaign more thought. And as time passed, along with showing resentment as the other children did—by alternately refusing to eat, brush teeth, take baths, go to bed on time, pick up toys— Cheryl became increasingly impertinent. The situation reached a climax of sorts one evening when Cheryl was slated to attend an old-fashioned tent meeting with a family friend.

The week before, Cheryl had made quite a scene at dinner by announcing there was a tent meeting that night which she wanted to attend. Patiently, Dale explained to her new daughter that it was far too late to make arrangements, that Roy, busy making a new picture, would be late coming in, that it was Virginia's night off, and that she herself couldn't leave the other children to take Cheryl. But the girl made a terrible fuss and wept copiously. Finally Dale placated Cheryl by promising that she could go the following week. It so happened that Roy and Dale were scheduled for a radio broadcast that particular evening and Dale went to no end of trouble to arrange for a friend to take Cheryl to the meeting. Dale suggested to Emily that they serve dinner early so the excited girl would not be rushed.

Late in the afternoon of the great day, Dale proposed that Cheryl get bathed and dressed before eating so she could be ready to leave immediately after dinner. "Get dressed for what?" Cheryl asked, all innocence.

"For the tent meeting," said Dale.

"Oh, that," Cheryl replied airily. "I've changed my mind. I'm not going."

As Dale Rogers admits, she finally saw red. And in anger it came to her that children need firm discipline as much as warm love. "I realized I was being unfair to all of us by letting the children think I was a spineless adult. And worse, that I was being unfair to Cheryl by giving her such free rein." Dale knew the moment had come to act, that she had already waited too long. And for the first time she faced one of Roy's children sternly. And although Cheryl sobbed that she didn't need a bath, that she wasn't hungry, that she had a terrible headache, Dale ordered the girl to get cleaned up and dressed, to eat every bite of her dinner, to don her wraps, and go to the meeting.

"We had meatballs and spaghetti that night too," Dale says with a sad smile. "And because I made Cheryl eat, I cleaned my plate also." But when the door had finally closed on the rebellious child, Dale's poise crumpled. She was reaching the end of the rope and was sick at heart.

Roy Rogers watched proceedings grimly. He realized that any interference by him would ruin Dale's every chance. If just once he sided with Dale, the children would feel she had robbed them of their father completely. "No matter how much it hurt, I kept my mouth shut," Roy says. "Love and respect are things you can't force on anybody, much less on children. I knew that nobody could win them for Dale but herself. And nobody could have tried harder than Dale."

Roy Rogers stayed on the sidelines—that is, until his daughters began a rash of lies. No matter what naughtiness was committed, neither seemed able to remember who the culprit was. Finally Roy invited his daughters into his trophy room and shut the door. He began by talking quietly and earnestly as he had always done. But the girls assumed exaggerated poses of boredom and disgust. "I raised my voice and began to lecture," Roy says. "I'll bet I talked for forty-five minutes. But the girls remained insolent, refusing to be reached. So I stood up and removed my cowboy belt. I placed one little girl and then the other across my lap and whacked each of them a couple of times on the place that was made for whacking when all else in the world fails." The girls backed away from their father, stunned. Then they fell into each other's arms, weeping as if he had broken every bone in their bodies. But Roy could detect relief in their crying too. Daddy was still Daddy, they were no doubt realizing. Dale hadn't changed him a bit. No matter how much he loved his wife and wanted peace for her sake, he wasn't putting up with dishonesty in any form. Lying was *out*. Roy hugged and kissed the girls after spanking them and said, "I'm sorry I had to whip you. But I'll add an extra lick every day until you learn to stop lying." It was the girls' last offense.

Later, when Roy sent the girls to their rooms, Dale was nowhere in sight. Unable to bear the sounds which were coming from the trophy room, she had fled from the house and was hiding in the garage.

As days turned into months, Dale was so occupied at home that except for her weekly appearances on the Roy Rogers radio show, sponsored by Quaker Oats, little was being heard of her in the entertainment world. She seemed to be forgetting even her career in her efforts to do everything possible to properly and affectionately establish herself in the new household.

"From remarks the children dropped, I decided they shied away from me because they didn't like the way I looked," Dale says. "So I threw away my hair bleach forever, the false eyelashes, and other stuff. I got to the point where I used no make-up except a bit of lipstick." One day Cheryl studied a filled ash tray. "What makes you so nervous?" she asked.

"And why do you think I'm nervous?" Dale wanted to know.

"Because you smoke so much. I wish you wouldn't. My mommy didn't smoke."

When Cheryl had left the room, Dale snatched her package of cigarettes and threw them in a wastebasket. She has never smoked since. "I kept hoping that if I did everything to please them, they'd finally want to please me," Dale says. "And I simply was determined to make Roy happy, to make a home for his heartbroken brood, and to make *a* marriage work for myself."

But Dale Evans, who had dedicated her life to making enough money to feed and educate a son, did not always know how to go about the domesticity for which she yearned. She suffered cake failures, burned a 10-pound roast to a crisp lump; and although she had a flair for fabrics and colors and knew a great deal about trimming perky hats, her first efforts at lengthening the little girls' dresses resulted in hems that sagged sadly. But Dale kept on trying. Most of her days were given to the children's clothes, food, and activities. She planned picnics for them when Roy was away, outings for the whole family on weekends. She took the girls shopping with her, consulting with them on choices, discussing prices. When she didn't join in their games, she supervised. And regularly she sat in on music lessons, conferred with teachers, accompanied the children to the pediatrician's office.

Of all the things she did, the one thing Dale didn't do was to try to bury the children's memory of their mother. Periodically Dale picked flowers in the garden with the children and took them to visit the cemetery. She often talked, especially to little Dusty, about Arlene. And from the day they moved in the house, Arlene's picture had been prominently placed in each child's room.

If, as time passed, the children seemed to be giving Dale less trouble, they still were giving her little love. Emily and Virginia, who today still compose the Rogerses' domestic staff, had only admiration and sympathy for Dale's efforts. And although Roy was insistent on no direct butting in, the housekeeper and nurse helped in every way they could. Tommy Fox, instinctively liked by the Rogers trio but later ignored when they found in him no ally, worried continuously about the situation that often threatened never to improve. Although he was relieved to see that no matter what happened, the love between Roy and Dale themselves seemed to deepen with each passing day, Tommy secretly prayed for guidance in helping them to find a way to enjoy that love.

Back in college again, having served his stint in the Army, Tommy was particularly interested in love and marriage at the time. He was planning a summer wedding with Barbara Miller, his long-time sweetheart, who played the organ at the church where Tommy directed a youth choir.

"I often tried to talk to Mother," Tommy says. "But she hated for me to worry, and she always put me off by assuring me that the children were settling down." But one afternoon, after a dreadfully trying day, Tommy found his mother staring into space in her room. He asked her if she wanted to talk about it. "I just don't know what else to *do*," Dale said. "I'm so confused I never know if I'm afoot or horseback. And what worries me most is that it's dangerous for little children to be filled with so much resentment. They aren't eating or sleeping as well as they should. And they cry too easily. If only there were some way I could *reach* them. Something new we could do *together* to give us a fresh start." Dale sighed wearily. "Well, I simply can't imagine what it would be. I've tried everything there is to try. And there's everything in this house to make people happy."

"No, Mother, you're wrong," Tommy said, as he faced Dale solemnly. "The loving spirit of the Risen Christ and the wisdom of Almighty God are not in this house. Why don't you start the children in Sunday school? That would be something new for you all to do together, as you say. And all kids need the kind of security that only real faith can bring."

Dale stared at her son, surprised. "I think *I* ought to know, Mother," Tom Fox went on. "I had some pretty mixed-up feelings before I realized that Christ could be a real thing in my life and I joined the church. I'll never forget how wonderful the pastor was to me and what a fine bunch of young people I met there." Tommy paused. "Think back over the years, Mother. Things might have been a *lot* different for me if I hadn't given over to Christ and started asking Him His will for my life."

The next Sunday, more desperate than confident, Dale dressed up the children and to Sunday school they all went. Shy at first in such strange surroundings, Cheryl and Linda stayed close to Dale. And when a larger child approached Dusty, the little boy cried, and flew into Dale's arms. Her eyes misty, Dale hugged Dusty as if she'd never let him go. It was the first time any of the children had treated her in any fashion as a *mother*.

But in the ways of children, Dale's small charges were reluctant to leave when Sunday school was over. "Why don't we stay for church?" the girls wanted to know. Dale smiled. "I think Dusty's had enough for his first visit," she explained, "but next Sunday we'll talk to him beforehand about staying in the nursery while we attend services." And the next Sunday they did.

The children always returned for dinner on Sundays bubbling over with exciting tales for their father and Virginia and Emily. Dale felt increasing surges of happiness when the children showed that their "we" included her, when they unfailingly turned toward her for confirmation of details. And in a matter of weeks a great change was creeping over the Roy Rogers household. "Whatever new the children learned at Sunday school and wanted to do at home, they turned to me as leader," Dale says. One day Linda asked if she might say grace. Then at the next meal, Cheryl wanted to take over. Even little Dusty howled to try. So to settle all arguments, Dale suggested that they try a sort of round-the-table grace, to give each member of the family a chance to say whatever words of thanks he chose. Dale began reading Bible stories to the children. And together they learned the Lord's Prayer and the Twenty-third Psalm. Evenings, the youngsters insisted more and more on gathering around the piano while

Dale played and led in the singing of hymns. And, eyes shining, they helped her arrange a small family altar where they gathered for bedtime prayers.

"Sunday school and church aren't just places to take children on Sunday," Dale soon confided to Roy. "They can last all week long. How about going with us sometime?"

Roy smiled at the woman who was beginning to look again like the happy girl he had married. "I'm afraid churches weren't made for the likes of me," he finally said. And when Dale tried to insist, Roy went on, "Look, honey, I work hard all week. Sunday is the only day I have to rest."

But Roy Rogers was neither unmindful of nor ungrateful for the changed atmosphere in his home. And one evening he tried to thank Tommy. "Son, that idea of yours seems to have worked. Worked amazingly."

"I doubt that it was really *my* idea, Dad," Tom Fox said. "I prayed for guidance and I guess I got it." When Roy looked puzzled, Tommy smiled. "Don't be so surprised, Dad. This certainly isn't the first time such a thing has happened."

One evening the minister of their church stopped by to see Dale and the children. Roy was very quiet at first, as he so often is with strange adults. But before the minister left, Roy had been drawn to him, and thus began a friendship and a series of long talks they had together. Before long Roy confessed that there was one thing that always had kept him from the church, that the answer to a question that had burned within him for years simply was not there. During all his years of working with children, on all his thousands of hospital visits, Roy had ended up with asking, Why, if God is loving and good, does He let so many innocent little children suffer afflictions?

"Why?" Roy raised his voice. Then he said, almost to himself, "And why didn't I get to be a doctor so I could help some of those kids?"

The minister saw gentle love for all mankind in Roy's questions. And he saw personal frustration too—a small boy trying to fix a

106

puppy's broken leg on the deck of a houseboat, a lad caring for stray animals on a farm, a youth gazing longingly at the buildings of a great university, a weary young man falling asleep in night school, a cowboy who finally had been able to feed the hunger of his body, but never the hunger of his soul. Roy Rogers still was consumed by the desire for the power to heal.

Finally the minister said patiently, "Perhaps, Roy, this is the life in which we see things from the back of the tapestry—the raw edges and loose ends—the life in which we ask questions but don't always receive clear, tidy answers."

Sadly, the minister soon was to have cause to remember those talks, to know that Roy Rogers had been much nearer to finding his answer than either of them had dreamed.

Breakfast is a favorite meal at the Roy Rogers home. And Roy, an early riser, often joins in the cooking. He has a special way of frying eggs, very fast in very hot grease, so that they turn golden around the edges but stay soft in the center. And anyone who has ever tasted his biscuits will vouch that they are the best. One Sunday morning when all the food was readied and the family had gathered at the table, and Dale, Tommy, the children, Emily, and Virginia each had had his turn at grace—saying in their own words anything they cared to say, thanking the Lord for His many blessings—Linda turned to her father. "What's the matter with *you?*" she asked. "Why don't you ever say anything, Daddy? Don't you know how to talk to God?"

Roy Rogers ducked his head, squirming. And then at that instant the telephone rang. Roger Cunningham, Roy's boating and fishing companion, wanted to know if he was ready to leave for the day. "I was saved by the bell that time," Roy recounts, "because when I returned to the table, Linda was busy finishing her breakfast, anxious to get off to Sunday school, and apparently had forgot her question. But I didn't forget it. And I thought about it all day. I had a sort of guilty feeling, as if in some way I was letting Dale and the kids down.

And I realized too that I was beginning to feel a little left out at home." And before his outing was over, Roy Rogers had made up his mind. He was going to church with his family the next Sunday to try to see just what it was they were finding there.

While Roy was fishing with Roger Cunningham, Dale was sitting beside Tommy and the children at church. During an organ solo Tommy leaned over to his mother. "The good Lord has done an awful lot for you and the kids, Mom. But don't you think you'd be even happier if you *joined* the church and gave yourself completely to God?"

Dale looked into her son's face that is so much like her own. "One doesn't have to *join* a church to work with God, honey," she said, softly. And she patted Tommy's hand. "You don't have to worry any more. Honest, I'm all right now."

"But is everything all right with your *soul*, Mother?"

Tommy's question hung in the air like a giant icicle. And then the congregation was rising for prayer.

After services Tommy met Barbara and went to her home for dinner. "But every hissing turn of the tires kept echoing Tommy's question as I drove home," Dale says. *Is everything all right with your soul?*

When finally she reached the house in the Hollywood Hills, Dale turned the children over to Emily and Virginia for the first time in many weeks. She went to her bedroom and fell face down on the corduroy spread. "The years of my life seemed to be peering at me from crazy angles," Dale says. "I remembered the early religious training my parents had tried to give me, the decision I'd made for Christianity when I was ten, in Osceola, Arkansas. And the way I'd strayed away after my high-school elopement. From then on I'd thought only of a successful career and financial security. I forgot that such things as the Bible and prayers even existed. And it dawned on me that my reasons for finally remembering were pretty selfish ones." Finally Dale wept. Then she picked up the phone and dialed Barbara's number. "Tommy," she said, "I've changed my mind, son. I've decided to join the church."

108

A few weeks later Al Rackin, Roy and Dale's publicity director, arrived at the Rogerses' home with Lee Green, the photographer, to shoot some stills. Later Roy worked with them in the back yard, posing for pictures with his dogs. When he returned to the house, he came upon Dale sitting on the porch. Wearing her cowgirl blouse, her divided riding skirt, her holster with its six-shooter around her waist, her Stetson pushed back on her head, she was sewing.

"Good night, honey, don't you ever rest?" Roy said with concern. "The children will run you ragged if you let them. There's no sense in their coming to you every time they need a button sewed or a hem mended. We can afford to hire a seamstress, you know."

Dale cast a firm eye on her husband. "Now look, sir, I had to listen to you for years about the way you wanted your children reared. Time and again you told me you wanted them to be healthy, normal, unaffected youngsters—untainted by fame and wealth. You said you wanted them to grow up with a proper sense of values, knowing how to be saving and self-reliant. Well, if I'm going to teach these things to the children, I have to set an example. I have to practice what I preach. Little people are mimics, Roy. They don't imitate what we *say;* they imitate what we *do.*"

Dale Evans knew full well that she was bringing no news to her husband, that there was little anybody in the world could teach Roy Rogers about the ways of children. And Roy knew she knew. "Bless that gal of mine," Roy says. "I could see her nimble mind working overtime. She was pitching for me to go to church regularly with her and the children, of course. And although she's too smart to ever press, she simply never lets go of an idea she thinks is right."

As time passed, Dale continued to cooperate with God in every way she could think of. One evening, as he prepared to retire, Roy found a Bible on his bedside table. "What's this for?" Roy asked his wife.

"Oh, since you've lost your old one, I thought I'd better get you a new one," Dale answered matter-of-factly.

Roy Rogers had never owned a Bible in his life. Sheepishly he picked it up and scanned a few pages. When he had closed the Bible, he said to Dale, "You know, honey, there's some common-sense stuff in there that I've been quoting for years. I never dreamed it came from the Bible." Dale smiled and kissed him good night.

"A turning point came," Roy Rogers says, "when Dale gave me a suggestion about speaking in public." The "King of the Cowboys" was dressing one night for a benefit performance when suddenly he confided to his wife, "I just think there's something wrong with me, honey. I risk my life over and over while making movies and performing in rodeos, and it never fazes me. But I seem to die a thousand deaths at the very thought of having to make a simple speech. I've always been like that. The musical part of a program, my shooting act, Trigger's tricks—I handle all that with no fear. But when I go to open my mouth—wham, I get sick all over."

"The Lord gave you a lot of talents, Roy," Dale said. "And if you want more, you'll have to ask for His help. Why don't you ask God to speak *through* you, honey?"

Roy Rogers was skeptical. Nonetheless, when Art Rush picked him up later, he discussed the problem with his manager and close friend. "Dale says I should just ask God to help me talk," Roy concluded.

Art Rush, a sincerely religious person all his life, said, "Well, why don't you try it?"

"But how will I know when I'm really speaking to God? How will I know when He's hearing me?"

"Buck," Rush said, patiently, "trying to tell somebody how they'll know when they're feeling the presence of God is like trying to tell them how they'll know when they're in love, or what it's like to hold your own baby in your arms for the first time. But I can say this much—when the time comes, you won't need anybody to tell you, you'll *know!*"

"I knew that both Dale and Art deeply believed in the advice they were trying to give me," Roy says, "and I knew that they really loved me and were trying to help. But I honestly had no intentions of taking their advice."

The occasion began as so many others had done. And when Roy heard the emcee introducing him, and the wild roar that followed the mention of his name, the cowboy's knees suddenly seemed filled with bubbles and the familiar pounding hit his chest. "This time I simply can't go out and face all those people," he said to himself, desperately. "I'll never be able to live up to their expectations." Then Roy felt the reassuring pressure of Art's hand on his shoulder, finally a gentle shove.

"As I emerged from the wings, bowing and smiling," Roy says, "I found myself saying silently, 'Now, Lord, You know as well as I do that I can't do this job on my own. Please help me to relax so what I say to these folks will mean something.' And when the crowd quieted and I began talking, I actually found myself getting out words in a way I'd never been able to do before. Now, don't get me wrong. I made no great speech, but I did manage to say the things I really wanted to say. And I felt so much easier, as if I weren't alone on that stage any more. It was just as if Somebody were talking *through* me—like Dale had said."

The Saturday night before Easter a group of friends, celebrating the completion of a picture, gathered at the Rogerses' home. "Dale had had a full day," Roy says. "The children had been so excited about Easter baskets and egg hunts and bunnies. And Dale had just put the last stitch on the girls' frilly dresses right before the company arrived. It was getting later and later, and the guests stayed on, and I kept watching Dale getting more tired and drawn." Then through the noise downstairs Dale heard a child crying. She flew upstairs and quieted Dusty and stayed until he was asleep again. When she finally came down, the crowd had gone.

"Well, at least they didn't stay for breakfast," Dale said, with a sigh. "I'm so tired and sleepy I could croak. And all that donkey talk! Really, I thought I was going to scream. They just can't talk about anything but who got top billing and how much a certain picture is doing at the box office in Cleveland. Honestly, I think every one of that gang lives by money values alone."

"Oh, I don't think they're quite that bad," Roy objected. "After all, you ought to understand about folks wanting a successful career."

Dale Evans was bone-tired. And Roy had said the wrong thing.

So before they realized what was happening, they were nearer than they had ever been to a real quarrel.

Later Dale tried to explain her feelings to her husband. "It's just that I want the children to have a kind of happiness that will outlast material things, honey. I want them not only to know Christ's teachings but to *live* them, *believe* them."

"After Dale was asleep," Roy says, "I still felt restless and unhappy. I got out of bed and went over and stood by the window. Everything was shiny with moonlight. I looked up at the sky and it came to me how many thousands of years it had been there, how fleeting fame and wealth were compared to God's heaven. I realized that no matter what careful provisions I made, everything I hoped to leave my children would wear out or become worthless. And finally I made up my mind that when the 'King of the Cowboys' was long forgotten, my kids would remember me as the man who took them to church and taught them to live close with God."

And so it came about that the next day, Easter Sunday, Roy Rogers received baptism.

CHAPTER TEN

By the time she had weathered the assorted diffi-
culties of her first two years as Mrs. Roy Rogers, marked changes had
taken place in Dale's appearance and attitude. Although she finally
appeared in eight of the eighteen pictures Roy signed for in his last
agreement with Republic—one entitled "Trigger, Jr.," which introduced to the world Trigger's son and heir—rumors reached her from
time to time of objections to the new Dale Evans. "They say Roy
always has been a cowboy and homebody to the core but you are
supposed to be a glamour girl," a friend confided.

Nobody was more aware of the changes in Dale, and Roy too, than
their old friend Pat Brady. After "The Sons of the Pioneers" left
Republic in 1948, a new musical group called "The Riders of the
Purple Sage" began appearing with the Rogerses. They were later
replaced by "The Roy Rogers Riders." Pat Brady, by that time, had
broken with "The Pioneers" to rejoin the Rogers troupe as the cowboy king's comic sidekick. And on the evening of April 21, 1949, he
was present for the momentous ceremony when Roy and Trigger
placed their hand- and hoofprints in the cement forecourt of Grau-
man's Chinese Theater.

"Well, Buck," Brady said, as he congratulated his old pal, "you've just reached the Hollywood pinnacle. Cowboys aren't usually invited to join the ranks of the all-time movie greats, you know."

"Roy just grinned at me," Pat Brady recounts. "But sometime later he seemed to take it very seriously when we learned that in a *Life* magazine survey, in which school children had been asked what person of whom they had heard or read they would like most to resemble, he had placed high with such men as Abraham Lincoln and Franklin Roosevelt."

Dale also noticed that Roy seemed serious, almost troubled, over this particular honor. "I don't know why you're so surprised," she told her husband. "Newsmen have been saying a long time now that if the kids of America could vote, you'd probably be president."

"But who am *I* to be the beloved hero of millions of children?" Roy asked. "I'm just a hillbilly, an ignorant farm boy from Duck Run. Honest, honey, when I look around, I wonder how I ever landed in this spot I'm in." Then a new and surprising realization dawned on his face as he said, "You know, Dale, for years the little boys and girls have told me that they pray for me every night. And thousands of letters from parents have said so too. Maybe those little prayers have had something to do with my success." And his wife saw tears glaze his eyes.

There were others, living and working closely with Roy and Dale Rogers, who became increasingly aware of what in retrospect they call "the seasoning process." One afternoon Roy stopped by the one-story building with an open center court that houses Roy Rogers Enterprises on North Highland Avenue in the heart of Hollywood. On his infrequent visits Roy always headed for the fan-mail department to gab with his sisters, to look over special letters they felt needed his attention, and to examine the walls covered with photographs of children from all over the world who no doubt had felt it was only fair to send Roy their picture when asking for his. But on this day Roy Rogers went directly to the office of Al Rackin, Dale's

114

long-time friend and press agent who became public-relations director for the Rogers team when they united their personal and business lives.

"Al, how many fan clubs have Dale and I got?" Roy asked with no preamble.

Al Rackin was taken aback. Except in matters that concerned ill children, Roy Rogers had never shown much interest in the affairs handled by Al's department. And when Roy pulled up a chair, indicating he was intending to stay awhile, Al could hardly believe his eyes. For it had long been agreed by members of the Rogers business family that unless their King was first settled down to a bit of whittling, all attempts at business conversation with him ended up resembling a ballet dance without music.

"Your fan clubs are countless," Rackin answered Roy's question. "You have them in most American cities and I don't know how many foreign countries. The club in London has 50,000 members. It's the largest individual fan club in the world."

"What do they *do?*"

Al Rackin smiled. He didn't know what Roy was up to but he played it straight. "A fan club consists of people who organize with one bond—they all worship the same idol. In this case many of them follow your lead. They foster the Western code and live by the credo set out in all your programs."

"Could we really *organize* them, Al? Help them to champion all that is good and suggest ways for them to do hospital, charity, and civic work?"

Al Rackin knew that to try to corral the millions of Rogers fans was not a practicable idea. But as he and Roy talked, another idea began to emerge. And thus were born the Roy Rogers Riders Clubs that today number 2,025 and have a membership of over two million children. With theater managers acting as "ranch foremen," the club meetings are part of special weekend matinees. The young members engage in assorted constructive jobs and high-level community activities and follow rules concerning matters from personal cleanliness to democratic principles. Meetings always open with Roy on the screen, leading his buckaroos in his "Cowboy Prayer," composed for him by his old friend Bill Alexander.

Lauded as weapons against juvenile delinquency, the Riders Clubs —whose membership rules dealt effectively with accident prevention and safety measures—soon led the Rogerses to cooperate with the National Safety Council in launching an annual safety award program. Today nearly ten thousand elementary schools compete each year for the Roy Rogers Safety Award. Schools plan their own safety programs and keep a scrapbook record of the results of their campaign. Judges include directors of the National Safety Council, educational leaders, and Hollywood celebrities. Roy and Dale Rogers always visit the school winning first place and make the award personally.

"We are looking forward to the day when it can no longer be said that more children in the United States are hospitalized by accidents than by illnesses," Roy said in 1949, at the John M. Patterson School in Philadelphia, first winner of the award.

It was about this time that Roy and Dale's recordings for RCA Victor began to include more and more numbers for children, even hymns and religious songs. "But the change that knocked me for a loop," says Larry Kent, now manager of Roy Rogers Enterprises, "was Roy's sudden interest in the products that carried his endorsement." One Tuesday Roy sauntered in during a regular weekly meeting of his executives. While products, manufacturers, prices, and advertising programs were being discussed, Roy busied himself examining some articles that had been submitted for endorsement. Suddenly he stood up and interrupted the meeting.

"This knife is a piece of junk, fellows. Or at least it *was* a knife." And he held out the pieces of a pocketknife in his open palm. "If I took it apart in two minutes, any kid in the world can break it up in five. And I refuse to have my name on *junk!*"

"We probably would have rejected that particular item ourselves," Kent goes on. "But at that time our business was suffering some pretty bad growing pains." When Roy Rogers began digging in, he dug fast. And he got to the point where he insisted on testing all items himself, restricting their number and type, cutting down the firm's list of licensees. "We were supposed to have been a bunch of well-trained business heads," Kent laughs. "But when Roy got personally behind the Enterprises even sales began to leap. And without his sense of responsibility to the parents and children that buy the articles bearing his name, I doubt that the business would ever have set the high standards and policies it has today."

Although this commercial facet of his cowboy kingdom provided a major source of his income, Roy Rogers always had refused to appear in a store to push his products. But in June, 1949, Roy relented and agreed to visit Bamberger's, a large department store in Newark, New Jersey, and Gimbels in New York City. Before noon on that summer day at Bamberger's, Art Rush realized he had allowed Roy and Dale to make a grave mistake. The excited crowd that swarmed in to see "The King of the Cowboys" and "The Queen of the West" when the store opened was frighteningly large. By lunchtime the store's doors had to be closed. And later it was estimated that the throng locked inside numbered 50,000, packing all floors, while 40,000 stood outside clamoring to get in. "Mothers were holding children up in the air to keep them from suffocating and being trampled," Art Rush says. "And although the police and fire departments were there doing their best, nobody could have done much if just one person had yelled 'Fire!'"

When the last child was out of the store, and miraculously no accidents had occurred, Roy and Dale Rogers bowed their heads and offered a brief prayer of thanks. Hiding their apprehension behind fixed smiles, they had stood without a break for nearly eight hours, shaking hands with children. Both of them suffered swollen, bleeding fingers, and later Roy developed a stubborn infection.

Although the president of Bamberger's called Gimbels and warned them to call off the Rogerses' appearance there, the New York store insisted on going ahead. Certain that some safety measures could be taken, Art Rush worked all night with Gimbels employees building a serpentine system of wooden pathways to control the crowd. And it was well that he had. For the next morning when Gimbels' doors opened, a crowd of 40,000 had gathered, waiting to get in.

Roy and Dale Rogers's career in commercial appearances was short lived. They've never so obliged a store since.

Although the memories of all parties concerned are a bit hazy concerning the subject, it was probably on this same trip East that the incident took place which severed the Rogerses' relations with night clubs too. It has been said that a celebrity may know he's really arrived when, on reaching New York, he receives a personal invitation from Sherman Billingsley to attend the famed Stork Club. And although Roy Rogers has seldom been known to visit night spots and Dale, after her marriage to him, had seemed to lose all interest in them, Art Rush was so pleased when his kids were favored with Mr. Billingsley's coveted summons that he nagged them into planning an evening at the Stork Club. In deference to such an occasion, Art insisted that the Rogerses don their finest white regalia. Beaming proudly, Art looked them over from the tip of their handmade boots to the top of their snowy Stetsons, bade them good-by, and settled himself to a bit of desk work. Twenty minutes later Roy and Dale were back.

Art almost did a double take. "What happened?" Then, noting the cold fury on their faces, he added tentatively, "Didn't you *like* the Stork Club?"

"We wouldn't be the ones to know," Roy said, kicking off his boots. "The bouncer wouldn't let us in."

"The bouncer?" Art cried, aghast.

"Okay, the keeper of the golden rope, if we must be fawncy," Dale put in. "He took one look at us and quietly informed us to 'Git!' It seems you have to be well dressed to enter the Stork Club, and he didn't think we were well dressed."

Art Rush wondered what the unknowing "bouncer" would say if he knew the cowpokes he'd turned away were Roy Rogers and Dale Evans, wearing a couple of outfits that had cost well over a thousand dollars. And the thought sent him into peals of laughter.

"I know that laugh, Art," Dale fumed. "It's the one you always use

118

when you don't know quite what to say. And it's usually followed by 'Don't worry, kids, things will work out the *right* way.' Well, for my money, this time things did work out the right way. Roy and I don't belong in night clubs. We've got more important work to do."

When Sherman Billingsley heard about the *faux pas* that had taken place at his front door, he was appalled. And his attempts at apology ranged from telegrams to flowers.

On their second wedding anniversary Roy Rogers presented his wife with a shotgun. "And it was no gag," Dale says. "My husband might be a thoughtful, even a sentimental, man, but he's no idle romanticist. By then I was a pretty good fisherman, but compared to Roy, I wasn't doing so well at hunting. He decided a new gun might improve my shooting record. And sure enough, it did."

At the time they celebrated the end of their second year of marriage, the Rogerses were in San Francisco for a holiday benefit appearance. Over a late supper after their performance, Dale remarked, "Wasn't that a lovely girl, the singer named Robin?"

"Yeah," Roy agreed. "And that's a mighty sweet name."

"Oh, honey," Dale mused, "wouldn't it be wonderful if *we* had a little girl named Robin? Dusty's getting to be such a man, and we don't have a baby any more."

Roy sighed. "There's nothing in the world like having a baby in the house, is there?"

A few days later when the Rogerses learned that Dale was six weeks pregnant, they remembered their conversation in San Francisco and laughed gaily.

On January 29, 1950, when Roy and Dale arrived at Houston, Texas, for their appearance at the Fat Stock Show there, a crowd of 5,000 adults and children met them at the Union Station. Roy was soon astride Trigger but Dale was whisked away to a convertible. Where's Pal, the fans wanted to know. Why isn't Dale riding Pal? They were to receive the answer when the Houston Fat Stock Show Rodeo opened on February 1 at the Sam Houston Coliseum.

On that opening night the house lights went down and four spot-lights stabbed the darkness, aimed at a gate on the far end of the rodeo arena. "The King of the Cowboys" came dashing out on Trigger and, as always, the audience went wild. A few minutes later "The Queen of the West" made her entrance. But the applause was as wavy as a question mark. She was riding in a small buggy—and slowly.

Roy grinned into the microphone. "Folks, if you're wondering why Mama is moving along so ladylike tonight, it's because we're expecting a little buckaroo at our house come summer." When the news had sunk in, there was a thunder of applause. When Dale reached Roy's side at the center of the arena, she jumped from her buggy to the tanbark. "Hey," Roy admonished her before 8,000 people, "don't let me see you jumping around like that any more."

Dale grabbed the mike from Roy and laughed. "That's just Pappy's way of bragging about soon being a father."

When the news spread that the Rogerses were expecting a baby, mail from fans all over the world flooded in. Not only had their King married their Queen but now there was to be a Royal Buckaroo!

At home the three Rogers children were beside themselves, talking constantly about the coming baby. There was a warm, strong relationship in the household now. And Dale spent more and more time in religious activities with the children during the last months when Roy carried on their career alone.

After he had joined the church, Roy had begun attending church regularly with his family. He served on many committees. And on Monday evenings the Rogerses met with the Hollywood Christian Group, an interdenominational gathering of stars and other people connected with the entertainment industry who, away from the limelight, met in private homes to discuss the power of prayer, to read from the Bible, and to sing hymns.

"I've never had enough education to really understand theology," Roy said at the Hollywood Christian Group one evening. "But when a fellow like our old friend Tim Spencer can stand here and tell us frankly how his belief in God and his love for Jesus Christ helped him climb back to a life of useful service after he'd hit the bottom with the bottle, then Christianity comes alive for me."

"Now I look back," Roy says, "and know that even then Dale and I and the kids were just getting our feet wet. For we were yet to learn that you have to walk closely with God a long time before you really get to know Him. But we'll always be grateful that He saw to it that at least we'd *met* Him before we really needed Him. For I shudder to think what might have happened to us had we not had at least a foundation to fall back on when our test came."

CHAPTER ELEVEN

Weighing 7½ pounds, Robin Elizabeth Rogers arrived at 2:20 A.M. on August 26, 1950. Dale's pregnancy had been completely normal, and so was the delivery.

"You have a little girl, Mrs. Rogers," a nurse said, holding the baby near.

Dale opened her eyes, smiled, and said, "Hi, Robin. You're beautiful."

When Dale was wheeled from the delivery room, proud and smiling Roy and Art Rush were waiting in the hall to follow the carriage. Just as they reached Dale's room a nurse called Art aside. "Mr. Rush," she whispered, "the doctor would like to see you at his office early tomorrow morning."

Alarmed, Art soon left Roy and Dale and sought the doctor immediately. Mrs. Rogers was perfectly all right, the doctor assured him. But there were indications, he sadly admitted, that the baby was not. Seven specialists had been called and at that moment were examining the child. Then the doctor hurried away to join them.

Unbeknown to the happy parents, Art Rush paced a hospital corridor until the group of doctors had finished their consultation. Was the baby minus arms, legs? Was she going to be blind, deaf, spastic? No, the doctors finally told him, the condition they suspected was even worse and completely hopeless. The Rogers baby had characteristics of Mongolism. There was evidence of a heart condition. She had been born blue, was being given oxygen.

It was almost daylight when Art finally turned into the driveway of his San Fernando Valley home. He unlocked the front door quietly, hoping not to disturb Mary Jo and their two sons. Walking directly to his study, he turned on a lamp, picked up the dictionary on his desk, and looked up the word "Mongolism." He read: "A congenital malformation, in which the child has slanting eyes, a large tongue, and a broad, short skull. Such children are often imbeciles."

"I was halfway up the stairs before it hit me," Art says. "The terrible thought—*Roy and Dale would have to be told.*"

Art Rush sank to the landing and buried his face in his hands. Secondhand pain, he realized anew, is the worst pain there is.

Even before she spoke, Art heard the rustling of his wife's taffeta robe. "Let's go down and have some hot milk," Mary Jo said softly.

Hours earlier Art had called her to report that the baby was a girl and that Dale had come through like a trouper. "Me too," Roy's elated voice had chimed in. But now it was obvious to Mary Jo that something had happened later.

"Even in the dimness I could see that Art was upset beyond talking," she says. "And I simply couldn't bring myself to ask any questions until we'd sat down at the kitchen table."

Remembering the tragedy that had followed the birth of Roy's son, Mary Jo braced herself and asked, "Is it Dale?"

"No," Art said. "The baby. The doctors think it's Mongolism."

"Think it's *what?*"

"I just looked it up in the dictionary. And the doctors explained a little. It means that for an unpredictable life span the baby will be physically malformed and mentally retarded."

"Mary Jo turned as white as a sheet but she didn't say a word," Art Rush recalls. "And we just sat there in awful silence for I don't know how long, doing our best to drink the hot milk she'd prepared."

The Rushes found it difficult to fathom the overwhelming sorrow that had befallen the two friends nearest to them in all the world. For truth is not quick to gnaw its way through the protective walls

123

that encase most human beings. Tragedy headlines newspapers, blares from radios, leaps from TV and motion-picture screens. Everybody cluck-clucks, "Oh, how terrible!" Yet underneath there's that old feeling: Other houses may burn, but not mine. Others may become alcoholics, be stricken by leukemia, have afflicted children. But not me. Never *me*. And then it happens. And finally the rodent truth makes its way through.

"The birth of a handicapped child," Art said at long last, "is bound to come as a great blow whenever it happens. And just because we love Roy and Dale so much, we have no right to feel that their case is so different from thousands of others."

"No," Mary Jo said, trying to match his brave logic, "we really don't."

Yet as they talked, they kept uncovering differences. And each one seemed unbearably ironical. "All her life," Mary Jo Rush says, "Dale had surmounted obstacle after obstacle, trying to find happiness. And it was a tormenting thought for us that she had it for such a short time. For months I'd watched her lovingly gathering a layette, preparing a little nursery. And with every bow of ribbon she'd tied and every inch of lace she'd stitched, it had seemed to me that she was trying to make up for all she'd missed when Tommy had been born. Roy had never mentioned it but we'd felt he sensed the situation too. And the whole time Dale carried Robin, Roy was her absolute shadow, lavishing the warmth, love, and security she'd lacked before."

As they spoke of Dale, remembering the early unhappinesses that had resulted in her possessive love and fears for Tommy, and her years of working with youngsters as Roy's partner, and her recent troubles at home, it just seemed to Art and Mary Jo that everything that had ever happened to Dale in her life had tended to magnify her feelings about children.

"And when I mentioned Roy," Mary Jo says, "Art just went to pieces. 'Nobody knows better than I,' he said, 'that for my kid the worst, the very possible worst, has happened.'"

Then, inevitably, the Rogerses' career was discussed. How on earth could they possibly go on visiting ward after ward in hospital after hospital? What would they think when they looked into the small faces that smiled on them all over the country? And what about the millions of fans and the newsmen that were waiting for the arrival of this particular baby?

"To me it all seemed cruelly wrong to have had this happen to Roy and Dale," Art Rush says. "And as we sat there, I'm certain I was knowing the lowest, most desperate, moments of my life."

When Mary Jo realized it was nearly time to waken Bill and Bob, the children of the household, and get them off to Sunday school, she rose and began clearing the table. "To have Roy and Dale go through so much," she said heavily, "God must have in mind for them a great destiny."

Over two years were to pass before Art Rush would recall those words.

The Rogerses' innocent happiness became more unbearable to watch with each passing hour. When Robin was first brought to her room, Dale kissed the baby hungrily and said a prayer aloud, thanking God for sending her and Roy such a beautiful, perfect baby. Roy Rogers stood before the glassed nursery, smiling broadly, proudly pointing out to everyone that Robin had tiny ears like Dale's and narrow, slanting eyes like his own. The doctors and nurses looked away, knowing that even those characteristics were typical of Mongoloid children.

When one doctor among the consultants expressed doubt about the severity of Robin's condition, Art Rush clung to the ray of hope with fierce tenacity and insisted that the others withhold their heart-breaking suspicions from Roy and Dale. "I looked at that baby and I looked at that baby, but I simply couldn't see anything wrong," Art Rush says. "She looked just like all other new babies to me. And as far as her eyes were concerned, I was sure they meant nothing. Roy has almond-shaped eyes and so do his sisters. And Andy Slye has them. I kept pointing out to the doctors that narrow, slanting eyes were a family characteristic."

The doctors and hospital personnel were familiar with this type of whistling in the dark, always born of love. And when they formally agreed on the dreaded diagnosis, they advised Art that the time had come. The Rogerses must be told the truth about their baby. "All right," Art gave in. "But let's wait now until Dale is stronger and on her feet."

The night before Dale and five-day-old Robin were to be taken home from the hospital, Art Rush phoned Roy. "I wish you'd delay your visit to the hospital this evening, Buck," he said. "Mary Jo and I want to stop by and talk to you a few minutes before you go to see Dale."

While Art Rush was talking with Roy at the home in the Hollywood Hills, Dale had a visitor, a nurse on duty elsewhere in the hospital, whose husband was a friend of Roy and Dale's.

"How're you feeling, honey?" the nurse asked, as she walked up to Dale's bedside.

"Why, I'm fine," Dale replied. "We're going home tomorrow."

"So you've decided to take the baby home with you, then," the girl commented sadly. And when Dale just stared, she added, panic-stricken, "Dale, haven't they told you *anything?*"

"It just took that little bit to topple my whole world," Dale Rogers says. "Because actually I'd been feeling something wrong in the air for days. Every time I'd tried to discuss Robin with any of the doctors or nurses, they'd put me off. And I'd noticed that the other babies were taken regularly to their mothers for long visits. I'd lie there listening for the sound of the carriage, but they never let me keep my little baby very long. I'd always had to ask, even insist, that Robin be brought to visit me. And then instead of squalling like the others, Robin seemed limp and drowsy. Yet nobody would listen when I tried to point out these things. And, of course, I *wanted* to believe it was all my imagination."

"When I realized what I'd done," the nurse says, "I was terrified. But then it came to me that perhaps I was saving Dale from an even more cruel experience. Because of the Rogerses' prominence, the news had swept the hospital like wildfire and spread beyond its walls. And there was always the possibility of a newspaper or radio leak.

You see, Roy and Dale weren't just names to us. We knew them and knew how good and kind they were. And the baby's condition was blow enough without the probability of hearing about it from some stranger. Or so it all seemed to me. And, of course, I had no way of knowing that plans were being made to tell Dale later that evening."

"I have no right to discuss the details of Robin's condition," the nurse finally told Dale. "Talk to your doctor." And then, weeping, she fled from the room.

Heartbreak is one word that means just what it says. A sharp, burning crash. A pounding in the site of injury. A choking. And finally a limp, sad quietness covers the victim. Automatically, Dale reached for the telephone. The doctor who delivered Robin was out for the evening. When she had located him and asked him to come to the hospital, she called home. "Darling," she said to Roy, "can you get over here right away?"

Roy replaced the phone and turned to Art and Mary Jo. "She knows."

When the doctor talked with Roy and Dale Rogers, he tried to break the truth to them as gently as possible. "It's true," he said, "that Robin hasn't responded well to tests. Her muscle tone is poor. And she's listless and is having great difficulty swallowing food."

Dale gripped Roy's icy hand and asked outright, "Doctor, what do people *do* with a Mongoloid baby?"

The doctor shook his head. "There really isn't much anyone can do, Mrs. Rogers," he admitted. "The few institutions for such babies are overcrowded. Waiting lists are overwhelming. And state hospitals can't take them until they're four years old." Then the doctor sighed. "As there are degrees of physical pain, perhaps there are degrees of heartache too. I can't help thinking of a patient whose baby was born the day after Robin. This mother is not married. And now that her baby has turned out to be a Mongol, the plans for adoption are gone. The problem is very urgent, for we have no place to put the baby and the mother has no home to take it to." The doctor rose wearily.

"But you people do have a home. And I hope you'll take Robin there and love her. Love will probably help more than anything else. Certainly more than anything else we know now."

When the doctor had gone, Roy faced a desperate Dale. "Why hasn't *somebody* done *something?*" she cried.

"I'm sure they're trying." Roy struggled to keep his voice even. "But it may take years of work and a miracle."

"Well, *we* know how to work, and *love* is a miracle! Maybe it's time *we* did something about the problem of handicapped children!" And as shock had turned to anger, anger dissolved in tears. Dale buried her face in her pillow and wept.

Roy knelt beside her bed. "Don't cry like that, honey, please. If we believe in God and love Him, we have to trust Him. He sent Robin and He'll take care of her. Let's pray now, so God will know we're putting our trust in Him."

So Roy and Dale Rogers began to *really* pray for the first time in their lives. They read the Bible as if they'd never seen it before. And quietly they took Robin home to the Hollywood Hills. The doctors had warned them against releasing the truth: "If Robin is ever able to attain any degree of normalcy, she won't have a chance in a world where she's been labeled Mongoloid." So the public merely was told the baby suffered a congenital heart ailment. Thousands of letters poured in. The fans were dismayed.

But the three Rogers children were not. Awed, Dusty touched Robin's little fingers and toes to make sure she was real. Cheryl and Linda laughed and cooed over her, thought she was wonderful. "They didn't see anything wrong," Dale Rogers says. "But then children seldom do. Their clear, sharp eyes look deep down and what they see is the beautiful."

Yet with the instinct of the young, they sensed the hurt in Dale. And suddenly they wanted to express their appreciation and affection. Cheryl picked some wild flowers, attached a note, "I love you," and laid them on Dale's pillow. At school Linda outlined her small hand on cardboard, sprayed it with silver dust, and printed "To my mother." Dusty painstakingly colored a large picture of Pal, Dale's mount, and left it on her dressing table. The following Mother's Day, Cheryl tried to sum things up in a postscript she added to an elaborate greeting card: "Thanks a lot for all that you've done for me. You've straightened me out on a lot of things that I was alone in. And when I needed a comforting or some experienced advice, you were always there to tell me what I wanted to know. You came to live with us at rather a bad time, with Daddy so sad, and two little girls who were naughty, and a little boy who needed a mother's love that he had never known, and that the youngest girl had had for only three years. The older girl who, when she was smaller always kept her sorrows and problems in her, and even when you had problems of your own you were always there by our sides and you helped make our Daddy a Christian. I can't find anything fancy to say, but thanks from all of us and we really, really love you."

Inevitably, Roy and Dale Rogers joined the heartbreaking caravan so familiar to the families of the handicapped. Specialist after specialist. Questions asked, tests given, therapeutics tried. But the verdict always was the same: "There is no earthly help. Your baby is in the hands of God."

There were doctors who felt the quick, cutting way was merciful. "You'll have to give this child up sooner or later. Do it before she becomes entrenched in your hearts. Mothers of such babies neglect the other members of their families, their careers, their own health."

Roy Rogers issued a firm *no*. "We'll keep Robin, do all we can for her." Dale added, "God must have had a reason in sending us this baby. We have no right to cast aside anything God sends." And much later Dale Rogers was to look back and comment, "From the minute Robin was born we began to appreciate the Cross."

But there were bad days when professional schedules had to be adhered to, when the mechanics of a large household snarled up. Then Robin's parents would succumb to human weakness and the sight of Robin's little left arm turning blue as she struggled to take her bottle, her wobbly head, her fretful crying sent them into the depths of despair. "Why? *Why?*" their aching hearts would insist.

129

And they would become terribly confused, trying again and again to figure out some answer, some reason for their baby's affliction. Then would come the tormenting question: Was it sent as a punishment for sins they had committed?

"It took us a long time to learn that anyone who thinks is bound to get confused," Roy Rogers says. "And to realize it's not thinking that's wrong—not the being confused."

When Robin was less than a month old, the doctors found that she had developed a definite heart murmur. They dismissed it as another symptom of Mongolism. But Dale doggedly investigated heart operations. And she was crushed anew when every doctor she talked with agreed it would be impossible to operate on Robin. Still Dale refused to give in. Becoming more and more wrapped up in her baby, she searched for any tiny spark of normalcy in Robin. Hour after hour Dale worked to get Robin to smile. She had learned that if a baby doesn't smile by the age of three months, it's an indication of severe mental retardation. And each time the doctor called he asked, "Has Robin smiled yet?" And the answer at the end of two months still had to be "No."

Later, to encourage Robin to try to hold her bottle, Dale sterilized a tiny perfume vial, filled it with milk, fitted a nipple to it, and tried to place it in the baby's weak little hands. Although she did seem better able to manage suction with the miniature setup, Robin's small hands, held in the upward, open position peculiar to Mongoloid children, just weren't meant to grasp.

"I was fighting myself as well as the doctors and the truth," Dale admits. "But I couldn't help it. I hovered over Robin day and night. And every time she cried I ran and picked her up. I was so afraid any exertion might be too much for her heart."

Finally everyone agreed that things would be better—even for Robin—when Dale went on tour with Roy. But Dale set her foot down against going. Emily and Virginia assured Dale that they could manage the household and older children without her help. And although Robin's nurse, Donna, had slipped and broken her wrist, the doctors pointed out that Jo, the new nurse, was equally well trained and competent. Roy resorted to the fact that he needed her as his partner. And Art Rush used every argument he could think of. But, as Dale puts it, she continued to buck like a steer at the thought of leaving home.

"We never have in our lives gone on such a tour before, why now?" she said to Roy and Art. "A western variety show booked for the smaller cities! Six weeks of one-night stands in the wintertime! Traveling by motor caravan! Why, the whole idea is awful!"

"Dale," Art said, trying to reason with her, "the tour was arranged long before Robin was born."

"Well, she's born now. And everything's changed. Cancel it."

"You know what kind of business we're in," Art answered. "We can't cancel." Tight-lipped, Roy picked up a Bible and left the room.

In the end it was stern Jim Osborne, the Rogerses' business manager, who told Dale the whole truth. The tour had been planned for several important reasons. And not the least of them was money. In February, Republic Pictures had claimed the right to telecast the Roy Rogers series of motion pictures. The studio had been advised that they had no such right. "But nobody knows what's going to happen," Jim said. "Roy's career could be ruined and the Enterprises destroyed. And you know you yourself haven't been able to work professionally in months."

Money was something Dale Evans could understand. Shocked, she thought of the household expenses that had soared since Robin's birth. And the baby's uncertain condition would be calling for more doctor bills, more medicines, more everything. "Of course I'll go on the tour, Jim," Dale said stonily. "I'm sorry I've been so much trouble."

It was decided that Robin and Jo should stay at the nurse's home in the valley, where it was warmer and drier than in the Hollywood Hills. And that settled, Roy and Dale rushed madly to finish up a series of tape recordings for their weekly radio show. Somehow they locked their grief in their hearts as they packed regalia in trunks, rehearsed new songs and routines, and posed for publicity shots with their touring company of thirty-five.

When the time came to leave, Roy and Dale put on bright Western outfits, went over last-minute instructions with Emily and Virginia, and lined up Cheryl, Linda, and Dusty for final hugs and kisses. Then they drove out to the valley for a last look at baby Robin.

On the way to the railroad station they stopped at a doctor's office for a consultation with the heart specialists who had recently examined their baby. "There is no doubt that the heart condition is very serious," one doctor said. "But we feel there's no immediate danger and you're safe in leaving at this time."

Back in the car, Dale broke down and sobbed. "If only just once somebody would give us some hope." Roy opened the glove compartment and drew out two small Bibles—which the Rogerses still carry everywhere they go—and handed one to Dale. "Our hope must come from God," he said solemnly. "Robin is in His hands. Let's leave her with Him."

Art Rush, Larry Kent, and Pat Brady left Los Angeles with Roy and Dale to travel by train to Kansas City. The tour was scheduled to open at St. Joseph, Missouri, on November 4. Friends met the party in Kansas City and drove them to St. Joseph.

"We arrived at St. Jo about ten o'clock the morning of the fourth," Larry Kent says. "Our troupe that had come from California in our chartered bus was already there. But we found them worried because Glenn, Trigger, and Bullet—Roy's educated German shepherd dog —had not arrived. All props and wardrobe travel in a section of Trigger's trailer. And the show was due to go on at 2 P.M."

When word finally came that there had been an accident near Hamburg, Iowa, the whole gang piled into the bus and hurried to the scene.

Later it was found that an axle had crystallized on the $25,000-air-conditioned truck-trailer that Roy had designed and presented to Trigger on the horse's seventeenth birthday some months before. The trailer—with a stable for Trigger, a kennel for Bullet, a tack room for riding appurtenances, space for props and wardrobe, and complete living quarters for Glenn—had thrown a wheel, lurched, and turned on its side.

"The instant I jumped from my truck cab," Glenn Randall says,

132

"I could hear Trigger stomping frantically, calling me. And I knew something bad had happened. When I got inside, I found Trigger was all right but Bullet had been thrown against a wall and was injured painfully. The first thing I thought of was poor Roy. He'd had so much trouble already. And he loves his animals so and had worked so long and hard training Bullet. We'd already used the dog in several pictures but this was to be his first personal appearance."

"When we finally located the van," Larry Kent goes on, "Roy jumped from the bus and flew to the trailer. Pretty soon he came out with Bullet cradled in his arms. The dog had a broken tail and his hind legs were temporarily paralyzed. He was moaning pitifully and licking Roy's hands."

A passing motorist rushed Roy and Bullet to St. Joseph to find a vet. And Dale joined the troupe in madly picking up the wardrobe that was scattered all over the highway. "We just heaped everything into our bus," Pat Brady says. "And I couldn't see how any of us were going to find the stuff for our acts."

The returning bus rolled up at the auditorium just as S.R.O. signs were being removed. The house was packed. Everybody scrambled out, carrying a load of costumes. Shortly, Glenn arrived with Trigger and the props. And then Roy came bearing the good word that Bullet would recover. "But the vet says it may take a long time and we'll have to leave him here in St. Jo for a while," he added, sadly. "So Bullet is out of the show for this tour."

"Gosh, and we've had so many letters from the kids up and down the line, excited about seeing Bullet for the first time," Larry Kent commented. "They're going to be very disappointed. What'll you tell them?"

"I'll tell them the truth," Roy said. "I've always found that children are the most reasonable of people."

And finally, with no rehearsal, the show was on—only ten minutes late.

By the time the Rogerses' tour was completed, they had covered 10,000 miles through the Middle West and Middle South, played in 26 towns, and grossed $278,000. Two engagements were missed in

Ohio because of a 16-inch snowfall. Trigger and Glenn were reported lost in the blizzard and newspapers across the country snared onto the story. But when the storm had settled, Glenn had arrived at his destination with a nonchalant Trigger ready to perform at curtain time. It was Roy and Dale and their busload of entertainers who were marooned in a nearby town and didn't make it.

Roy Rogers, unlike some stars, believes in really appearing in his shows. And during the tour he was onstage with his own acts for forty minutes and emceed the whole performance. The second week out he developed a severe cold and for a few days lost his voice. So Dale took over the mike. "Before things happen, we look ahead and vow we can't pull them through," she says. "And afterward we look back and wonder how we did. But at the time, somehow we manage. And it was on this tour, I think, that Roy and I realized the Lord fits the back to the burden."

In many places where the Rogerses appear, schools close for the occasion. And at their hotels and dressing rooms the team is besieged by squealing, robust small fry, many in Western attire, for autographs and handshakes. There are always many phone calls from parents whose upset youngsters, after great plans to attend the Rogerses' show, have at the last minute come down with ailments ranging from measles to appendicitis. Roy and Dale always talk to these children and usually manage to get them to hang up smiling.

"But on this tour," says Pat Brady, "I noticed a difference. It just seemed that there were so many more pleas for Roy and Dale to talk with or visit critically ill or fatally stricken children. And the stretcher cases that were brought backstage were simply heartbreaking. Although we were doing matinee and evening shows daily and traveling in between, the Rogerses somehow managed to visit hospitals everywhere. Often they skipped meals and ate sandwiches in cabs in order to make their rounds. It was at St. Luke's Hospital in Aberdeen, South Dakota, I think, that the whole polio ward broke into tears when Roy and Dale left. None of us, knowing about Robin, could understand how they could bear so much. But when I tried to talk to Roy, he just patted my shoulder and said, 'Patrick Aloysius Brady, what you need to do is to trust more and worry less.' And every day he and Dale quietly read their Bibles and turned more and more to prayer."

Finally Pat Brady talked with Art Rush. "I think I understand the changes in Roy and Dale," he said. "But is it my imagination that the youngsters are looking at them with a new kind of worship in their eyes?"

"No, I've sensed a difference too," Art answered. "Since their marriage, the children seem to think of them not only as 'The King of the Cowboys' and the 'Queen of the West' but as a mommy and daddy also."

And Art Rush was right. For everywhere the Rogerses went they were quizzed about their family. And there always were special questions about Robin, the Royal Buckaroo. Dale broke down only once. "Please, let's don't talk about her," she begged of a reporter. "It makes me so homesick."

Every night Roy and Dale made two phone calls to California. One to Emily and Virginia and the older children. And one to Jo and Robin. On Sundays they talked with the Slye and Smith families too, and with Tommy and Barbara—married now and expecting a baby of their own in Yreka, California, where Tommy had a teaching position.

One glorious, memorable night Jo answered the phone with great excitement. Little Robin had *smiled*. "She not only smiled, she laughed out loud!" the nurse reported breathlessly. "And she's not yet three months old!"

Roy Rogers was too overcome to talk further. And sobbing, Dale notified friends, relatives, and business associates. There were calls and telegrams and prayers of thanks. "Now Roy and I look back and know it was then that we lost all pride," Dale says. "There's nothing like a handicapped child to strip parents of pride and pretense. A handicapped child strips people of many things and their real selves begin to show."

Happiness for Roy and Dale Rogers was short-lived. When their show played the city where one of the greatest medical centers in the world is located, they arranged to talk with the head pediatrician there. They showed him many pictures of Robin that Roy himself had taken. And they answered all kinds of questions.

"Is she an unusually good baby?" the doctor asked finally.

"Oh, yes." Dale beamed.

"And relaxed and limp?" the doctor probed.

"Yes," Roy admitted. "Almost always."

The doctor sighed heavily. "I know enough without your bringing the baby here. The trip would be trying for you and a risk for her. And there's no use. For we could do nothing. *There simply is no earthly help for your child.*"

The doctor tried to console the parents with the truth: This affliction can strike any family, any time, any place. And nobody knows why. "One of the pediatricians on our staff has a Mongoloid baby," he said. "And he cannot help his own child any more than he can help others."

When they prepared to leave, the doctor said kindly, "For your own sakes I advise you to put your baby in an institution." But Roy and Dale refused to consider it.

The tour ended in Birmingham, Alabama, on December 3. The Rogerses parted from the members of their troupe to stop in Texas en route home to see Dale's parents. When they called California from Dallas to check on the children, they learned that Jo, Robin's nurse, was ill with a virus infection. Frantic with fear that the baby too would be stricken, they got on the first available train to Los Angeles.

A certain amount of confusion inevitably greets people returning from a trip. But Roy and Dale immediately were submerged in bedlam. Both of them love Christmas and ordinarily start preparations early. This year, of course, nothing whatsoever had been done. And they had a deadline to meet with more recordings for their radio program. But the problem that urgently overshadowed all others threatened to be insurmountable. No doctor, no friend, no relative,

136

no hospital, no agency could find a new nurse for Robin. The Rogerses were very upset because their baby needed constant and expert attention. Still unable to hold her head up, she was hard to handle. And she was very difficult to feed. Her throat muscles failed to coordinate properly and her tongue protruded.

Then Art Rush called to say that he had located a nurse capable of caring for Robin. But she would take the case only in her own home. The nurse felt that such babies fared better away from fearful, anxious parents.

Roy and Dale said "No!" But try as they did, no other nurse seemed available. And finally they partially gave in. They arranged for "Cau-Cau," as Robin later was to call her, to visit a few days in their own home so they could observe her care of their baby. In the end, Roy and Dale let Robin go home with Cau-Cau. She was excellent with her and the baby seemed to respond to the nurse immediately.

Unable to let go of the cherished fact that they had ultimately succeeded in getting Robin to smile, Dale Rogers searched endlessly for other signs of normalcy in her baby. Day after day, hours on end, she struggled to improve Robin's coordination, tried to teach her to pick up a tiny rattle. A response to music—often apparent in Mongoloid children—was also frantically encouraged. And a little red radio was set up by Robin's crib; a toy horse with a music box inside was placed on Robin's pillow. When the baby became fretful, Dale walked the floor with her tirelessly, patting the small back, crooning.

Cau-Cau disapproved of this behavior. She tried to impress on Dale that Robin was really God's child, that Dale should relax, release her possessive, tight hold on the baby, giving God a chance. She said Dale should never think of Robin as imperfect but as a child perfect in the eyes of God. "And actually," the family minister was to say much later, "Robin was the most exquisite little thing I ever saw. She was so perfect in her imperfection."

One day when Dale was writing down a telephone number, Robin grabbed at the pencil, scribbling a stroke across the writing pad. Heart beating wildly, Dale rushed out for crayons and a drawing book. But it was no use—hope always ended in disappointment. "It's her little hands," Dale said, weeping. "If only she wouldn't hold them in that strange way."

"Robin's hands are loving, stretched out to give," the nurse replied. "They're not earthly, grasping hands."

By Christmas Robin was settled at Cau-Cau's home. And the radio recordings were finished. Roy brought home a giant tree and somehow had managed to shop for simple gifts for the children and other members of the family. On Christmas Eve, Dale stayed up very late working on her special surprise for Cheryl, Linda, and Dusty—a cake with colorful gumdrops sprinkled through it, representing Christmas tree ornaments, topped with marshmallow icing and grated coconut, representing snow. Painstakingly she outlined it with greenery and other decorations symbolic of the great occasion. "Why, Mama's made a birthday cake for baby Jesus!" Linda exclaimed when the cake was presented to the children. And they were so overjoyed with her gift that every year since, Dale has baked the cake for them at Christmas.

All the members of the Slye family came for Christmas dinner. And the Smith family was there from Texas—Dale's parents, her brother Hillman and his wife Bennie Merle. And Tommy and Barbara came from Yreka. "It was a different kind of Christmas from those we'd had before," Tom Fox says. "Everything seemed so quiet, so holy. Mother and Dad read to us all from the Bible and we sang many carols and hymns."

"For the first time in their lives," Virginia, their nurse, says, "the children seemed more interested in somebody else than in themselves. They kept running to me with different gifts, wanting to know if I thought them suitable for Robin. And at dinner, during round-table grace, each of them, with no prompting, prayed for the baby—asking God to send her back home again soon."

After dinner everybody drove out to visit Robin at Cau-Cau's. They remarked that she showed more recognition, seemed stronger. Her little head was steadier, and she smiled broadly when Roy and

Dale showed her the new doll Santa had left for her under their tree at home.

But the visit soon proved too much for the baby. The noise upset her and the nurse had to ask them to leave. They lined up to kiss her. It was difficult to leave little Robin behind.

CHAPTER TWELVE

The Rogers family was so unhappy about Robin's living away from them, and Roy and Dale spent so much time driving back and forth to see her, that even Cau-Cau began to realize that a change would have to be made. For many reasons Roy and Dale felt the Hollywood Hills home was not ideal for Robin. But when they talked about buying a roomier, quieter place in the country, Jim Osborne set his foot down. "Roy's contract with Republic expires on May 27," he explained. "And your careers are going to be so unsettled that I can't let you spend a penny unnecessarily."

Fate took the matter in her own hands, however, about midnight one spring evening when Roy's pet raccoon escaped from a pen in the Rogerses' back yard. "Roy had about twenty dogs at the time," Dale says. "And when I woke up, I couldn't imagine what was happening. I'd never heard so many dogs barking at once in my life."

When Dale roused Roy, he quickly grabbed robe and slippers and hurried outside to investigate. For over an hour the cowboy chased his coon, through one neighbor's gate and out another, loudly encouraged by every dog in the vicinity. And when finally he captured the animal and returned home, Roy's robe was almost in shreds and he was wearing only one slipper. Worse, his dogs and all others in the neighborhood were still yapping, excited to fever pitch. The racket continued till daylight and the Rogerses got little sleep. Unhappily, so did their neighbors.

"Roy Rogers's menagerie is a nuisance," Art Rush was informed by a representative of the indignant neighborhood. "Either the animals leave the Rogerses or the Rogerses leave us. And if you don't see that such steps are taken immediately, we shall all sign a petition and take legal action."

"Poor Roy was deeply hurt," Rush remarks. "Of all the things success has brought him, I think he gets the most joy out of knowing he can have all the dogs he wants. And it's hard for him to understand that everybody doesn't love his animals as much as he does."

Finally Jim Osborne was made to see that a move was really necessary, that the Roy Rogers family needed the open spaces. So Roy and Dale set out to look for a ranch in the San Fernando Valley and decided on an unpretentious place near Encino. The ranch covered 5 acres and included a rambling ten-room stucco house. Cau-Cau agreed to move with Robin, at least for a while. And Roy, Andy Slye, and Andy's brother immediately began the work of building a small noise-protected house behind the main one for the baby and her nurse. There was a large bedroom—done in blue with white organdy curtains—for Robin, a smaller bedroom for Cau-Cau, a specially equipped bath for the baby's care.

When Robin was ten months old, the move was made. It was an occasion of great happiness and relief for the whole Rogers family. Robin's control over her wobbly little head, her tongue, and throat muscles seemed improved by then. And she was able to be strapped in her stroller for frequent tours of the ranch to see the many animals quartered there—chickens, ducks, geese, horses, foxes, raccoons, and countless dogs. Roy Rogers has two prized gray Weimaraners, a rare and highly intelligent breed of dog, named Lana and Joaquin. Lana quickly became Robin's favorite pet and faithfully the dog followed the baby wherever they took her.

Robin's interest and love for animals inspired Dale and Cau-Cau to turn to the reading of animal stories to the baby at feeding times.

Patiently they tried to divert her attention with the colorful illustrations as they struggled to get some food down her throat. Dale decided that Robin might enjoy meals better if she held her own spoon. And they resorted to trick after trick trying to teach her to feed herself. But nothing really worked. And they usually ended up upsetting the baby as well as themselves. Robin simply didn't care for solid foods.

Roy and Dale Rogers tried hard to include their baby in the family routine. "At our mealtimes," Dale says, "we'd pull her little highchair up to the table. If Robin made any sounds at all during round-table grace, the other children were so pleased, sure she too was praying in her own little way."

Of all the attractions inside the house that she found interesting—from Roy's large pool table, his animalskin rugs, to his movies taken of the family—Robin was most enchanted by the piano in the living room. And during the day when Roy could be home, he drew up the piano stool with the baby on his lap and let her pound away. Evenings after dinner, Robin sat with Dale or Cheryl at the piano. She was quite still as long as the music lasted, but when they removed their fingers from the keys, she grabbed at their hands, silently pleading for more. Among Robin's few words was "pa-pa"—her version of "play piano." "When I once told a doctor all this," Dale says, "he explained to me that children like Robin nearly always respond to music."

"I believe they just march to a different song from ours," the doctor told Dale. "Someday that indication may lead to cause and cure."

Despite her frailness, the handicaps that plagued her every moment, her nervous restlessness, her inability to tolerate the slamming of doors and other loud noises, Robin was an affectionate, loving baby. Although her wide blue eyes often had a faraway look, she sometimes tried hard to enter the world of her brother and sisters. Happily she sat in her stroller on the lawn, watching Dusty, Linda, and Cheryl as they played ball. And she squealed with delight while they chased each other around. When they stopped their game and brought the ball over to her, as they frequently did, gently closing her little fingers around it, she gurgled with satisfaction, and did her

142

best to talk. As they cooed over her, kissing her tiny doll-like toes and head of blond curls, she strained and struggled to pucker her lips as they did, trying to kiss too.

"Whenever Roy approached her little house," Dale says, "she seemed to become all alertness at the sound of his footsteps. Usually he'd whistle softly as he stepped onto the porch and her delicate face would break into a grin."

By this time Dale Rogers, as she still does, was devoting an hour of each day to religious reading. Often she spent this period beside Robin's crib, reading many of the Bible passages aloud. The older children loved these sessions and frequently grouped themselves on the floor by Dale's chair. Robin seemed especially interested in pictures of Jesus in an illustrated book of Bible stories that Dale had got for the other youngsters. And Dale set to work trying to teach her to say the Master's name. Every time she came to it in her readings she would emphasize the word *Jesus*. One day Robin moved her small lips until she almost made it. "Tay-tay," she said, "Tay-tay."

Dale was so overjoyed that she wept. Dusty misunderstood Dale's tears. "Don't worry, Mama," he patted her hand reassuringly, "Jesus understands all little babies and when Robin said 'Tay-tay,' He knew she was calling Him."

As the treasured days passed, all too swiftly, Roy and Dale tried not to remember the doctors' warnings that their baby's time on earth was inevitably limited. And as they watched the other children unselfishly and unceasingly winding Robin's musical toys for her, they knew that the baby was winding herself tighter and tighter around the hearts of the entire household. Cau-Cau was devoting her life to Robin's care. Virginia tirelessly held Robin before the television screen, encouraging her to sway her little body with the rhythm of the performers. Patiently Emily taught a routine which the baby perfected well. "What time is it, Robin?" the pretty, gray-haired housekeeper would ask. And in answer Robin would extend a tiny wrist, as if it bore a watch.

"We were all working for Robin," Dale says. "But what we didn't realize at the time was that Robin was working for us."

And strangely, although many of their hours were filled with an undercurrent of anxiety and fear, the Rogerses began to sense that Robin had not only brought a new kind of love to their home, but she had brought a sort of peace too. "I'd come in at dusk after hard hours of tape recording or working on location," Dale says, "and I'd go straight to her little house. There I'd always find that peace. Robin was so lovely to look at and she smelled so sweet. She was so undemanding, so meek, so free of evil, so quiet and loving."

"Robin is *in* this world but somehow she just never seems *of* it," Dale remarked to Roy one evening when she came in from the little house.

"Yes," Roy agreed, "she seems more like an angel than a human being."

To the men who worked closely with him, Roy Rogers's love for his baby was a heartbreaking thing to watch. But his increasing concern for sick children everywhere was heart-warming. Set on answering as many appeals as was possible, Roy drove many miles to visit bedridden tykes in their homes. When a personal visit was out of the question, Roy made long-distance calls. And he wrote letters by the dozens. Thus the last hours of many fatally ill children were made happy by Roy's songs. And those who had a chance to live often were pulled from their lethargy by his encouraging words. Always Roy Rogers told the young patients and their parents about Robin, referring to her more and more as "our little angel."

"In retrospect," comments Dale Rogers, "I see that trouble is simply a school. Some people work hard and pass test after test, gleaning much knowledge. Others give up and fail along the way. Now I know that it was easy for us to do well during that period because, relatively speaking, Robin was doing well. And actually it was her progress that was seeping through all of us. But, of course, I didn't realize it at the time, and I was growing quite proud of myself, my deep faith and fortitude. Then something happened, as it usually does in such cases, to pull me down a couple of pegs, to abruptly remind me that I was a mere human being after all. And I was shown that although I'd developed enough faith to pass the test of bearing my own heartache, I still had not developed enough to pass a much harder test—that of bearing the heartache of someone I loved."

Dale's setback, as she terms it, came about a short time after they had moved to the ranch. Tom Fox's teaching year at Yreka, California, had ended, and he, Barbara, and their infant Melinda, arrived for a visit with the family. A doting mother, Dale quickly got herself dubbed by Roy "a double-doting grandmother." And teasingly he called her "my little old woman in the shoe," as happily she walked around carrying Robin in one arm and Melinda in the other, with Cheryl, Linda, and Dusty following close behind. Roy took candid shot after candid shot of his family. And one day, when everybody decided to dress up for more formal photographs, he smiled proudly at his wife. "Well, Miss Evans," he remarked, "you might be a grandma but I'll bet you're the youngest and purtiest grandma that ever was!"

Then without warning came the never-to-be-forgotten day when Tom and Barbara Fox took their little Mindy to a pediatrician for a routine checkup. "Tommy and I have always been so close," Dale says, "that we can almost read each other's mind. And when they got back that day, I had only to take one look at my son's face to know that something was gravely wrong."

When Barbara went to the kitchen to prepare Mindy's lunch, Tom joined Roy and Dale in their bedroom and closed the door. "We've had some very bad news," he said. "The doctor found that Mindy was born without a hip socket on one side. He said that we can expect serious trouble with that hip and leg. And he advised us to get her placed in an orthopedic hospital at once."

"And *leave* her there?" Dale asked, white-faced, stunned.

"Yes. He says she'll have to go into a cast immediately. And that we'll have to resign ourselves to leaving her in a hospital for . . . for an indefinite period."

"And if you do," Roy asked hesitantly, "then what?"

Tommy's voice broke. "He didn't mince words, Dad. He said the prognosis was very uncertain." Struggling for composure, Tom went on, "At first Barbara and I decided against telling you. You two are

145

carrying a heavy enough load already. But we realized we had to. The doctor said that waiting lists at crippled children's hospitals are long. What would you advise?"

Dale Evans Rogers controlled herself somehow until her son had left the room. Then she flung herself on the bed, weeping wildly. "I can't bear it, I can't bear it, I can't bear it," and she pounded her tight fists. When Roy tried to console her, she faced him with unanswerable questions. "Tommy has brought only happiness to everybody and everything he's ever touched," Dale cried. "And he and Barbara are the most devout people I've ever known. *Why* would God want to punish them?"

"As Dale asked why, why, *why*," Roy Rogers says, "she was questioning the wisdom of God, and when we do that, we find ourselves suddenly bereft of His presence. And when you have got used to His closeness and comfort, it's a mighty bleak and lonely feeling to find yourself without it. Still, I knew no way to help Dale regain her faith. I felt it would have to be returned by God."

But if Roy did not know how to help his wife at that desperate moment, he thought he might be able to help Mindy. For years Roy and Art Rush had been hard-working Shriners. And Roy knew that the doctors at Shrine hospitals for crippled children are among the best in their field. So he walked to the telephone and put in a long-distance call to a Shrine hospital in San Francisco.

When at last arrangements had been made for Mindy's admission there, Tom and Barbara began packing their car, preparing to leave at once. And Dale found herself torn between loves. "I'll be here with Robin and the others," Roy told her. "And when Tommy and Barbara walk out of that hospital without Mindy, I think they're going to need you more than any of us." So hurriedly Dale packed her bag.

"Tommy did most of the driving," Dale says. "And Barbara sat in front beside him. I sat in the back, sometimes holding little Mindy, sometimes watching her sleep in her car-bed. If any of us said one sentence an hour all the way to San Francisco, I don't remember it. And for miles and miles I just sat numb, rigid, tormented by my

146

earth-bound questions. Then I happened to notice Tommy's jaws moving. I thought with a pang that he was crying, and I reached over to put my hand on his shoulder. But I quickly saw that my son wasn't crying; he was *praying*. And I felt very ashamed. I leaned back and closed my eyes and tried hard to pray too. I didn't ask God for a miracle for my grandchild. I just begged Him to show me the way back into His Kingdom. All I wanted then was the kind of faith my son has—the grace to know God's wisdom and the courage to accept it nobly."

When the group arrived at the hospital, Tom Fox took his baby in his arms and briefly bowed his head. "Oh, Father," he prayed, "when we enter and depart from this hospital, where so many of Your servants are at work, please help us to do so relying on Your will, never to rebel against it. . . ."

As little Mindy's case history was being taken, her parents answered countless questions. And there were examinations by doctor after doctor, X rays, and more probings by expert fingers. Then finally came the moment when Dale, Tommy, and Barbara sat by while Mindy lay on a treatment table, being examined by a chief of staff. In silence he had reviewed the many reports on Mindy's condition, studied her X rays. At long last he picked up the baby and handed her to a nurse. Returning to his desk, he faced the family. "Everyone here agrees with the diagnosis you've had concerning this baby's trouble. But progress is being made everyday, and as specialists in this field, we are more familiar with these cases than your pediatrician. And we highly disagree with everything else he told you." The doctor smiled. "We are going to put a lightweight temporary brace on this young lady, and because of her age and the pliability of her bones, we expect this condition to right itself in a short time. We certainly find no reason for you to leave her here, and we certainly find no reason for anybody to expect permanent handicap from this condition."

Wordless, Dale stared at the doctor. Then, hearing a muffled sob, she turned and saw Tommy, radiant with new hope and the glorious answer to his prayers, take his baby from the nurse.

CHAPTER THIRTEEN

The summer of 1951 continued to be an encouraging, progressive period in the life of little Robin Rogers. "And God was good to have made it so," Dale says, "because careerwise those were the most hectic months her father and I had ever known. Even when I called Roy from San Francisco to tell him the wonderful news about Mindy, I thought I detected a new worry in his voice. But all I thought of was the children, and he assured me they were fine."

When Dale returned from San Francisco, she found her husband's bags packed, waiting for her to go East with him. Roy's agreement with Republic Pictures had terminated on May 27. And Roy refused to sign a new contract without the right to do television. Friction between the cowboy and his studio began coming to a head. On June 8 (and again on June 19 and 20) Republic, through its subsidiary Hollywood Television Service, Inc., offered the Roy Rogers series of motion pictures to advertising agencies and television stations for immediate telecasting. The Rogers forces demanded a withdrawal of the offers and were refused. Consequently, through his attorneys Roy sought and was granted a temporary restraining order, then a preliminary injunction forbidding Republic and its subsidiary the use of his name, voice, or likeness for commercial purposes. That meant, of course, that the issue would have to be settled in court.

"Nevertheless," Roy told Dale, "Quaker Oats didn't renew our radio contract because of the possibility of the old pictures being on TV. And apparently they've lost all interest in sponsoring us on TV for the same reason." Then Roy managed a grin. "You sure better love me a lot, Mama, because pretty soon we may have to live on love."

"How bad is it really, honey?" Dale wanted to know.

"Well, to put it bluntly, I have no motion-picture contract and no radio contract. Of course TV is the hot thing now. But while other cowboys have been riding the TV range, I've had to sit on the sidelines. So we have no TV contract either."

"But it won't be hard for us to find a sponsor, will it?"

"I honestly don't know. If the studio wins this suit I've filed, that'll mean I'll have to compete against myself on TV, against eighty-some-odd of my own feature-length pictures. And that's a load! But the thing that makes me sickest of all is the idea of my pictures' being peddled promiscuously. Everything I believe in personally, and everything I've built my professional reputation on, is based on clean living and follows the Western code. Suppose those pictures end up being sponsored by manufacturers of cigarettes or liquor, or some product dangerous for little children to handle? Where will I be then?"

Dale smiled. "Now, surely, honey, nobody would be silly enough to tie up the name of Roy Rogers with that kind of stuff. There are too many good items made."

"Yeah," Roy came back, "and I'm endorsing over a hundred good items right now through the Enterprises. I can't have any overlapping there. I don't want our licensees to have to bear the brunt of this."

"Come to think of it," Dale pointed out, "we do still have the licensees—the Enterprises."

"And how long do you think newspaper strips, cartoon books, and royalties from endorsed merchandise will hold up if we aren't active in the entertainment mediums?" Then Roy's voice turned low with serious worry. "We're in a real jam, Mama. Millions of dollars

149

and the jobs of thousands of people are tied up in this. And if we go down, they go down with us."

"Well, what are we going to *do?*"

"First, we're going to Chicago and New York. Art's already up there seeing what he can do for us in radio and TV. I want to talk to some of our licensees. And Art wants us to meet some of the network and agency people."

"It's a funny thing," comments a member of the Rogers organization, "but when any of us gets in a tight spot—even Art Rush—we always holler for Roy and Dale. No matter what end of the business we handle, in one way or another we're actually selling Roy Rogers and Dale Evans. And the quickest way we've found to do that is to call in Roy and Dale and let them take over and sell themselves. I don't know if it's their simplicity and sincerity that impresses people in all walks of life or whether it's that magic they seem to have over an audience. But whatever it is, it usually works."

But on this trip East—at a time when most choosy sponsors wanted their entertainers for both radio and video—even the easy-to-see if difficult-to-describe charm of Roy and Dale Rogers was overshadowed by the looming possibility of the King's old pictures being used on television. And after a short stay it was decided that the team should return to California to start breaking ground for a television production company of their own. Art would have to remain and somehow find a sponsor.

"As impossible as it sounds, with crews, scripts, and all the other stuff necessary for producing our half-hour Western TV films still unsettled, we wanted to start actual shooting by July 1," Roy says. "Because a deal had jelled for Trigger and me, under our new independent status, to make a picture for Paramount, with Bob Hope and Jane Russell, called 'Son of Paleface.' Production on that was supposed to begin August 1, and I knew I'd be tied up there two or three months."

Meantime, at the small building that houses Roy Rogers Enterprises, executives and secretaries had been pacing the floor and tearing their hair. And rumors were spinning like a tangling web. The one that later proved to be nearest correct was that the National Broadcasting Company had advanced the money for Roy's television productions. This was done with the invaluable help of John West, vice-president of NBC and a close friend of Art Rush's. "But working as we were, on an hour-to-hour basis, what was true one minute wasn't true the next," Al Rackin recalls. "New York would call California and a decision would be made. Then California would call New York, and the decision would be changed. Actually, for a while there, none of us knew if we were coming or going."

Riding herd over everybody, as usual, was the keeper of the purse strings—Jim Osborne. As part of his economy wave he insisted that the offices of Art Rush, whose financial affairs he handles as well as those of the Rogerses, be moved to the Enterprises building on Highland Avenue. "With Art in the East, that job was up to me," says Larry Kent, vice-president of Art Rush, Inc., who manages the Roy Rogers Enterprises. "And our attorneys kept cautioning me not to let a single scrap of paper in our files get misplaced because eleven years of records had to be gone through in preparation for Roy's impending suit."

Helen Young, Art's long-time Girl Friday, was appointed guard of the filing cabinets. "I even rode with them on the mover's van," she says, with a smile.

But if the world of business had gone mad around them, and if it often looked as if the King and Queen would be hung by red tape, Roy and Dale still had their private world, and there they found refuge. "When we'd get home," Dale says, "the gates at the entrance to the ranch seemed almost symbolic. Because inside them there was so much beauty, peace, and quiet. If we could manage to return home before their bedtimes, our brood would be waiting for us on the lawn, the older children grouped around Robin's stroller. And the very sight of those smiling faces and outstretched arms made the rat race we'd been fighting all day seem a little ridiculous. Cheryl, Linda, and Dusty were understanding more and more about Robin. And they were so patient and generous with her, and so cooperative with the rest of us, that I knew God was blessing our home—that the kind

151

of love that was pervading it could only be His. And Robin herself was coming along fine. Her little legs were so much stronger that often in her crib she kicked them over her head in an incredible way. Roy told her she was doing the 'splits' and predicted that she'd be a dancer. He knew that could never be true, of course, because our baby at ten months was just beginning to sit alone. But we were so grateful to our Lord for granting her relief from many of her earlier discomforts that we couldn't ask for more."

"In reality," commented a doctor-friend of the family, "things were not going as well for Robin as her parents seemed to feel. A Mongoloid child is a source of constant concern and worry and presents many problems of care. And Robin was a poor eater, and her heart condition kept her always weak and frail. No, it was not Robin who was changing so much; it was those around her who were changing. By this time Roy and Dale had developed a humble sense of appreciation. And they were presenting such a magnificent example of courage and faith against all odds that theirs was a case at once heartbreaking and heart-warming to watch. You see, this family wasn't *talking* religion; it was *practicing* it. And it was that inner spiritual strengthening which was bringing them a new sense of values, changing their attitude. So actually the troubles weren't easier; they just *seemed* easier. One day when I spoke to Roy about this, he just smiled shyly. 'Well, Doc,' he said, 'a shared burden is a lighter burden, isn't it? And Mama and I are sharing ours with God.'"

Day by day Emily and Virginia noted differences in their charges, the three older children. They were quieter, more affectionate, easier to handle. And whether or not their parents could be at home, the round-table grace, evening prayers, Bible reading, and hymns went right on. "Their compassion for Robin," Virginia, their nurse, says, "soon spread to all creatures weaker or smaller than they. They adopted stray animals and fed and tended them. And they showed an increasing interest in all sick children. They begged to accompany their mother and daddy on hospital visits. And when a call would come for Roy from the parents of an ill child, they tracked their father down until they found him." By this time everybody in the personal family and in the business family knew that wherever Roy Rogers was or whatever he was doing, those calls were to receive top priority.

Throughout that summer Roy and Dale Rogers were to work as they had never worked before. And business problems were to spring up like weeds. No sooner would they rid themselves of one than two more would sprout in its place. While they were making TV films—which they hoped would help lure a sponsor—they were up at five every morning in order to be on location ready to start work at seven. Because both time and money were strictly budgeted, they often kept at the job till nine or ten at night. Many a time, during the remaining few hours in which they slept, they were awakened by thin, complaining wails coming from Robin's little house. If the fretful cries continued, they would tiptoe outside to peep through the windows or sit on the porch of the small white house. Although it took much self-discipline, they seldom entered to further disturb Robin unless it became obvious that Cau-Cau needed help in making the baby comfortable and getting her back to sleep again.

But as their troubles grew, Roy and Dale Rogers grew. And in retrospect it can be seen that things were working out as Dale still often says, "If you'll just give Him a chance, the Lord will fit the back to the burden."

Art Rush remained in the East three weeks. "I had a ball rolling with NBC," he says, "but they too were insisting on an escape clause to cover them in the event Roy lost his suit."

During his last week in New York, Rush had daily appointments with advertising agency after agency. "But as far as a sponsor was concerned," he says, "it simply was no soap. The possibility of Roy's pictures' being used on TV was like a psychic poison in the air. As a last resort I contacted the Benton and Bowles agency. They had turned me down once before. But I saw no harm in trying again, and I was desperate. This time Walter Craig, their vice-president, came to my hotel. He is a wonderful man, and we talked a long time. General Foods was their client, and I told him we'd be mighty proud

153

to have such a sponsor. Mr. Craig said he would work on it and let me know."

The day Art left New York he was beseiged by telephone calls from Hollywood. Nobody, apparently, could wait until he got home to hear the verdict. "When Jim Osborne, our pessimist, called to find out what I'd been able to do, I had to tell him *nothing*. Because if deals aren't down in black and white, Jim is always very sure they'll never work out. I smiled wryly, though, because I knew if Jim spent money on a long-distance call, he was *really* worried!"

Larry Kent was worried too and with cause. The Rogerses' uncertain position was already affecting the Enterprises. And Al Rackin was beside himself, needing information for the press. But as Art Rush said over and over, there simply was no concrete information to give. "Everybody I have any business with at all on the West Coast called that day, I do believe," Art says, "except Roy and Dale. It was their careers that were at stake, yet they were the only ones who weren't pressing me."

But it is one of life's oddities that the greatest pressure one human being can put on another is no pressure at all. And when Art Rush boarded the *Century* for Chicago, heading West, he could think of only one question: What will I tell my kid when I get home? And it came to Art with a pang that this was the first time in their association that he was returning to Roy Rogers empty-handed.

The trip to Chicago was passed in a haze of depression. "For a while I kept trying to figure out a quick personal appearance tour," Art says. "Then I realized that even that idea was impossible. Roy and Dale were too tied up risking money, making TV films, for me to put them on the road to make any. And Roy was soon due to check in at Paramount for his picture there. Too, I remembered that none of us could afford to get very far from home base because of the impending trial."

Just before seven o'clock, in the fading light of that end-of-June day, Art Rush got on the *Super-Chief,* bound for California. "I knew I couldn't swallow any food," he says, "so I went on back to my bedroom. I sat there, whipped, pondering that same question: What will I tell my kid? When the train began moving, I decided I'd never be able to sleep either, so I opened my brief case to look over some mail that had been forwarded from my office. But when I spied my Bible, which I always have with me, I took it out instead, turned on the light, and leaned back and started reading."

It was half past nine when Art heard the buzzer and realized he had fallen asleep. Groggy, he took a telegram from a porter. The message was signed by Walter Craig of Benton and Bowles: GREAT SEEING YOU. HAVE TALKED TO SPONSORS. VERY INTERESTED. YOU MUST GO TO BATTLE CREEK ON JULY 11 FOR PRESENTATION FOR RADIO AND TV. BELIEVE DEAL WILL JELL.

"I read the wire several times," Art says, "before the unexpected good news began to sink in. Then I realized I was still clutching my open Bible, that the telegram had been read atop its pages." When Rush picked up the telegram his eyes were caught by another message: "Your Father knoweth what things ye have need of, before ye ask him." (Matthew 6:8.)

"For a minute I was simply stopped in my tracks," Art says, "and then I felt terribly ashamed for having displayed so little faith." Art Rush bowed his head briefly in prayer. Then he rose, splashed his face with cold water, and struck out for the diner. "They were just closing in there," he says, "but I talked the steward into serving me. I told him I hadn't tasted food in weeks. And actually I hadn't. I was suddenly starving."

Early next morning Art Rush sent a telegram to his wife: CALL ROY AND DALE THAT I HAVE GOOD NEWS AND MUCH FAITH. And the following day when he stepped off the train at Pasadena, Art was full of plans for the General Foods presentation. Smiling, Mary Jo, Roy, and Dale were at the station to meet him.

Earlier in the year Al Rackin had hatched an idea for a half-hour commercial sound-movie—to be called "Presenting Roy Rogers, King of the Cowboys"—which would dramatically show the scope of the Rogerses' fabulous empire and the workings of its many phases. "We have miles of film that we've shot at rodeos, parades, during Roy's training sessions with Trigger, and so on," Al told Connie Krebs, sales manager of the Enterprises, "and I think we could work out a keen merchandising promotion with it." Connie had talked with Larry Kent, and Larry had talked with Art Rush. Everybody agreed it was a whale of an idea. But because it was a costly one, and because, as usual, there were other more urgent projects on the agenda, the film was forgotten.

On the train, however, as he tried to figure out an effective presentation for the date at Battle Creek, Art Rush remembered Al's idea. He wished desperately that one of the Rogerses' proposed TV pictures could be readied in time to serve as a pilot film. But he knew it could not. And he had decided that although the commercial movie might seem an improbable task to finish in less than a week, it wouldn't be a downright impossible one.

At the Rogers building in the heart of Hollywood, before even a secretary is hired, it is customary for her first to be interviewed by every member of the existing staff. The prospect then is discussed in a meeting of the close-knit "family." If it is agreed that she's okay, she's passed muster. But if there's a serious objection by any one of the dozen members of the organization, she's out. And so it is with new ideas.

These meetings are held in Art's office—originally decorated for Roy in his personal mixture dubbed "cowboy modern" but occupied by Rush since the move—and Art presides in a high-backed, over-sized desk chair strikingly upholstered in unborn-calf skin, above which hangs a grouping of photographs, centered by the faces of Will Rogers and Hoot Gibson, the mutual favorites who unknowingly helped Roy and his agent get together.

At such a meeting, called when Art returned from the East, the sound-movie idea met great favor with everybody but Jim Osborne. "It could never be readied in such a short time," he said. "And even if you had the time to be conservative, such a project would cost us around fifty thousand." He tightened his thin lips decisively. "No, a movie for the General Foods presentation is out."

Art's eyes swept the room. "Uh, . . . would you let us have five thousand?" he asked, as a sort of test.

Osborne thought a moment. "Five thousand? Well, yes." Then he rose with finality. "But mind you, not a penny more." Later Osborne was to smile sheepishly about the matter. "With things in the shape they were in, I would never have agreed to even that amount, but I simply had no idea they could pull it off."

But, incredibly, pull it off the Rogers gang did. There is great and varied talent among them and, even normally, everybody doubles in brass. For no matter what his present title, each member has had experience in some phase of show business. And, as Art Rush says, with a smile, they all have friends.

"For five days and five nights," Larry Kent remarks, "every one of us worked like dogs. We went through acres of old films, cutting, selecting. And we dreamed up new shots, as simple as possible, and tied everything together with appropriate background music and sharp commentary. We hired a few technical experts, and everybody in the industry who could help us was wonderful."

On July 8, an exhausted Art Rush boarded a train for Battle Creek, Michigan, to present his cause to the brass of the Post Cereals Division of General Foods. He was armed with a motion-picture screen, a projector, and the dream-come-true film, which in a personal and convincing way answered all possible questions concerning the facts and figures that are used to measure the penetration an entertainer has made into the hearts and minds of the public. And it proved beyond doubt that the penetration of Roy Rogers and Dale Evans was among the deepest in the history of show business. The office had packed several large boxes of display gear for Art to take along too, including life-size natural-color cut outs of Roy, Dale, and Trigger. And in his bag Mary Jo had carefully folded what is known in some circles as "sincere" clothes—a handsome navy-blue suit, white shirt, and black knitted tie—and a love note in one of the suit pockets, as she always did when packing for Art.

Like all members of the Rogers organization, Art Rush finds it depressing to embark on or return from a trip unattended and unheralded. "And when I arrived at Battle Creek on July 10, I wasn't met," he says, sadly. "It was simply one place where I didn't know a soul." Later in the day, however, Art was joined by Conrad Krebs, who had been in Chicago working with licensees and retailers.

"After we had dinner, I stayed up very late," Art says, "working on a speech that would tie in the film with our other exhibits and reports." At two o'clock in the morning Art went to bed, leaving an eight-o'clock call. But before six o'clock he was up, reviewing and arranging things, pacing the floor. "I had never been so nervous in my life. But when I dressed, I found one of Mary Jo's inevitable notes saying 'I love you. Don't worry. It's in God's hands.' "

At the Post Cereals plant the pair was shown to a conference room. Immediately they got out a diagram and set to work. They pushed the long conference table against a wall and on it arranged their exhibits. Twenty-five chairs, soon to hold twenty-five executives, were arranged theater-fashion, filling the center of the room. Facing them were the screen and a podium for Art.

"Gosh," Art said as he laid out the sheets of his working script, "I feel just like I'm back at Bethany College."

"And I," retorted Connie, setting up the projector at the rear of the room, "feel like I'm back at the hospital waiting for my wife to have our baby."

"Maybe that's what's wrong with me." Art managed a smile. "Labor pains."

Connie looked up, alarmed. "Are you really sick, Buck?"

"No, not sick, but I sure am having some goofy pains." Then, noting Connie's serious concern, he added quickly, "There's nothing wrong with me that a good contract for those kids won't cure. I'll be okay once the meeting starts. It's probably just jitters."

A few minutes before ten o'clock the expected men began filing in, and at the stroke of ten the chairs were filled and an austere quietness covered the room. A figure rose and with the verbosity of a Calvin Coolidge introduced Art: "Gentlemen, Mr. W. Arthur Rush, manager of Roy Rogers and Dale Evans."

"As I got to my feet," Art says, "I turned on my brightest smile. But the instant I faced the audience my eyes caught on a man who'd been seeming vaguely familiar. Then in a flash I remembered. He was the one who'd turned me down flat the first time I'd gone to Benton and Bowles."

Panicky, Rush shuffled his papers, trying to compose himself. Before he could open his mouth, another figure rose.

He was Ed Ebel, a top executive of General Foods. "Excuse me, Mr. Rush, gentlemen," he said. "But perhaps this is the best time for me to read a telegram I received from Florida this morning: THE FACTS AND FIGURES THE ROGERSES' MANAGER WILL PRESENT TO YOU ARE INCREDIBLE. I HEREBY VOUCH FOR THE AUTHENTICITY OF ANY WORDS MR. W. ARTHUR RUSH MAY SPEAK. It is signed by Walter Craig, vice-president of Benton and Bowles, our advertising agency." Mr. Ebel resumed his seat and a low murmur swept the room.

With overwhelming relief, and no doubt a revived sense of showmanship, Art Rush glanced toward the rear of the room at Connie Krebs. He began to speak. Then shortly the room was darkened for the motion picture. And soon there was only the whirring sound of Connie's projection machine.

Suddenly a boom of music stabbed the darkness and swelled as from nowhere. The title flashed across the screen: PRESENTING ROY ROGERS, KING OF THE COWBOYS. As the music softened, Roy, in magnificent regalia, came riding out on Trigger.

The half-hour motion picture was good. So good, in fact, that it was going to be used for years to present the Roy Rogers merchandising program to retailers throughout the country. And in 1952 it would win the first award from the National Visual Presentation Association and the Sales Executive Club of New York.

Yes, it was all there. The results of over eleven years of work together. And Art Rush knew every beloved figure by memory. He had leaned back in his chair trying to ignore the mysterious pains, while the familiar sights and sounds tugged at his heart as they always did. And obviously it was happening again. That thing called audience reaction, which is as warm and unmistakable as love. Not seen, not heard, but felt. His kids, as always, had taken over.

The film had less than five minutes to go now. And soon Roy would come riding out on Trigger, waving his legendary farewell,

"Until we meet again, on the screen, radio, in person, and on *television,* good-by, good luck, and may the good Lord take a likin' to you."

It would be up to Art to take it from there, to strike while the iron was hot, to effectively summarize that success story, to point out that those who hitched their wagon to these Western stars were going to find mighty smooth riding.

But, unfortunately, Art Rush did not get his chance to strike. The last minutes of the picture were destined to be lost in great commotion when two dreadful discoveries would be made—almost simultaneously, but later determined unrelated. First, it would become painfully clear that the Rogers organization had committed one glaring error in selecting their material. Second, when twenty-five shocked men, all talking at once, would turn to Rush for an explanation, they would see that he was slumped over in his chair, apparently unconscious.

"Everything had gone as smooth as oiled silk," Connie Krebs explains, "until in a closing sequence, which showed how exacting the Rogerses are in their selection of items for sponsorship, the commentator mentioned that our products ranged from six-shooters to *cookies.*"

Like a bolt from the blue, a man's voice pierced the darkness, "Why, gentlemen, I'm afraid we've been wasting our time. These people are already endorsing foods. And foods is *our* business."

"Actually, the cookies were a new and very minor item with us, and the only edible one we had," Connie Krebs goes on. "And I knew we could dispense with them easily. We had made a stupid error, to be sure, but it didn't have to be a fatal one. So, as everybody else in the room did, I turned to Art, sure he would rise and say just that. But Art didn't say *anything.* He didn't *move.* And then I realized he'd fainted. To tell the truth, in the excitement I forgot about the pains he'd complained of earlier and I jumped to the conclusion everyone else did—that the shock of the cookie deal had knocked him out."

By the time Connie had gathered his wits, the film was ending, unnoticed. One man was switching on the lights and another was pouring water for Art. "When I got to Art, he was rallying," Connie says. "He was miserably embarrassed and trying hard to smile."

Kindly, Ed Ebel grabbed the reins and said, "Gentlemen, I suggest we disband for lunch." As the room emptied, Ebel started to the phone to call a doctor. But Art Rush struggled to his feet, insisting he was quite all right. And he gave Connie a look that was half plea, half command.

"He was frankly pulling rank on me," Connie says, smiling. "And all I could do was follow his lead. As we made our way to the nearby dining room, it became plain to me that Art had little, if any, recollection of the cookie episode, so I went over it with him, explaining the unimportance of the item to Mr. Ebel."

Somehow Art Rush sat through the luncheon. But he was in violent pain and Connie watched with growing apprehension. "I knew that no matter how badly he wanted to, he'd never be able to return to that conference room and stand on his feet speaking for an hour," Connie says. "And I had that desperate, helpless feeling like you have in a nightmare. If only this were a scenario, I remember thinking, a miracle would save us."

And as it turned out, a miracle of sorts did happen. At the end of the luncheon, Art Rush was told, in effect, that the men had agreed they had heard and seen enough, that if he could iron out the cookie difficulty, and would agree to an escape clause, to protect the sponsor in the event Roy Rogers lost his impending suit, he would not even have to present a pilot film of the TV series now in production. General Foods was sold—they wanted Roy Rogers and Dale Evans for radio and television.

For a fleeting instant Art's spirits rose. Then, even in his weakness, it came to him: The crisis wasn't over; it was just delayed. Everything, *everything* now hinged on the outcome of the trial.

Their departure from the Post Cereals plant, even their departure from Battle Creek, is unclear in the memories of Art Rush and Connie Krebs. "All I remember," Art says, "was that sickening pain and being half-carried from place to place by a series of taxi drivers, bell-boys, and porters."

At long last a Chicago hotel doctor was examining Art Rush. "He's seriously ill and needs immediate surgery," he told Connie later in the hall. "In layman's language, it's a rectal inflammation. And there's indication of a growth. At any rate, it's the worst case of its kind I've ever seen."

"Mr. Rush has been under a great strain, Doctor," Connie said lamely.

"Well, stress sets off the trigger for many ailments. But this particular condition has been years in the making." The doctor hesitated. "I'm sorry to have to tell you, but it's not unlikely that it's cancer."

Connie Krebs knew at once what he must do. He had to get Art home. "The doctor gave Art some pain-killing pills," he says, "and by the time I got him on the *Super-Chief,* headed for California, he was feeling more comfortable. He had flatly refused to let me accompany him, reminding me of the Chicago work I'd left unfinished to join him in Battle Creek. So, not wanting to alarm or upset him further, I had to be content with just settling him in his bedroom and waving a prayerful good-by."

The last leg of Art's journey was the worst. The pills were used up long before he reached Los Angeles, and then his only relief came when from time to time he passed out.

Before Art's train reached Los Angeles, Larry Kent received a rather cryptic telegram from Connie Krebs: ART NOT FEELING WELL. SUGGEST YOU HAVE DOCTOR READY TO SEE HIM ON ARRIVAL.

Larry alerted the family doctor but didn't mention the matter to anyone else until he and Mary Jo were driving to the station. "By the way," Kent told Mrs. Rush, "Connie says Art's been pretty bushed since that Battle Creek deal. I hope he got some rest on the train, though, and is feeling better."

But even Larry Kent, much less Mary Jo Rush, was not prepared for the shock they received when Art was carried from the train. Recognizing the comatose figure, Mary Jo, with pure reflex, screamed

162

shatteringly. And people from every section of Union Station swarmed to the scene.

At the doctor's office Art was given a hypo. "He's far too ill to be examined properly now," the doctor told Mary Jo and Larry. "My nurse has called an ambulance. A specialist and I will meet you at the hospital shortly."

Five days passed before the doctors felt Art was able to stand surgery. And Mary Jo was warned that their findings might be grave. Art Rush was to be ill for many weeks, but happily it was determined that his condition was not malignant.

At the end of his second week in the hospital, Art was allowed to have a telephone at his bedside. The step was a bad one. Local and long-distance calls soon were jamming the hospital switchboard. And on a day when Rush had already received thirty-two calls, NBC telephoned. They had decided to accept his deal. Such a decision was in direct conflict with that of General Foods. And Art Rush found himself tangled in a net of his own weaving.

The doctors removed the telephone. But too late. Art suffered a severe hemorrhage, was given several blood transfusions, and finally was rolled back to the operating room for more surgery.

For ten days Art lay isolated. And then, feeling better again, he began begging Mary Jo to manage another telephone. "But, Doctor, I'm afraid you don't understand," Mary Jo said, following her husband's instructions against her will. "Several careers are at stake."

"Careers are not my business, Mrs. Rush," the doctor replied. "But human lives are. And I'm afraid that it is your husband who does not understand. His life is at stake!" The doctor's voice became lower, more kindly. "Mrs. Rush, I must urgently advise you to take him away from here to recuperate. He can have no visitors and no telephone calls, no business messages of any kind. Otherwise, I'm sorry, but I will have to relinquish all responsibility for the case."

So Mary Jo rented a cottage at Santa Barbara. And a few days later she and Art disappeared. Nobody knew where they were except Art's faithful secretary, Helen Young.

163

Before his second operation, Art's last words to Mary Jo had been "Tell Larry Kent to go to New York and see what he can work out with NBC, Benton and Bowles, and General Foods."

"But I had had no briefing from Art," Larry says. "And I didn't know what was what in any direction. When I got there, I decided that a joint deal could probably be worked out amicably, and I called home for Fred Sturdy, one of our attorneys, to join me."

So, at the Rogers building, with Art in seclusion, Larry in the East, and Roy and Dale on location, all the others could do was to wait.

For weeks now, since the moment they had left Art in New York, Roy and Dale Rogers had been up to their necks in television production. Shooting from sunup to sundown, able to return to their ranch in the valley only briefly, the Rogerses had not been told about the severity of their manager's illness. "Art and Mary Jo have gone on a little vacation so Art can rest up before the trial begins," Jim Osborne told them. "And Larry is in the East finishing up a deal with NBC and General Foods to sponsor those pictures you're making. So hurry them along. Everything's in the bag."

"We had been allotted a hundred thousand dollars to make four half-hour films in four weeks," Roy says. "So with us spending about eight dollars a minute, Mr. Moneybags saw to it that we weren't upset."

Starting from scratch, with both time and money closely budgeted, the Rogerses had to perform some pretty magical feats in organization before they could begin actual shooting. "We didn't have any plans or rules to guide us," Roy says, grinning, "so we just sort of made them up as we went along."

It had been early decided that the format of the shows should follow closely their other Western ventures, with each picture presenting a different story. The locale would be mythical Mineral City in mythical Paradise Valley. Roy, living on his Double R Bar Ranch, would be a prosperous rancher with both time and inclination to help anybody and everybody in distress, a sort of law-abiding Robin Hood. Dale would be the proprietor of Mineral City's Eureka Café, whipping up coffee and cakes for the citizenry when she wasn't out helping Roy on his missions of mercy. In true Western tradition, there would be no romance between them on the screen, just camaraderie.

That settled, they had to decide on the permanent members of the cast: Roy, Dale, Trigger, Bullet, Pal—and there they hit a snag. A few trial shots showed plainly that Pal, Dale's mount, so closely resembled Trigger that the use of two Palominos would only prove confusing. Word went out for another horse. And Roy presented Dale with Buttermilk, a small, feisty buckskin gelding with black mane and tail—soon to be considered a beloved member of the Roy Rogers family in the minds of children all over the world.

The problem of Roy's comic sidekick, and a mount for the funster, caused a much greater stir. The Rogerses' advisers wanted a well-known, established comedian—the usual older man riding a broken-down steed. But Roy Rogers preferred his long-time friend Pat Brady, aboard a temperamental jeep named Nellybelle! And in the end Roy was firm: A vehicle would be a fresh twist and Pat Brady would have his chance in television.

Actually Roy Rogers, treading on unsure ground himself, was taking a great risk to help a friend. And hues and cries rose even from the would-be sponsors. For months to come, Pat Brady was to worry frantically, afraid this time Roy might have been too loyal. But there was no cause for anybody's alarm. Pat and Nellybelle were destined to be rated tops by the Rogers fans. And, ironically, for his selection Roy was to be credited time and again with "story sense" and "foresight," not loyalty.

Next, Roy and Dale needed script writers, a producer, a director, cameramen, sound men, electricians, grips, wranglers, prop men, make-up experts, hairdressers, wardrobe men, carpenters, maintenance men, doubles, stand-ins—a whole working crew gathered according to union requirements. Jack Lacey, who drove a truck on the lot where Roy's first picture was made, and had risen to a production manager, was picked as producer. In fact, the majority of the thirty-five people they assembled to form the Roy Rogers Production Company were old friends. "As far as getting people to work for them goes," says the young woman who served as Dale's stand-in, "the Rogerses had no trouble. They have a knack for forming lasting friendships, and as they are always so kind and generous, we all leaped at the chance."

Iverson's ranch—whose rocky, hilly terrain has been hired as a ready-made background for westerns since 1914—was chosen for the company's exterior shots. The old Western street at Goldwyn lot was revived and rebuilt. A portion of Goldwyn Studio was rented for interior shots. The little house-trailer Roy and Dale had bought for weekend outings with the children was to serve as a dressing room on location, half to be used by the men, half by the women. There everybody could rest between takes or sit out short rains. An indoor set would always be standing by at the studio in the event of heavy rains, so that shooting sequences could be switched and little time lost.

Roy Rogers always had loathed memorizing lines and he decided that now, his own boss, he was going to do something he'd always wanted to do—read over a script, get a good general idea of a scene, and then "wing" it. "The conversation is more natural that way," he explains. Dale and Pat Brady immediately fell in with his scheme but one bit player, a poor study, had doubts about the wisdom of ad-libbing before the cameras. "Oh, come on now," Dale said, with a laugh, "we don't have exactly what you'd call Noel Coward dialogue!"

The first day on location Roy and Dale began setting other unusual policies for their company. Coffee and doughnuts were served free to everybody on arrival. And at lunchtime, the stars refused to sit alone and be served at the cloth-covered table with lovely appointments that had been provided for them by the caterers. "Naw, Mama and I like to grab a place in line with everybody else," Roy said. And from then on, the table disappeared and the Rogerses were served with the rest of the gang from the chuck wagon's deep pans, cafeteria style, on paper plates.

Before eating, Roy and Dale bowed their heads in silent prayer. "That was the moment I realized just what the change in Roy and Dale was," comments Jack Lacey. "I've known them both for years and they've always been basically fine people, I think. But from the minute Roy had come to me on this television filming deal, I sensed a difference in him. And I hadn't been able to put my finger on just what it was. But the instant I saw the look on his face when he bowed his head in prayer, I knew. It was a calm, quiet spiritual quality possessed only by those who live close to God."

During one period, Roy and Dale Rogers were away from their family for two long weeks. When finally they were driving homeward, Dale said to Roy, "You know, honey, this is all kind of silly. Why do people work so hard just to make money and die? Do you think that's what God intends for us to do with the time he gave us on this earth?"

"No," Roy said, "I don't. I think at the close of a day if we cannot feel that the world is better because we have lived in it, then I think we can only ask ourselves, 'Why have we lived?'"

"What do you think Christ would do if He were in our position?" Dale mused. "Don't you feel that no matter where He was or what He was doing, He'd find an opportunity to work for God? Then why can't we? All this hard work would be really worthwhile if we could use it to spread God's message, especially among children."

Roy smiled at his wife. "That's a pretty big undertaking, honey, for the likes of us." But as the miles sped by, and they talked on, the idea took root. "We'll pray over it," Roy said finally. "The decision will have to come from God Himself."

"Yes," Dale agreed. "He's the only One who knows all the answers."

The Roy Rogers Production Company finished its four films in time for Roy to check in on schedule at Paramount for "Son of Paleface." And back at the ranch again with the children, Dale began preparations for Robin's first birthday. In special little shoes made for her tiny, narrow feet, Robin was by then able to stand up for short intervals in Cau-Cau's lap. She was growing so beautiful that those who loved her found it difficult to remember that physically and mentally she was hardly growing at all.

167

Dale and Roy's gift to Robin was to be an exquisite birthday dress which Dale herself was making. The three older children had saved part of their allowances and had decided to pool their funds for a large picture of Jesus to hang at the foot of Robin's crib. And the baby was to form the habit of talking in her own little way to the picture the first thing in the morning and the last thing at night when she opened and closed her wide blue eyes. "Tay-tay," she called, "Tay-tay."

"I think Robin loves Jesus better than anybody," Linda said one day.

When Robin's birthday would arrive, the Roy Rogers family would have a party, and the honoree would laugh and kick her tiny feet while the older children sang "Happy Birthday" to her and opened her presents for her and blew out the large candle that centered the beautiful cake that Dale and Emily had made. But before that happy date, the clouds looming over the Rogers business horizon were to start settling in storm formation.

The warning flash was to reach the Rogerses' ranch, Larry Kent, and Fred Sturdy in New York, even Art Rush at Santa Barbara— and send everybody scurrying to the Rogers building for shelter, to huddle there in organized confusion until September 13. The opening date of the hearing of Roy's suit filed against Republic had been set!

CHAPTER FOURTEEN

On the morning of September 14, 1951, those who
live by the jargon of *Variety* read its headlines: TESTING PIX COS.' TV
RIGHTS.

Headed "Roy Rogers' Suit Vs. Rep Opens; Will Key Future Of
Old Pix on Video," the account stated:

The matter of film companies' television rights in their libraries of
pictures is getting a severe test in what may be one of the most portentous
court cases in the history of Hollywood—Roy Rogers' suit against Republic seeking to prevent the studio from selling or leasing his theatrical
pix to TV.

Hearing opened yesterday on Rogers' action before Federal Judge
Peirson M. Hall in U.S. District Court, with Herman Selvin of Loeb
and Loeb repping Republic and Frederic Sturdy of the firm of Gibson,
Dunn and Crutcher, attorney for Rogers.

The piece then briefly summarized the claims of the opposing parties and the highlights of the opening proceedings, ending:

Case is of great significance and is being closely watched by talent and
studios alike. It may provide the key to the future of theatrical films
on TV.

For weeks before the hearing had begun, the midnight oil burned
at the Rogers building. When they had finished their job of combing

eleven and a half years of records, Roy Rogers and Art Rush gave depositions of over three hundred pages.

During the trial Roy Rogers—caught in the middle of his picture for Paramount and forced to commute between courtroom and movie set, often appearing on the witness stand in bright regalia and make-up—would only comment, "If I'm right, I want to be right. If I'm wrong, I want to know that too. I firmly believe that *right will out.*"

For four and a half wearing weeks Judge Peirson M. Hall—an impressive man with salt-and-pepper hair, bushy eyebrows, and slow, deliberate speech—clad in a black robe, seated in a high-backed red-leather chair, presided over the hearing in a courtroom located on the second floor of Los Angeles's Federal Building.

Finally on October 18, 1951, Roy Rogers, Art Rush, Jim Osborne, Larry Kent, and Fred Sturdy entered the courtroom together. The time for the decision had come. "As the group settled in their places," recounted one reporter later, "Roy, in his colorful trappings, shone like a lighted Christmas tree in those hushed, austere surroundings."

"And then, just as the judge prepared to render his opinion," tells Art Rush, "a jingling noise suddenly broke the vast silence. I looked out of the corner of my eye at my kid, and sure enough, he was the culprit—sitting up there as nonchalantly as you please, twirling his large key ring and chain. I kicked him a couple of swift ones, but through those heavy boots of his he felt nothing. So I reached out and placed my hand over his to stop the racket."

Much hand squeezing was to follow shortly among the members of the Rogers forces because the main portion of the court's decision was in their favor.

The following day the Los Angeles *Times* reported the story under the headline ROY ROGERS WINS BATTLE TO BLOCK FILM TELEVISING.

Cowboy Actor Roy Rogers yesterday won a court fight to prevent Republic Pictures from televising 81 of the western films he had made for the studio over a period of years.

U.S. Judge Peirson M. Hall handed down a ruling granting a permanent injunction restraining the studio from selling the films for television purposes. In his ruling Judge Hall held that under his former contracts with Republic Rogers has the right to control the association of his name with any commercial product or advertising.

In addition, the judge ruled the Rogers films may not be used as a "sustaining" program because this in effect advertises the station televising them.

Rogers' request for $100,000 damages was turned down by the judge, however, on the grounds that while there was indication that Rogers had been damaged, the evidence failed to show in what amount.

Meyer H. Lavenstein, New York, general counsel for Republic, said the ruling will be appealed.

Variety, the Hollywood *Reporter,* and other newspapers, covering details of the case and its far-reaching importance, expressed the opinion that the battle would ultimately reach the Supreme Court of the United States.

But on that day, Roy Rogers was the winner. And after he left the Federal Building, he insisted on stopping off with Fred Sturdy at the attorney's office to personally thank everyone there who had played a part in the vast preparations for his suit.

"Before you leave us, Roy," Fred Sturdy said, "I want to tell you something and ask you something. In all my years as an attorney, I'm sure I've never seen a better witness than you. I know you don't realize it, but no matter what anybody did or said, you remained completely unruffled. It was your first time on a witness stand. How on earth did you manage it?"

Roy Rogers's face turned bright crimson and his mouth crinkled into his shy grin. "Aw, shucks, Fred," Roy said, as he dug his boot into the carpet. "I don't know. I reckon I just did what Mom and Pop taught us to do when we were kids back at Duck Run. When somebody asked me a question, I just rolled it around in my mind real good before I answered. Then I looked 'em square in the eye and told the truth as best I knew it."

Following a brief visit with all the members of their business family at the Rogers building, Roy and Art Rush finally climbed into the cowboy's station wagon and headed for their homes in the San Fernando Valley. When Roy pulled up in front of the Rush residence, he turned to his manager. "Buck, I didn't tell Fred Sturdy everything back there, with all those people gawking at me. But I would like to tell you. I said a prayer every time I went on that witness stand. And I asked God to help me to keep calm and to speak the truth."

"Just one more thing, Buck." Roy stopped Art as he stepped from the car. "This I've been wanting to say for a long time. I'm awful sorry for the trouble I gave you in the early days. And I'm ashamed of the years I wouldn't listen when you tried to talk to me about God and tried to get me to read the Bible and go to church."

When Roy reached his ranch, he and Dale closed themselves in his office to discuss the details of their victory. "But Republic has announced they're going to appeal for a reversal," Roy said. "This thing could drag on for years." (It did, until June 4, 1954, when the United States Court of Appeals for the Ninth Circuit reversed a portion of Judge Hall's decision, stating in effect that where a motion-picture actor relinquished all his rights in movies in which he appeared he could not thereafter contend that the producer's use of those motion pictures in competition with the actor was unfair competition.)

Soon it would be announced that *The Roy Rogers Show* was going on radio and television in December, under a dual contract agreement between the National Broadcasting Company and the Post Cereals Division of General Foods Corporation. And almost immediately "The King of the Cowboys" and "The Queen of the West" would be set back to work producing more TV films and tape-recorded radio shows.

The Rogers team wouldn't be on television long before the tabulators would report that theirs was the number one Western video show. And more, that their penetration in all fields was deepening beyond anybody's wildest dreams. For among the multiple millions who weekly would be following the Rogerses' action-packed Western dramas, new types of fans were to join the legions. Tiny tots, too young to attend theaters, would soon cheer excitedly in their living rooms as Roy and Dale came riding up on Trigger and Buttermilk, always in the nick of time to save some poor person in trouble.

And delighted with a warm, good world in which bad folks inevitably lost, the youngsters would insist that their parents watch too. Parents, grateful for the wholesome entertainment the Rogerses' show provided for their children, would eventually give in and promptly be smitten themselves.

Late one afternoon, soon after the court case was finished, Dale Rogers finished work on the movie set before her husband did and decided to go home alone. "The minute I got there I knew something was wrong," she says. "The gate to the ranch was wide open and a strange car was parked in the driveway."

Noting the "MD" on the license plate, Dale jumped from her car, heart pounding. At that moment Lana, Robin's favorite dog, rushed across the lawn, barking urgently. When the gray Weimaraner reached Dale's side, she turned and swiftly led the way to Robin's little house.

Emily stood on the porch, the three older children huddled near. At the sight of Dale, the trio burst into fresh tears. "Mama," Cheryl cried, "our baby's real bad sick!"

Finally inside, a trembling Dale found Cau-Cau and Virginia efficiently following the instructions of a doctor who was working over Robin. The baby had suffered a severe convulsion.

For nearly a week there were to be many times when it seemed as if little Robin Rogers just couldn't make the grade. And her anguished parents maintained an almost constant vigil of prayer.

Then at last came the glorious morning when the doctors agreed that the baby had successfully passed the point of immediate danger. And with prayers of humble appreciation, the members of the Roy Rogers household struggled to recede to normal living. But as they did so, they began to see the ravages of Robin's illness and their hearts broke anew. The baby had been left too weak even to stand in their laps any more.

A short time later it was decided that Robin might benefit from physical therapy. And somehow, despite her working schedule, Dale herself managed to take Robin for regular appointments at an orthopedic clinic. "Mrs. Rogers did everything but stand on her head to keep the baby interested during these sessions," a therapist says, "while we worked to restore strength to that poor little body."

The climb back was difficult and slow. But gradually Robin improved to the extent that when supported, she could stand for five whole minutes. Then returned the proud grin to the delicate little face and the happy kicking of tiny legs high over her golden curls as she lay in her crib.

But the greatest disappointment of all was yet in store for Roy and Dale Rogers. The orthopedist soon had to tell them that Robin's trick of doing "the splits"—of which they'd long been so proud—was in reality a seriously dangerous one. "The way she kicks her legs around, she could throw her hips out of joint. We hate to do it but we'll have to fit a brace between her feet," the doctor explained, sadly.

Robin Rogers objected strenuously to the brace. And she became increasingly nervous and fretful. So until their baby could become adjusted to new restrictions and discomforts, the Rogerses found themselves thrust back into heartaches similar to those they had known in the first months of their daughter's life—endless days when Cau-Cau walked the floor with the baby, crooning; nights when Robin seemed unable to sleep; desperate moments when they felt that come what may, they simply could not leave their baby, that their own show could not go on.

But leaning more and more on their Heavenly Father, the Rogerses did go on. And those who lived and worked closely with them were almost awed to realize how much this couple had grown in a year's time, how much better equipped they were to bear heartaches. "For by then we were learning that there really can be such a thing as 'tribulation without and peace within'—'the peace of God, which passeth all understanding,'" Dale says. "But we were not to know the balm of that peace, of course, until we'd discovered the key to perfect prayer, the secret of complete surrender. No longer were we begging God to grant *our* will. We were asking only for strength to know *His* will."

"And actually, finding God through Jesus Christ is not such a diffi-

174

cult thing to do," Roy Rogers goes on. "We soon saw that learning to have real faith was not too unlike other processes we'd learned. Take water sports, for instance. We all know that when we flip over on our backs in a swimming pool, if we'll relax—really yield—the water will hold us up. So it is with man and God. But the all-important trick is relaxation—or blind faith. And over and over I read the words in my Bible: 'Except ye be converted, and become as little children, ye shall not enter into the kingdom of heaven.' In short, I guess it might be said that Dale and I finally learned that we couldn't have complete faith until faith completely had us."

So, day by day, little by little, the Rogers household grew relaxed again. And once more Robin was able to enjoy her stroller, to join the family at their dinner hour, to remain for the singing of hymns and bedtime prayers that followed.

One evening, their beloved brood safely asleep, Roy and Dale Rogers sat up very late talking. "Honey, have you ever considered the possibility," Dale asked musingly, "that the retarded child has a prominent place in God's plan for slowing down the rest of us? The whole world is tense, frustrated, rushing, always rushing. Quietness is almost a lost art. We've made so many noisy efficient machines to do our work that we have too much leisure, so we get into mischief, worry, quarrel, invent newer, faster, deadlier weapons of war with which to destroy each other. Then, in the midst of bedlam, along comes a little child who is different. She doesn't conform to our fast pace. No matter how much we strain and worry, try to push her into the accepted mold, she progresses only as fast or as slowly as God wills." Dale sighed. "This last spell of Robin's brought me up short, made me take a real soul-searching look at myself. And it taught me a lot. After all that hurrying and worrying we did to strengthen those little legs, what did we then have to do? Put a brace on them to protect them from that strength. It's almost as if the Master's voice was filtering through our befuddled, modern consciousness to say, 'Peace, be still. Be still, and know that I am God.'"

Dale tried to smile through threatening tears. "Maybe you'll think this sounds mixed up, honey," she went on. "But it just seems to me that it is only when we learn to slow down, when we learn to be still, that we finally begin to *progress*. And if that is true, then a retarded child bears fruit. Afflictions are direct links with Christ. And through the afflicted, God reaches us. I think I am beginning to see that actually God is granting a privilege to those He entrusts with the care of His 'special ones.' Come to think of it, even the medical profession speaks of them as 'exceptional children.'"

Roy's eyes shone with love akin to solemn wonder, as they invariably do when he gazes at his wife. "Honey, I can only say to you what the Good Book has said to me, 'Trust in the Lord with all thine heart; and lean not unto thine own understanding.'" He rose and began preparing for bed. "Only God knows the final answer to our problem. And if and when He wants us to understand, I guess He'll let us know."

Halloween soon turned into Thanksgiving, and Thanksgiving into Christmas. It was Robin's second Christmas with the family and there was much discussion about what Santa would leave her under the tree.

"I know, I know," Dusty said, as he clapped his hands one day. "A piano, a little red piano, small enough to go in her crib. If she could talk, I know that's just what she'd say."

So Cheryl, the eldest, was granted the privilege of writing Robin's letter to Santa Claus, with Linda and Dusty hovering near. And then the letter was added to the others and given to Roy to mail.

On Christmas Eve, Roy and Dale Rogers attended a midnight service at their church. Earlier that day Roy had stopped by for a talk with the family minister. "I think I have found an answer to my lifelong question, sir," Roy confided. "I am beginning to see that it is not so much the afflicted children who suffer as it is those around them, while they are learning to become obedient to God's will." He paused. "Dale and I are coming to church tonight to say a special prayer of thanks to God for sending us Robin."

"I simply couldn't answer him, I felt so humble in the presence of such faith," the minister admits. "And I've never been more touched than I was that Christmas Eve when I saw Roy and Dale Rogers enter my church to say their special prayer of thanks."

Christmas, as always, saw a family reunion at the Roy Rogers ranch. But on this day two guests who had just returned from a long stay in San Francisco were invited to join the intimate group. They were Margie Hamilton and her then nine-year-old daughter Nancy, who was recovering from a thirty-fifth operation on her legs. The presence of the Hamiltons, counted among the Rogerses' most treasured friends, has become traditional at the ranch on Christmas. "If it is possible for human beings ever to attain perfect faith," Dale Rogers comments, "I'd say Margie and Nancy Hamilton are among those who have. And they've provided such inspiration for Roy and me that we can only feel their coming into our lives when they did was an act of God."

Margie Hamilton was an average woman with an average job in the business world when abruptly one way of life ended and the curtain rang up on the barren stage of another. Shortly after a whirlwind wartime courtship and marriage, Margie's husband was killed —never even to know his child was on the way. "I guess you might say I was crowded to Christ," Margie admits, "for I had nobody else to turn to that day in a hospital ward when the doctor told me my baby had been born with a rare and dread lymphatic ailment, similar to elephantiasis, which could result only in shocking deformity and an unpredictable life span."

Margie Hamilton was to go through her Gethsemane before she ultimately found her serene strength through deep religious faith. "I see now, of course," she says, "that always I was led by my child. And just as she led me to God, she led me toward the worthwhile things on earth, even to friends like the Roy Rogerses.

Everywhere in the hospital where Nancy stayed, Margie Hamilton continually heard the names of Roy and Dale Rogers. She decided to try to uncover the magic secret of such hero worship. And through ward after ward, from bed to bed, she took her question. "But after I'd conducted my poll," Margie says, "I couldn't have felt sillier. And

I was very glad I wasn't working for Mr. Gallup. Because, incredibly, over and over I'd receive exactly the same answer. There were counterparts, of course, but in the majority even the phrasing was the same. And there was no mistaking the matter-of-fact tones and direct looks I got—they most certainly were the same."

Margie Hamilton laughed outright when it dawned on her how uncomplicated the world might be if it were run by children. "Why do you love Roy Rogers and Dale Evans?" she had asked her profound question. " 'Cause they're good," each child had answered simply.

Margie's curiosity about the "King of the Cowboys" and the "Queen of the West" turned to real interest because of a particular case. "I'd seen it happen dozens of times," Margie says, "but this time it really hit. The little fellow had cancer. He was an orphan and had been in the hospital almost a year. Toward the last he was so very ill, and then one day out of a clear sky he received a mysterious package—a Roy Rogers outfit from soup to nuts. I've never seen such a change in a child in my life. We had to put all the riggin' on him, of course, and his happiness had even the nurses in tears."

Inevitably, the morning came when Margie entered the ward and found the little boy's bed empty. "Our little cowboy rode away in the night," a nurse said. Then she sighed. "But at least this one was happy to the last. He died with his boots on." The girl's voice changed. "I wonder, Mrs. Hamilton, if those Rogerses realize how many sick children there are almost living through their spirits. How many small lives are actually being prolonged by the wonderful gifts they send. How many families are even burying little bodies in Roy Rogers and Dale Evans outfits because they know that's the way the kids would want it." She paused. "In fact, I wonder what kind of people those Rogerses *really* are."

Margie Hamilton didn't know it at the time, of course, but it wasn't going to be long before she could answer almost any question about the Rogerses. "Because by then my Nancy had caught the Roy-and-Dale bug too," she explains. "And one day while we were staying in Los Angeles, during a waiting period between her operations,

Nancy asked me to write a letter for her to Roy Rogers. I wrote it just as she dictated it and smiled to myself when I realized what a designing female I had on my hands, for she even included our telephone number."

Making her way back and forth on small crutches, Nancy Hamilton haunted the mail box for several days. "I became deeply sorry that I'd ever written the letter," Margie admits, "when I saw how genuinely concerned she was over a reply. So I set in impressing on her what a busy man Roy Rogers was, how much he traveled, and how impossible it would be for him to read and answer all the thousands of letters he no doubt received."

And as Nancy Hamilton loves to tell the story, "Mommy was right. I never did get a letter from Roy Rogers." Then she pauses dramatically and adds, beaming impishly, "Because he *telephoned* me instead! And he gave me his address and invited us to come to see them."

Naturally, Margie Hamilton was hesitant about visiting famous movie stars. But one day when she had Nancy out for a drive and they realized they were near the Rogerses' home, she gave in to her daughter's pleas. "Dale herself answered the door," Margie remembers, "and when I tried to apologize for not calling ahead, she waved my excuses away. I saw immediately that formalities had no place in that home." When the Hamiltons entered the living room they saw Roy sitting on the sofa with Cheryl on his lap, teaching her to play his guitar. Dusty was on the floor, which was littered with toys. And then, as many visitors to the Rogers home do, Margie particularly noticed Linda. "She seemed so unbelievably calm and sweet and understanding," Margie says. "And she took Nancy over immediately—but as an *equal*. There was no noisy self-consciousness about her, no quiet pity, no apparent notice whatsoever of Nancy's condition. Later I was to learn, of course, that almost from the moment Robin was born, Linda had made up her mind to be a nurse. And that her idea of a great occasion was to be allowed to accompany her parents on their hospital visits. It might not be fair to say that Linda is the most unselfish of the Rogers children and the most devout.

But she is amazingly poised and articulate. To hear that little girl pray is a memorable experience."

"Actually," Dale comments, "we showed the Hamiltons no more courtesy that day than we often show other fans. Then after we'd learned a bit about them, our primary interest was in seeing what we might do to help them. It was quite a while before it dawned on Roy and me that perhaps God had sent them to help *us*."

By anyone's standards, Margie Hamilton really is a remarkable person. And she has withstood dire poverty as well as sorrow. "But Margie doesn't talk easily about that part of her story," Dale says. "And finally when I got up enough nerve to ask her about it, she replied, 'My touch-and-go experiences with Nancy have left me with a great detachment for material things.'"

"Margie's philosophy consists of many such answers," Dale goes on. "She has taught her child—and me—that the human body matters little, that only the spirit counts. 'Deformities mean nothing, they are just mud around the gold,' is her way of putting it. And evidently she has talked to Nancy about death from the beginning. Nancy is an extremely bright child, and I'm sure many of her questions have been difficult ones. But they often speak casually about leaving this earth, calling it 'going upstairs.'"

Even the Hamiltons' unshakable religious faith seems a special kind to Roy and Dale Rogers. "As long as people love God and follow His word," Margie has told them on many an occasion, "the church they attend is of no significance. Believe me, because I *know*. There have been times when Nancy and I had not one slice of bread in the house, times when she had to have expensive medicine and I had not one penny in the world, times when blood was needed to save her life. Always God sent help. Sometimes through Catholics, many kinds of Protestants, Jews, Negroes, Latin Americans. To Him they were all the same. And that is what all of us in the whole world must see—that people are people. And if we want Him to love us, we must first love each other. The trouble is that people are so busy carrying banners they never stop to read what's on them."

"And of course just the sight of the Hamiltons' serene, happy faces

180

lifted us many times when we were feeling down about Robin," Dale says. "The first time Margie saw Robin she told me, 'Your baby is straight from heaven, Dale. I see it in her eyes just as I've always seen it in Nancy's. God has loaned us these children for a short time but for a big purpose. And we are blessed to have a part in His work, to learn many things other parents never learn.'" Dale smiles. "Then at times when I'd continue to buck like a steer—as Roy says no steer on earth can buck, Margie would inevitably bring out what I think is her most important motto of all: 'Let go, Dale. Let go and let God.'"

Because of their work, Roy and Dale Rogers are most often compelled to maintain a nonstop pace that is not conducive to ordinary friendships. And actually it was their children who, after the first meeting, kept in touch with the Hamiltons. The little girls often talked on the phone and wrote letters back and forth whenever the Hamiltons returned to San Francisco for Nancy's stays in the hospitals there. And so it came about a few weeks before that Christmas in 1951, that Linda ran to Dale one day waving a letter. "Mama, Mama!" she cried, "Nancy's done with her thirty-fifth operation and she's going to be out of the hospital for Christmas. May we invite them to spend Christmas Day with us?"

"Darling," Dale replied, "we know so many, many people and have such a flock of friends and business associates that Daddy and I long ago decided to confine our Christmas guests to our own folks—Daddy's family and mine. Remember?"

"But Mama," Linda pleaded, "the Hamiltons don't have any family." Then she thought a minute and the thought brought tears. "Just think, Mama, it'll be Christmas and Nancy and Margie won't have any place to go. Don't you think we can find room for them at our inn?"

Dale smiled as she told Roy about it later. "So, what could I say then but yes?"

"You did right, honey," Roy answered. "And we can be very proud of Linda. I think, too, that the Hamiltons will turn out to be the kind of people who are worth breaking rules for."

It was nearly noon on Christmas Day when the Hamilton pair arrived at the Rogers ranch in their ancient coupé. Before she got out of the car, Nancy tied to one of her small crutches a beautifully wrapped package—her Christmas gift for the Rogers family—so she could carry it in herself. "The house was full of Christmas sounds and Christmas smells," Margie says. "And many relatives were gathered in the trophy room where the tree was set up. Roy was busily helping the children clean up the debris left from their attack on packages. Emily told us that the excitement had been too much for Robin and that Dale had taken the baby back to the living room. We walked on back and found Dale in her favorite chair there—an old-fashioned rocker—singing to Robin. Dale is such an energetic, capable woman, always insisting on doing things for herself and so much for her husband and children—even to part of the cooking and other household chores—that I simply forget what a tiny person she is until I see her as she was then, very tired, in repose. She was wearing a gingham apron over a housecoat and no make-up at all. And I remember thinking that she didn't look much like a rootin'-tootin' cowgirl at the moment, but more like a weary child rocking her doll."

Dale brightened immediately at the sight of her guests, however, and showed proper interest in the package Nancy was proffering. "Here, Margie, you take Robin," Dale suggested, "so I can get to the insides of this wonderful-looking package."

"No, please let *me* hold Robin," Nancy begged. And with a nod from Dale, Margie took her daughter's crutches and helped her settle herself in the rocker. Then she placed Robin in Nancy's arms.

"The picture of those two little angels together in that rocker etched itself on my heart," Margie says. "And something seemed to tell me: Look quick! This will never happen again on another Christmas." Margie sighs. "To tell the truth, I thought it was Nancy's stay that was about up, for the doctors already had scheduled her thirty-sixth operation—complete amputation of one leg. And because of her frail condition, they weren't too hopeful about the outcome."

At that moment Dale was staring at another picture, the one she had found beneath Nancy's elaborate wrappings. And tears sprang to her eyes as she realized the profundity of the child's gift. For to the house of Rogers, Nancy Hamilton had given her most cherished possession—a picture of Jesus in modern dress, surrounded by afflicted children.

Automatically, Dale started to protest. But Margie's quiet voice intervened: "Always remember, Dale, there's a way to give and a way to receive." Then, somehow, Dale quickly thanked Nancy with a bright smile.

Today Nancy Hamilton—who has successfully recovered from the amputation of both legs—has discarded crutches for a wheel chair in which she is sometimes seen whizzing around the Rogers ranch while playing with her dear friend Linda. Her Christmas gift—which Roy and Dale always point out as the picture a little girl loved enough to give away—now hangs on a wall in their bedroom, a prominent part of the Rogerses' family altar.

The "King of the Cowboys" and the "Queen of the West" were slated to open a twelve-day, eighteen-performance engagement as stars of the Houston Fat Stock Show and Rodeo on January 30, 1952. "And we decided that before we left for Texas, we wanted to have Robin christened," Dale says. "At that particular time it just seemed to us that the most important thing in the world was to have our baby dedicated to God, to let Him know that we had really surrendered, that we were willingly placing her forever in His hands."

"And that was when it came out that little Robin had 'reached' even Jim Osborne," says a member of the Rogers organization. "For when Jim heard about Roy and Dale's plans, believe it or not, he hurriedly left his ledgers to go shopping for a baby's christening dress. Later we learned that he spent most of a day making his selection, going from store to store before he carefully decided on a lovely white organdy pinafore with a wide pink satin sash."

On the always-to-be-remembered day, Cau-Cau painstakingly curled the baby's blond hair—which Dale always refers to as "Robin's golden halo"—and finished off the job with a tiny pink bow. With the dress Jim Osborne had sent for Robin, she wore new white shoes and socks on her doll-like feet, happily freed for a short time of their hated brace. "I'll never forget the looks on Roy and Dale's faces when they handed me their baby during the ceremony," the minister says. "They seemed completely at peace, happier than I'd ever seen them."

A few days after Robin's christening, Dale Evans Rogers received what she later realized was a strange telephone call. "I had just walked in the house from the studio," she explains, "and only because the phone rang at the precise instant I passed it, I did something I seldom get to do—I answered it myself. A woman's voice told me that she needed money desperately, that she was an artist and wanted to do Robin's picture in her christening outfit." When Dale was to look back and realize how automatically she had agreed to the woman's proposal, she could only ask herself these questions: How on earth did the woman secure their telephone number, which of necessity is unlisted? Why, with the odds so against it, did she happen to answer the phone herself? How did the artist know about Robin's christening when there had been no publicity about the private ceremony? Why, when Jim Osborne had long before set a strict rule that all appeals—which arrive in an endless stream—had to be properly investigated, did she so unhesitatingly make an exception? And why, if the idea of a picture of Robin in her christening dress had been brought to her mind, did she not then instead call Lee Green, their own photographer?

"I honestly didn't know the answers to those questions then," Dale says. "But I know now, of course. There's only one answer for all of them, and it's the same as that to the many others that puzzled me through the years. Now that Roy and I have learned that a master plan exists, we know it's the answer to everything that ever happens, big or little, to any of us in our whole life. *The answer is God*. In this instance, God crossed the lives of strangers so all things could 'work together for good.' The woman, I learned much later, did need money desperately for a very worthy reason. She must have prayed for guidance, and God sent her to us to get the money. For she did more than take a photograph; she made a wonderful color etching of our baby. And today, as any parents could understand, it is our priceless treasure. Sometimes I shudder to think that if that woman hadn't called, we might not have a really good picture of Robin. So, as God provided an urgent need for the artist, He provided a future need for Roy and me. That lifelike etching, you see, was going to serve a very significant purpose later on."

Before the year was to be over, the color etching of Robin Rogers would be hung to center the family altar. And sitting at the desk in her bedroom one day, Dale would gaze at it and find inspiration at what she considers one of the most important moments of her life. And, as it has turned out, a moment important to the lives of countless others all over the world.

Before they could leave California for their date at Houston, Texas, Roy and Dale had to rush madly to tie up many loose ends while also making all the necessary preparations for a fresh show. New regalia, for street wear as well as stage—which they design for themselves—had to be cut and fitted by their Western tailor, Nudie. New numbers had to be dreamed up, worked out, and rehearsed—solos, duets, acts with Pat Brady and with "The Whipporwills," a Western musical group. And tape recordings of their radio show, plus a TV film—their twentieth—had to be completed. "So, as usual," Art Rush says, with a sigh, "we got off on one leg."

But, also as usual—as anyone who's ever spent much time with the Rogerses can testify—to leave home for a road engagement was merely to go from a hot frying pan into a hotter fire. "You'll do eighteen shows in twelve days," Art said, as he went over plans with his clients on the train. "Things begin with your leading a big parade with Governor Allan Shivers, lots of radio and press interviews have been set up, requests for personal appearances have simply flooded in, and. . . ."

"Just be sure you leave some time for us to visit hospitals and see the other sick children," Roy interrupted firmly. Then, curling his lip, much like an underprivileged child himself, he added, "I sure would like to get in some good coon hunting while I'm down there."

"Well, *I* am going to spend some time with my mother and daddy if it harelips every cow in Texas," Dale announced. "They're meeting us in Houston."

When the stars arrived on the *Sunset Limited* at 8:40 A.M., January 26, an even larger crowd than usual was gathered at the railroad station to meet them. And the Rogerses soon noticed that the mob of children—many dressed in facsimiles of Western splendor—were anxious-faced as they screamed excited welcomes. Then, as children do, the teeming throngs soon made it plain that they had insisted on dragging their parents downtown at such an early hour not only to see their hero and heroine but also to inquire about and protest against a rumor that had flashed from coast to coast: that Roy Rogers was considering selling Trigger!

"Right before we left home," Roy explains, "I received a telegram signed by a J. B. Ferguson, offering me two hundred thousand for Trigger. We were rushing around so that I didn't even investigate it or think of answering. But when we got to Houston, I learned that the offer was authentic and already had hit the papers, that Mr. Ferguson was not just a wealthy Texas oilman trying to satisfy the whim of his little boy, but that he was a great lover of horses, and had a stable full of thoroughbreds and quarter horses. He thought it would be a profitable business deal for him to have Trigger for breeding purposes."

From time to time Roy Rogers had received many offers for his wonder horse. But never before had one exceeded twenty-five thousand dollars. And, as the newspapers had a wonderful time pointing out, two hundred thousand might be a sum that would make a cowboy, whose horse was nearly nineteen years old, stop and think. Besides, the consensus ran, Roy has Trigger, Jr., and we hear by the grapevine that a whole string of Palomino colts are constantly being trained at the Rogers stables.

When Roy and Dale reached their suite at the Shamrock Hotel, they were met by a deluge of calls, telegrams, and letters, all pleading with Roy not to sell Trigger. And soon the Fat Stock Show, Houston newspapers, and the whole Shamrock Hotel were feeling the storm. The Rogers building in Hollywood was simply besieged. And crowds

186

of children began making pilgrimages to the ranch. Even the team's sponsors, network, and licensees called.

When finally Roy met and talked with J. B. Ferguson, the cowboy's words were typical: "Gosh, two hundred thousand *is* a lot of money, sir. And please don't think I don't realize that and appreciate your offer. And I'm mighty proud of anybody thinking that much of my horse. But old Trigger is a part of me, Mr. Ferguson, and we've ridden a lot of miles together. And, well, I just couldn't sell him for all the money in the world." Roy grinned and then came the quote that was repeated all over the nation, "Not even for all the money in *Texas!*"

When a reporter laughingly mentioned that the latest rumor was that Trigger had been offered a million dollars for his master, the man wanted to know, "And what do you think your horse will say to that, Roy?"

Roy smiled. "I think he'll say 'neigh.'"

And so the excitement died. In Houston, that is. But in Hollywood the Rogers organization had to continue to cope with the matter for days. Thousands of children had written letters, emphasizing their pleas by enclosing coins that ranged from pennies to silver dollars. Evidently, if Roy Rogers needed financial help to hold on to Trigger, the small fry of America was prepared to give it. "So all that cash had to be carefully returned," Al Rackin says, with a laugh. "It was a mess."

And to make sure that such a situation would never have to be met again, Roy soon announced that Trigger belonged not only to him but to all the children of the world. To substantiate that fact, he had certificates of ownership printed which state that the bearer is an honorary shareholder in Trigger. And today, all over the world, those certificates are proudly carried in many a small pocket.

While in Houston, despite their overwhelming professional obligations, Roy and Dale Rogers somehow managed to telephone California daily to talk to their children, to get in some coon hunting, and to visit with Walter and Betty Sue Smith, Dale's parents. "It was on this trip," Betty Sue Smith says, "that I began to realize the extent of their conversion, to see real evidence of the changes Robin had made in their lives. I had worried many times in the past when I'd seen a hospital visit or a telephone conversation with a dying child or an unsightly stretcher case leave both Roy and Dale completely unnerved, frustrated to the point of almost screaming their *whys*. But now it seemed they were finding an answer. Sorrow indeed had come with a gift in her hand. The gift was faith, of course. A faith that brought wisdom and understanding to the point of inner peace. And perhaps the most heartening thing of all was to see that their new-found attitude was not only helping them face this most difficult part of their careers—their work with sick children—but they were transmitting this peace somehow to those heartbroken parents always standing nearby."

One day when Betty Sue Smith talked with her daughter on the subject, Dale smiled. "Now, Mother," she objected mildly, "please don't go around talking to people about us. You make it all sound—well, a little too pat. And don't let even yourself think for a minute that Roy and I believe we've found *all* the answers to anything. Sometimes it takes years to understand why God does certain things. And sometimes we never understand. And who can say? Maybe we aren't supposed to. But the important thing is not so much to *find* answers as to learn that there *are* answers. And it's that sure knowledge that gives us a goal, so to speak. Nobody can feel confident and secure when he's merely floundering. But to know there really is a God, and through Christ to live closely with Him, is to know you're not traveling alone, that no matter what or where, He's always beside you. And in these travels when you get glimpses of His love and His power, you're spurred on to see more. Because when you see parts of anything, you can be sure that somewhere there's a whole. And to know that *whole* exists—that's what makes the difference."

At the opening performance of the Fat Stock Show Rodeo, 4,000 underprivileged and handicapped children filled one-half of the hard-to-get seats at the Sam Houston Coliseum. Several hours before each future performance, Roy asked Glenn Randall to station himself, Trigger, and Trigger's trailer outside the show grounds for the convenience of any child who wanted to ask questions or just gape. Asked about it, Roy explained, "If they had the money, those kids would be inside." Toward the end of their engagement, when it became clear that the Rogerses were breaking even their own box-office records, and that it was going to be an absolute impossibility ever to meet the clamoring demand for tickets for their final performances —the Coliseum was simply sold out—Roy and Dale hit upon an idea. And with the stock show officials and the General Foods Corporation giving them a go-ahead, they made special arrangements to have their entire rodeo performance televised for the first time. "And we'll dedicate it to the disabled veterans, shut-ins, and all children who have been unable to attend our show," Dale said.

"But of all the things our children did during their stay in Houston," Betty Sue Smith says, "the most surprising was their decision to include their religious faith even in their wild-and-woolly rodeo. Dad and I couldn't believe our eyes and ears at first, when Roy came out for a solo, and there before thousands of people, instead of doing 'I'm a Buckeye Cowboy from O-h-10,' or one of his usual kind of numbers, he began to sing 'Peace in the Valley,' a hymn-ballad. Never in all the years we'd known him had we ever heard Roy Rogers sing so beautifully and with so much feeling. Suddenly I realized that the whole booming-zooming Coliseum had become as quiet as a church. And then Roy talked to the children in the audience about the importance of going to Sunday school. Dad and I were simply dumbstruck, because neither Roy nor Dale had told us a word about it beforehand."

Actually, the Rogerses had not told anybody their plans beforehand. "I did hear Roy rehearse the song," Art Rush says. "And I was quite surprised too, because so many times in the past I'd tried to get him to do heavier stuff and he'd always refused. Roy had an inferiority complex and he just was afraid to trust his voice." So, delighted with the new confidence Roy's switch displayed, Art Rush complimented his kid profusely on the way he sang "Peace in the Valley" and only once casually ventured to ask him why he'd chosen that particular number.

189

"I guess, Buck," Roy answered quietly, "because Dale and I feel we're at last learning *how* to have peace in the valley."

Later, discussing the matter with Jim Osborne, Art Rush shook his head. "I'm telling you, Jim, that kid of mine is changing so much I doubt soon if I'll have any problems to deal with at all."

"Yeah," Jim agreed. "But I still think the most incredible thing is the way he's learned to speak in public. Next I guess we'll be hearing that he's making speeches of his own accord!"

But little did Jim Osborne or Art Rush dream that a speech of his own accord was exactly what Roy Rogers had in mind when he decided to sing "Peace in the Valley" at the Houston rodeo. "Honey," he said to Dale one day before leaving California, "I've received a letter from a little boy that I somehow can't get off my mind. This kid says that he likes to go to Sunday school but when he does, all his little friends call him 'sissy.' He asked me outright, 'Roy, is it or is it not sissy to go to Sunday school?'"

"Well, is that such a difficult question to answer?" Dale asked, with a smile.

"Ordinarily, no," Roy conceded. "But I've got a sort of fuzzy hunch that the answer could be important to a lot of other youngsters besides that one little boy." He hesitated. "Mama, what do you think of my answering that question publicly?"

Dale was not at all sure what Roy was getting at. Many requests recently had come in from magazines and newspapers wanting articles about the couple's new-found faith. And Roy had flatly turned them all down. "But you've been so emphatic about our keeping our deepest personal feelings out of our professional lives," Dale pointed out finally.

"Well, maybe I've been wrong. Maybe God has been trying to open a door for me and I've been too dumb to realize it. Maybe I still need what our whole world needs—more faith in faith itself."

"Yes," Dale agreed. "It's pretty silly to continue to pray so hard for guidance and then refuse to recognize it when it comes."

"That's exactly what I'm getting at." Roy picked up a Bible from a nearby table and turned to the Book of James. "I'm sure a lot of

190

people would call it mere coincidence, but I ran across this the very day I received that child's letter. Listen to these words: 'Faith without works is dead.'" Roy closed his Bible and his face was solemn. "I know that text applies to a lot more than this situation, honey. But still, when you think about it, what good really is thought without action?" Roy sighed. "I don't know what to do, Dale. I honestly don't. The only thing I'm sure of is that I haven't been able to shake the idea that God might have had this letter sent to me for a concrete purpose. It's been like a force, almost pushing me. And I simply can't get rid of it."

"Then that settles it, honey," Dale concluded, in her quick decisive way. "I learned long ago that a nagging idea deserves to be heard." Then, as usual, Dale Evans Rogers lost no time in getting down to brass tacks. "How are you going to handle this, Roy? Through a regular press release?"

"No," Roy replied, shaking his head. "I'm going to answer that question in person so I can talk to the children face to face. And in a setting they know me best—right smack in the middle of a rodeo arena."

Dale's green eyes opened wide with surprise. And then, to hide deep emotion, she smiled broadly. "You know, Mr. Rogers, there are times when I think you are downright wonderful."

Roy's face crinkled into a grin. "Well, it just might be that some of our worthy advisers wouldn't share your approval at this moment, Mrs. Rogers. Perhaps we better keep this plan under our Stetsons— between you and me and God."

And so it came about that on February 6, 1952, Charlie Evans head-lined his Houston *Chronicle* column A SERMON BY A COWBOY and commented:

One of the best sermons we have heard in some time was one delivered Sunday.
And it wasn't from the pulpit of a church. It was from the center of the Coliseum rodeo arena, delivered by Cowboy Star Roy Rogers.
At the Sunday matinee and night shows Rogers asked how many of the youngsters in the stands had been to Sunday school or church that

191

morning. Then he advised: "All you little cowboys and cowgirls out there, be sure to go to Sunday school. You might hear some of your little friends say it's 'sissy' to go to Sunday school.

"But don't you believe 'em! Going to Sunday school is the best way in the world to get started right in life," Roy told the youngsters.

And when he had finished, we heard a couple of youngsters sitting next to us talking. Said one: "You see, we better start going to Sunday school again. Roy Rogers said for us to."

And we imagine many another youngster thought the same thing.

If Roy Rogers really expected objection from his managers, he was disappointed. Because they made no comments either way. "We simply still didn't see the handwriting on the wall," Jim Osborne was to admit much later. "We just figured that the kids received a letter that snared their interest. And that after they'd answered it, that would be that."

But, as now is common knowledge, that was not exactly going to be just that in the case of Roy Rogers and Dale Evans. One Sunday during their stay in Houston, they would be asked to talk at a church there. They would accept the invitation. And soon such requests would start pouring in from churches and clubs all over the nation. "Now we can look back and see how it all happened, step by slow step," Dale Rogers says today. "How, through Robin, God opened a whole new life for us."

By the time the Rogers troupe got back to California, everybody was alarmed over a high temperature and deep cough Roy had developed on the trip homeward. For over a week he had been silently battling what he calls "walkin' flu." But on the train he became so ill that even the hearty cowboy had to admit that perhaps at last he had met up with a nasty varmint he couldn't lick singlehanded.

"All the newspapers had lauded Roy for keeping up his good works twenty-five hours out of every twenty-four while he was here," comments Paul Boesch, a Houston radio man. "And there's simply no telling how many hospital visits he and Dale made, how many handicapped children they saw, how many times every day they signed their names and posed for photographs, how many thousands of little hands they shook—over and above their countless radio, television, and press interviews, their personal appearances, and the hours they performed in their show itself. But the last straw on this trip, I think, was piled on the day before they left. Roy heard about a little girl named Ronni Ryan, a patient at the Hedgecroft Polio Clinic, who wanted for a birthday present only to see the Rogerses' rodeo. But because this child is one of polio's greatest examples of destruction, she'd been unable to go with many other youngsters at the hospital or even to see the show on TV. Roy and Dale couldn't rest when they heard about her, of course. And they arranged for a fabulous birthday cake to be topped with a replica of a rodeo arena and trimmed with the symbols and characters of their show. Roy insisted on taking the cake to the child himself, and on the way he picked up enough ice cream for the whole hospital. Roy made Ronni the happiest kid in the world, of course, and to this day, if you mention his name at Hedgecroft, it had better be with reverence. But, unhappily, it happened to be pouring rain that day and Roy got drenched. So, knowing about the bad cold he already had, I was not very surprised to learn that by the time he reached California, Roy had developed pneumonia and had to be hospitalized immediately."

For a few days the condition of Roy Rogers ran nip and tuck. And then when the doctors were sure he had safely passed the crisis, they firmly announced that their patient would have to rest quietly for several weeks. Only those who know him well can understand the effect such news had on Roy's associates. "Mercy, I'd sooner try to hold back Trigger when he gets an S O S from Roy than try to keep that kid in bed when he's able to get out," Art Rush said. But finally Mattie and Andy Slye came up with an idea to keep their son quiet, and an urgent call went out from the Rogers building for a supply of something called "vining maple prongs."

"They're found on a tree that grows in Oregon," Art explained to his mystified secretary who was put in charge of the search. "Roy thinks they make the best slingshots in the world."

Today Art Rush adds, chuckling, "I didn't actually count them, so I don't know how many slingshots Roy whittled during that rest period. But it was dozens. And we still use that trick today. Whenever we have to keep him still to talk over lengthy business matters, we just first hand him whittling paraphernalia and let nature take its course. And when he has enough slingshots on hand, he whittles trigger-four-deadfalls, which are traps to catch varmints on his ranch."

With working schedules canceled, and her husband out of danger, Dale decided suddenly one day to do something that had been in the back of her mind since Christmas. "Margie Hamilton had told me about a doctor in San Francisco who had helped some children like Robin," Dale explains. "And I'd simply been unable to forget it. Roy and I talked it over, and although every doctor we'd ever seen had told us absolutely nothing could be done for our baby, we decided we should try again. It wasn't that we were looking for miracles or magic cures any longer. But we just felt we wanted to do everything possible to help Robin's condition, make it easier. We had learned by then, of course, that God takes care of all results, but we felt—and still feel—that He expects us to meet all situations to the best of our ability. And we had constantly prayed that somewhere there might be a doctor whom God would guide to relieve our baby of at least some of her discomforts. Our doctors at home were very concerned over Robin's heart condition, but they seemed to understand the way Roy and I felt and they okayed the trip."

Dale decided that she and Cau-Cau should take time off to take Robin to San Francisco.

"And here you have a perfect example of the kind of thing that someday may put poor Art Rush and Jim Osborne in padded cells," says a member of the Rogers business family. "When Roy and Dale get a bee in their bonnet, they move at the pace of a fire fighter, consulting no one but each other, bypassing all channels. In this instance, instead of notifying us at the office so we could smooth the way for her through our travel agency, Dale simply threw a few things in a bag, pulled on her hat, wrapped a blanket around Robin, and took off for the railroad station. None of us has ever been able to figure out whether they simply don't realize they're celebrities—

194

entitled to many privileges and obligated to take some precautions —or whether they just refuse to acknowledge, even to themselves, that they are wealthy, important people and prefer to go around behaving like any John and Mary Doe."

Be all that as it may, on this day Dale Evans Rogers was rushing to make the *Daylight* to San Francisco. And when she arrived at the station, she learned that all space was filled, that not even a chair was available on the popular train. But always a person difficult to discourage, Dale took a place on a bench in the crowded station in hopes that some accommodation might turn up in the forty minutes that remained before the train's scheduled departure. By this time little Robin was quite upset and was complaining at the top of her weak, thin voice, refusing to take notice even of her favorite toy—the small red piano which she loved so dearly that Dale had brought along. "Finally I got up and walked the floor with my baby," Dale admitted much later. "And I patted her little back and sang. But underneath I was praying. I asked God, if He felt the trip was right for us, to open the way."

And less than five minutes before traintime, the way was opened for Dale, Cau-Cau, and Robin. A ticket agent's telephone rang, a cancellation was reported, and the three passengers were allowed to board the *Daylight* just as the final "all aboard" was being called.

"I learned about all this only because I just happened to call at that particular time to check on Roy," Art Rush says. "And when I heard what Dale had done, I slammed down the phone, jumped in my car, and flew to the railroad station. I simply didn't know what I might find. Any parent who's ever traveled even with a well baby knows there are few greater tasks. And Robin was so far from well. The very thought of Dale, and the nurse there in that crowded station, with no reservations, trying to manage luggage and that baby, made my blood run cold."

By the time Art Rush reached the train station, however, the *Daylight* had gone. And seeing no sign of Dale and Robin, and anxious to know their exact whereabouts, Art inquired from window to window if anybody had seen Mrs. Rogers. But nobody, it seemed, had.

Determined, Art explained further: "She's five feet, two inches tall, weighs about one hundred and ten pounds, and has reddish-brown hair. And she was carrying a little girl, a year and a half old, with blond curls."

"Was that baby kind of sickly?" one man asked.

"Yes."

"Then I saw her. I handled her ticket. A cancellation came through and she was able to get on the *Daylight* at the last minute."

"But are you sure?" Art asked, in his careful way. "Did she *say* she was Mrs. Roy Rogers?"

"Oh, heavens, no." The man misunderstood Art's motive. "This was a nice kid, not at all the type to pull anything phony like that."

Art gave up and walked away. "I realized then that he thought I was a detective looking for an imposter," he explains sadly. "And there was no point whatsoever in my telling him that the nice kid he saw really was Mrs. Roy Rogers. He probably wouldn't have believed me anyway."

Dale was just getting Robin settled in a San Francisco hotel room when one of the worst possible things that could have occurred happened. The city staged an air-raid warning. "Robin had been completely unable to tolerate noise from the moment she was born," Dale explains. "And all those sirens, whistles, bells, horns, all the rushing around and shouting and confusion sent my poor baby into an absolute frenzy. I was so worn out from our train trip I simply couldn't walk the floor any more so we placed her, stomach down, on the bed and turned her head so one little ear would be against the mattress. Cau-Cau held her hand over her other ear. And I patted her back."

At long last the terrible explosion was over. Cau-Cau changed the baby's perspiration-soaked clothes and Dale quickly warmed a bottle. "She was simply exhausted, as limp as a little rag doll," Dale says, "and in a few minutes was fast asleep."

The doctor in San Francisco was very frank with Robin's mother when he had finished a thorough examination of her child. "He prescribed glandular extracts and vitamins, with the hope that they might improve her appetite and muscle tone," Dale says. "And he told me that if the medications worked as they had in other cases, in time, with the added help of constant massage, our baby might even walk."

"But," the doctor added firmly, "for her heart condition, I'm sorry, I can do nothing. *Nothing.*"

In silence Dale Rogers bundled up her precious cargo once more and went out to the street. "I don't know how long I stood there before I recovered enough to hail a cab," she says. "And I asked the driver to take us to the city square."

And it was there, at the sight of all the pigeons, that Robin perked up and smiled for the first time since they had left home. "She called to the birds with the noises that were her strange language," Dale tells. "And she waved her little arms as if she too were trying to fly away. I remember very well saying to her, 'Well, young lady, Robin was surely the right name for you. You're a little bird, that's what you are. No wonder you won't walk. What you really want, I think, is a pair of wings.' "

Dale shakes her head, reliving the scene. "But little did I know then, little did I know."

Back home again, Dale insisted that Cau-Cau continue her vacation, and for the remaining time of Roy's rest period she took complete charge of Robin. "Everything went well for a few days," Dale recalls, "and we all had a lot of fun. But then the more I cared for my baby alone, the more I realized what constant attention she needed. And before I quite knew what was happening, an old fear I'd suffered years before—when Tommy was a baby—returned to plague me. But this time, magnified a thousandfold. I became obsessed with the terrifying thought that someday Robin might have to get along in this world without me."

Suddenly Dale's peace was gone. All her prayers turned to mere frantic pleas. And soon she found herself unable even to eat and sleep. Day and night she could think of nothing but begging God to let her stay on earth as long as Robin did, so that she could guard and take care of her.

197

"But the dear Lord helped Dale find her way back into His Kingdom just as He helps all His lost children," Roy Rogers says. "And this time he used his most powerful reminder—Easter itself."

All during Holy Week the family read frequently from the Bible. "No longer for any of us could Easter mean just new clothes and bunnies and baskets and colored eggs. The children enjoyed all that, of course, but this year we had so much more. Robin had taught us what it means to really love. And through her we had gained an understanding of Christ and suffering humanity. We understood the miseries of the Crucifixion and we felt the glories of the Resurrection."

When Roy and Dale returned from church on Easter Sunday, the certainty of eternal life was strong within them. "So much so," says Dale, "that I could actually smile again as I bundled up Robin and took her on the lawn in her stroller to watch the older children hunt for eggs. Roy teased Robin, telling her she looked just like an Easter bunny herself in her white woolly cap with a peak over each ear. And he took snapshot after snapshot of us all, as usual."

That night when Dale retired, it was with a renewed desire to really pray. "I told God," she says, "that once more I was ready to obey His will. I knew then that someday our baby would live in heaven in a better condition than she was on earth. And that everything was going to work out all right."

When Dale finally closed her eyes, she slept a night through for the first time in nearly two weeks.

The first thing Roy and Dale Rogers did when the cowboy was set free by his doctors was go to San Francisco with their baby. "The doctor there had advised us to bring Robin back for a checkup so he could determine what good, if any, the new medicines had done," Roy explains. "But what a trip that one was! The racket of the train and the city noises upset the baby terribly, and during one of our nights at the hotel, Robin developed a high fever. Finally the doctor had to give her a shot of penicillin and some rest medicine. He found her muscle tone improved, but he said her heart condition was worse.

198

So all in all, it was decided that such wearing trips were doing her more harm than good."

"But if no good was to come from taking her to San Francisco," Dale asked her husband later, "then why did God open the way for Robin and me that first time?"

Roy thought a long while before he answered. And when he spoke his voice was low. "I think God took care of that question for us at Easter, honey. Perhaps these trips were to teach us once and for all that there will be no help for our baby on earth. That we must let her rest in the hands of our Lord."

Of all the nightmarish hours the Rogerses experienced until they finally got back home again with their baby, those on the returning train were the worst, and during the short period that Robin slept, they discussed a new problem that had presented itself. Cheryl, the eldest of the Rogers children, who had been adopted at Dallas, Texas, was nearing adolescence, and recently she had confronted her parents with questions that made them realize she was brooding about her background.

"Cheryl's happiness the rest of her life may depend on the way we handle this problem," Dale said. "And I honestly don't know what to do."

"Well, I think there's only one thing *to* do," Roy replied, "and that's to see that her questions are answered truthfully."

"But we don't *know* the answers."

"The officials at the adoption agency do. And I think we should see if they won't allow Cheryl to visit them there so she can see and hear for herself."

"School will soon be out," Dale agreed. "I'll make arrangements just as soon as it's feasible."

Then the Rogerses turned to another problem. But this one, concerning Dusty, was not going to be so easily solved. Reports from school indicated that the little boy needed companionship. The two older girls, naturally, were together a great deal and Dusty was showing signs of being unhappy alone. "Perhaps all things about the children seemed magnified to us then," Dale comments. "But because we had to be away from them so much, we worried constantly that in some way we might overlook or neglect a serious need."

But if troubling reports had come in about Dusty, he certainly was loving and kind with little Robin. He never seemed to tire of entertaining her and endlessly he played peekaboo and other simple games that sent the baby into peals of laughter. And on her birthday he had carefully wrapped his most treasured toy and carried it out to her little house.

"If Robin had a favorite among the children," Virginia, their nurse, says, "it was surely Dusty. And when Cau-Cau returned from her vacation and it was decided that she should start taking a day a week off, as Emily, the housekeeper, and I did, Dusty was a great help to me with Robin on those days. He is a shy, quiet child and deeply compassionate. Mammy and Grampy Slye say that Dusty not only looks exactly like his father but that he acts as Roy did at that age."

As the weather grew warmer, Roy and Dale began taking baby Robin into the swimming pool with the other children. And she showed much delight in kicking and splattering the water. "You may look like a water lily, my beautiful angel," Roy told Robin many times, "but you behave more like a frog." And he took reel after reel of color movies of these happy moments which today the Rogers family often view along with the countless others Roy has shot through the years.

"Of all the records that can be kept of children's growth," he says, "I think moving pictures are among the most rewarding. And it seems to me that parents are letting themselves miss a lot of future pleasure if they don't take them. Maybe Dale and I are behaving kind of like squirrels, but we are constantly gathering every possible reminder of these wonderful years with our kids that we can. And when the time comes that they are grown, and Mama and I have had to trade our saddles for rocking chairs, we hope to be able to enjoy many an hour reliving the fun and happiness we're having with them now."

As she neared her second birthday, Robin Rogers weighed just a bit over 17 pounds. The soft spot on her head still had not quite closed. And most of the time she seemed tired and frighteningly drowsy. Nevertheless, there was evidence that the glandular extracts and potent vitamins which had been prescribed for her in San Francisco were improving her muscle tone. "She got to where she could turn herself over in her crib," Dale says, "and sometimes even managed to get into a crawling position. She had eight teeth by then and had added a new word to her small vocabulary—'cack-cack,' which meant 'crackers.' Somehow, by that time Roy and I seemed to understand that God did not mean for our baby ever to walk. But Cau-Cau would not give up. Faithfully she kept hoping and praying, and patiently she continued to exercise Robin's thin little legs, rubbing and massaging day after day."

In early June, Roy and Dale were slated to speak at a large religious meeting at Houston, Texas. But when the time came, they realized that to do it, and still maintain their working schedule, they would have to fly. But Dale balked at the idea. "I had not been on a plane since Robin had been born," she explains. "I was plain scared. Afraid that we might crash. And of all the tests I'd managed so far to pass, it looked like this was one I was doomed to flunk."

Finally the Rogerses decided that Roy should go to Houston alone. And in troubled silence Dale drove him to the airport. "I slept hardly a wink all that night," she says. "It was as if somebody were asking me over and over, 'Which comes first, *your* Robin or *God*'s Robin?'"

The instant Dale opened her eyes the next morning she seemed to clearly understand that question. "I knew then that it was more important to tell people what God had done for us all through Robin than it was for me to be so frantic about being beside her all the time," she says. "And perhaps one of the greatest things Robin did for me was to help me win out over fear. My decision to fly to Houston seemed to remove the last vestige of it. And I don't think I've ever been downright *afraid* of anything since."

Because Roy and Dale Rogers were invited to appear at the meeting as representatives of the Hollywood Christian Group, Dale immediately called Tim Spencer. "I've changed my mind, Timmy," she said. "I've decided to go to Houston *for* Robin instead of staying *with* her."

"I knew what a difficult time Dale must have had to reach that decision," Tim says. "And I was very proud of her indeed. I told her to hurry and get her things together, and that I'd call the airport and try to get her on the next plane."

When Tim Spencer called back, Dale could tell by his voice that he was smiling. "Your trip is blessed, honey," he said. "You got the last available seat on the plane. They told me in another five minutes it would have been no soap."

Just as Dale was preparing to leave the house, she received a long-distance call from Italy, Texas. Her father had suddenly been stricken ill by a cerebral hemorrhage. "The doctor thinks it was a mild heart attack," Dale's mother told her. "And I think maybe you'd better come home."

"Well, I'm leaving for the airport now and I'll be home by dinner-time."

"You mean you're going to *fly!*" her mother exclaimed. And then came a logical afterthought, "But can you get a reservation?"

Dale laughed. "God works in mysterious ways, Mom. And I'll explain when I see you. But I've already decided to fly and I've already got my reservation. Just have Hillman meet me when the Houston-bound plane stops in Dallas. I'll get off there."

After spending the night at Italy with her parents, and relieved to find her father doing nicely, Dale drove back to nearby Dallas with her brother Hillman and his wife Bennie Merle, to board the *Rocket* for Houston. "We got to Dallas a couple of hours before departure time," Dale says, "and I decided to run out to the adoption home to talk over Cheryl's problem with officials there. They were highly in favor of Roy's idea to have Cheryl visit them, and I said I'd send her as soon as possible. Then just as I got ready to leave, I had a strange urge to see the babies there. And the supervisor consented to take us through the nursery."

As the party walked down the aisles between the cribs, Bennie Merle suddenly squealed. "For heaven's sake, Dale, look at this!"

"When I turned, I saw a little black-eyed, dark-skinned baby girl with a wad of coal-black hair," Dale goes on. "And when I spoke to her, she pulled herself up on her elbows and gave me the once-over but good. Then, just as if she approved of what she saw, her fat little face broke into a wide grin."

As Dale moved on from crib to crib, she kept stealing glances at the vividly brunet child. "I couldn't help myself," she smiles. "Those ripe-olive eyes were following every move I made."

When Dale inquired about the baby, she learned she was two months old, three-quarters Choctaw Indian, and called Mary. Then, despite the fact that she knew she was breaking a rule, Dale begged permission to hold Mary before leaving the nursery.

"All right," the nurse agreed, "for you, Mrs. Rogers, I guess we can make an exception."

"When I picked her up," Dale tells, "she held her little head away from me and inspected me again with the solemnity of a judge in court. But quickly her formal dignity was gone and she grabbed at my hair, roughhousing like we were old friends. I had to put her back in her crib soon, because time was running out on me by then."

"All Dale talked about until she finally got off for Houston was that baby," Hillman Smith says. "But Bennie Merle and I paid no serious attention. Anybody who knows my sister and her husband knows they simply go off the deep end at the sight of any child. And they cuddle thousands every year. So it didn't dawn on us that God had something special in mind about this baby. But looking back, of course, we can see His many reasons for sending Dale on this trip. And I guess it's only in retrospect that we're ever able to understand some of the intricate ways He works."

When Dale joined Roy in Houston, it seemed to her husband that she was bubbling over with happiness. "It's just that I've seen so much evidence of God's loving-kindness the past thirty-six hours, honey," she tried to explain. "The way He managed everything about my trip was wonderful, and Dad is going to be O.K., and the supervisor at the adoption home feels sure she can help Cheryl settle her worries." Dale smiled. "And believe it or not, I even *enjoyed* flying!"

Roy laughed fondly. "Well, young lady, you've had a busy day. You didn't just happen to wipe the whole slate clean by running across a six-year-old boy for Dusty to play with, too, did you?"

"No," Dale said, as she shook her head sadly, "no little boy." Then she brightened. "But guess what I saw at the adoption home—a real papoose!"

"A papoose?" Roy repeated, surprised.

"Yep. A little Choctaw Indian girl. I simply could have eaten her up. She was a pistol if I ever saw one." Dale's voice turned serious. "She'll be ready to be placed soon, and I want us to pray that that baby gets a good home."

At the religious meeting, attended by 45,000 people, Roy Rogers and Dale Evans spoke extemporaneously, as they always do on such occasions. "There's a difference in accepting Christ and in giving him your whole heart," Dale said. "I've missed a great deal by learning that so late, I know. But I have given Him what life I have left and asked Him to bend it, break it—I don't care, just so long as He *uses* it." Then for the first time, publicly, Dale mentioned Robin. "God sent us a little baby who is sickly," she continued. "At first, Roy and I were shocked, almost outraged. Then frantically frightened. But now we are beginning to see the many riches she brought with her—a new kind of love that binds our family closer together, patience, understanding, and tolerance for all forms of suffering, a real appreciation of the Cross." In closing, Dale cautioned, "Our country, our world, depends on its youth. If we as parents don't give our children their rightful heritage—love of God through Christ—then who will be to blame for what might happen in the years to come?"

In the main, Roy's speech was a tribute to his wife. "Dale worked with God to bring me something I had longed for all my life—peace," the cowboy said. "Materially speaking, for years I had nothing. Then for years, I had much. But I soon learned that having too much is worse than having too little. I bought something new only to cast it aside soon. Nothing ever seemed quite right. I was restless, confused. But the power of prayer, the feeling of spiritual blessedness, and the love of Jesus have no price tags. And now that I've found these price-less possessions, I'll never cast them aside." As he often does, Roy quoted freely from the Bible. "No matter what problem I meet up with, if I'll look long enough, I'll find an answer for it in my Bible," he added. "It has happened for me so many times." Then Roy grinned. "And while I'm talking, I'd like to let off a little steam about discrimination among various denominations. Thank the dear Lord, in our country we can worship in the church of our choosing, so why can't we all appreciate that freedom and respect each other's choice? If every man, woman, and child in this whole world went to church regularly and realized we all have the same Heavenly Father, I think we'd have few worries about future wars. Sane people simply don't go around shooting their own brothers and sisters."

Before he finished, Roy Rogers scotched a rumor that had begun in religious circles and was swiftly spreading across the nation—that he was forsaking show business for evangelism. "Personally and pro-fessionally, I have always lived by the Western code," he explained, "and perhaps I myself am just beginning to realize how near that way of life is to Christ's teachings. But if I'm going to be an evan-gelist, I guess I'll have to be one in the entertainment medium on horseback, because being a cowboy is all I really know. Just why God put me where I am today, only He can know. There are others in my business with more talent, more education, even more ambition. Yet somehow I made the grade. And so did Mama—much against her own will. We feel now that He must have had His reasons. But what they are we don't know. So until we do know—or until He does something to stop our careers—we intend to go on praying for guid-ance, giving our laymen's testimony on what He means to us."

When Roy prepared to leave the microphone, a battery of cameras flashed. And his picture was swept across the country, often captioned THE KING SAYS A WORD FOR HIS KING.

After the Rogers team had sung a duet, "He Is So Precious to Me," Dale closed their part of the program with "Over the Rainbow," a number particularly suited to her excellent voice and for which she had written special religious lyrics.

"Roy and Dale didn't know it at the time," Tim Spencer says, "but sound movies were being made of their portion of the meeting. And in the past two years those pictures have been shown at countless churches and missions all over the world. There is simply no telling how many decisions for Christ have come about because of them. Because ministers and missionaries alike have reported that the consensus is 'If it's good enough for Roy Rogers and Dale Evans, it's good enough for me.'"

Maxine Garrison joined the Rogers organization as assistant to Al Rackin a short time after Roy and Dale returned from Houston. "The kids were scheduled to appear at Madison Square Garden in September," Al Rackin explains. "Although it was to be Roy's fifth engagement there, he was returning after an absence of seven years. And Dale, making her New York debut, was going to be the first woman ever to receive star billing in the twenty-seven-year history of World Championship Rodeos. They were slated for a personal-appearance tour following their forty-three performances in twenty-six days at the Garden. So all in all, I had a lot of groundwork to lay in the East and I took off in July, leaving the Hollywood office with Maxine."

"Much later Roy and I would be able to see that God was wonderfully supplying another future need for us when He sent Maxine Garrison into our lives," Dale says. "Maxine, of course, had no inkling of Robin's condition when she joined our business family. And it was going to be a long time before any of us learned that she had a small son, Garry, who is a victim of cerebral palsy. Nevertheless, Maxine's expert knowledge in the field of retarded children, and her burning personal interest in the problem, would be ready and waiting to help us make many important decisions in the months and years to come."

One of Maxine Garrison's first duties with the Rogers organization was to set up a buffet party Al Rackin had planned for the press and all people concerned with the team's newly launched TV and radio shows. "As I drove to the studio that day to talk with Roy and Dale about the party," Maxine says, "I was remembering the last time I'd seen Dale—in 1946 when I did a piece on her for the Pittsburgh *Press* concerning her dilemma about remaining in westerns. I knew none of the details of just what had happened in the intervening seven years, of course. But I smiled to myself, remembering how deeply perplexed she'd been, and how she'd fought to go into musical comedy, when all the time her destiny was to marry Roy Rogers and be his leading lady for always."

When Maxine talked with Roy and Dale, she pointed out that August 26 was open on their calendar and seemed a good date for the buffet party. "No," Dale said, "that date was left open purposely. It's our baby's birthday, and we'll be having a family celebration."

Maxine studied their jam-packed schedule. "Well, I don't know quite what to do. Unless we have the party on a Sunday. Would Sunday evening, August 24, be all right?"

Roy and Dale agreed that should be fine. "We had no way of knowing, of course," Dale was to say much later, "what that day held in store for us—that August 24, 1952, was going to be a date we would remember the rest of our lives."

The "King of the Cowboys" and his "Queen of the West" worked continuously all summer long. "We not only were preparing wardrobe and numbers for our stint at the Garden and the tour that was to follow," Roy Rogers explains, "but before we can ever leave on any trip, we have to get far ahead with recorded radio programs and TV films to cover our absence."

But underneath everything, Roy and Dale were uneasy about having to leave home again. Obviously Robin had reached a point where she was showing no progress whatsoever. And it was impossible not to see Cau-Cau's increasing signs of wear. Finally they decided that the nurse had contributed enough, that for her own sake she must leave. "Cheryl, Linda, and Dusty had all had the mumps," Dale says "and because we always had to take every precaution with Robin, she had been isolated from them. The baby missed her brother and sisters terribly, and for days she had been restless and fretful. Cau-

207

Cau loved Robin intensely, but she looked worn to a frazzle and she was worrying more and more about Robin's inability to walk. The day the orthopedist told us it would be at least six months before Robin could possibly even put on walking braces, Cau-Cau looked as if she might break into tears."

Sunday, August 17, was Cau-Cau's last day with her little charge. And many tears were shed by Dale when she said good-by to the good nurse. Up to the last minute the devoted nurse continued her faithful massaging of Robin's tiny legs. "Perhaps God felt that the coming week would have been just too much for Cau-Cau," Dale says, sighing. "At any rate, she was gone. And when Roy and I left for work Monday morning, we realized with a thud what a great void she had filled. All the way to the studio I kept worrying, 'Should I go to New York with Roy, after all?' And between scenes I tried to work on a song I was writing for my debut at the Garden, 'Yippee-I-O, Broadway,' but I was so upset I couldn't concentrate."

Robin Rogers cried a great deal the first two days Cau-Cau was gone. And Dale began to fear they had made the wrong decision. "No," Roy said, as he reassured his wife, "we prayed and prayed over it. It was the right decision because it was the only fair one for Cau-Cau. Cau-Cau had been with Robin almost constantly her whole little life. It's natural that she should miss Cau-Cau, and crying is the only way she has to complain. We must be patient. She's just a baby, and she'll become adjusted soon."

On the third day, Wednesday, about noon, Dale received a telephone call on the set at Goldwyn Studio. "I know what's wrong with Robin, Dale," Virginia said. "One side of her face is swollen. I've already called the doctor, but I'm pretty sure it's the mumps."

"Roy and I went into an absolute tail spin, naturally," Dale says. "Our poor little baby was fighting enough of a battle already without being expected to handle more foes." But, happily, by Friday the puffiness was receding nicely. "And Virginia and I were so sure Robin would be all right," Dale adds, "that we insisted on Emily's going ahead with her plans for a weekend trip."

By Friday evening, however, the other side of Robin's face swelled, this time much worse. And her temperature rose. "We were scheduled to finish up a TV film on Saturday," Dale relates. "And I knew I had to work. But we shot my scenes as fast as we could. And I told Jack Lacey to have me written out of Monday's script. I was reaching the end of my rope, having to be away from Robin when she was so sick."

Late Saturday afternoon Robin's fever reached 106 degrees. Roy and Dale called one of the doctors who had been consulted when Robin was born. He explained that the baby's temperature had hit her brain, that she was crying so much because she was suffering an excruciating headache. And he administered a drug to deaden the pain.

Before the doctor left he talked with Robin's anguished parents. "You did the right thing, keeping your baby at home and giving her so much love," he said. "My wife and I are expecting a baby ourselves soon. And if God sends us one like your Robin, we intend to follow your example and keep it with us too. I have seen a great deal of this problem and I have learned that with heartache God always sends love. And I am becoming increasingly sure that it is wrong to deny that love." Finally the doctor rose wearily. "I am so sorry to have to tell you this," he spoke quietly, "but as a doctor I must. Robin's weak, tired little heart may give no warning. I don't know exactly what will happen or when. But you have to prepare yourselves, be ready."

Roy and Dale Rogers walked up and down, up and down, outside Robin's little white house. Anyone who ever has had a sick baby knows the monstrous ache that these two were suffering, the kind that begins in the region of the heart and slowly spreads to every bone and muscle in the body, the almost unbearable heaviness that dims out the whole world and makes each step as one on the road to Calvary.

"Robin is God's baby," Roy told Dale over and over. "She has always been in His hands, and we must continue to trust His wisdom. He will call her when He's ready. We've got to rely on His will."

Dale could make no answer.

About midnight, the nurse who had been called in to help Virginia

209

persuaded Roy and Dale to go to the big house to try and rest. Before retiring, they knelt together at the family altar, praying silently. And then finally they both managed to fall asleep.

"I woke up about three o'clock," Dale says. "Lana, Robin's favorite dog, was howling mournfully. We had been unable to get poor Lana to move from the porch of Robin's house, even to eat, for two days."

At six o'clock Dale knew she could lie there no longer. She rose and slipped on a quilted cotton peignoir and slipper socks. She would not change for twenty-four hours.

"When I got to Robin's room," Dale says, "the nurse had propped the baby up on pillows to aid her labored breathing. Her little body still was as hot as fire and I noticed that her stomach seemed swollen." In a short while Dale returned to the main house to call the doctor. Roy was up by then and dressing. And once again they knelt together in prayer.

When the doctor arrived and examined Robin, he had to tell Roy and Dale Rogers that their baby had developed mumps encephalitis, a rare and terribly dangerous complication. They knew by the look on his face, by the pressure of his hand when he said good-by that he held little, if any, hope for the child's recovery. "Please check with me every hour," he told the nurse when finally he prepared to leave.

Dale went back to her bedroom then and called Frances Eilers, a fellow member of the Hollywood Christian Group. And together they prayed on the telephone. Frances said she would call others of the group and ask them also to conduct special prayers.

"Cheryl, Linda, and Dusty were getting up by that time," Dale continues, "and I remembered that Emily was away, so I tried to pull myself together enough to go to the kitchen and prepare some breakfast for them. Their young eyes betrayed their heavy hearts, but it was obvious that they had agreed not to bother me, and they asked not one question. I had to bite my lips to keep from crying out, however, when I heard their pitiful little prayers during round-table grace. Each one begged God to please, please let us keep our baby."

Despite every effort known to medical science, Robin's temperature

210

rose steadily all that Sunday, August 24. And by late afternoon it had reached 108 degrees. The baby was unconscious.

Roy and Dale were sitting on the steps of the little white house trying to coax the grieving dog, Lana, to drink some water the children had placed nearby when Dale suddenly remembered the buffet party Maxine Garrison had planned for them at the Brown Derby on that evening.

"I forgot too," Roy said. "But Art reminded me when he was by this afternoon and I told him to go ahead with the party but that we wouldn't come. It would have been impossible for Maxine to have reached all those people and canceled it."

"Honey," Dale said after a long pause, "I hate so badly to have to ask you to do this, but I really think you should go. So many people have been invited as our guests and they're arriving right now. They don't know anything about what's happening out here and neither does poor Maxine. This is the first big thing she's ever handled for us, and she's worked so hard and made such elaborate plans. Trigger will be there and Bullet and Pat with Nellybelle. The photographers will be waiting, and Maxine really is not prepared to answer all their questions. Could you possibly jump into your regalia and go make a quick appearance? You wouldn't have to stay long."

Roy Rogers sighed and went to the big house to get dressed. When he came out a few minutes later, he was the "King of the Cowboys." Countless times, through the years, Roy had somehow picked himself up from the tanbark after a nasty spill during rodeos and managed to finish shows with blurred vision and a throat tight from fighting nausea. Many miles of many parades he had ridden, in both snow and rain, waving and smiling for thousands of cheering youngsters, ignoring the aches and fever of flu. But Dale knew, as Roy bent over the baby's crib for a quick kiss before leaving, that this time her husband was doing the most difficult thing a man can do. And though he made no sound as he climbed into his station wagon, tears were streaming down his cheeks.

"When I walked back from the car after Roy was gone," Dale says,

"I saw Cheryl, Linda, and Dusty huddled together on the kitchen steps. They looked so forlorn I could have wept. But I tried hard to smile and persuaded them to come inside for a bite of supper. I sat down with them and tried to drink some coffee, but it simply wouldn't go past my lips. So finally I went back again to Robin's little house."

Dale stood awhile by the baby's crib. Virginia and the nurse were sponging Robin with cool cloths, still trying to reduce her fever. The baby's breathing was deep, rattling. Dale kissed one tiny, burning hand and then turned, blinded by tears, to go back to the porch.

Unable to resume her station on the steps of the little house, Dale walked past the patio, past the greenhouse, across the tennis court—taking the path they had so often covered with Robin in her stroller on her beloved tours of the ranch. Finally Dale reached the animal quarters near the barn, Robin's favorite spot in the whole world. And there in the moonlight, still in her cotton peignoir, she fell to her knees. "Oh, God," her lips moved, "if You will just heal my baby, I'll spend the rest of my life telling people about it all over the earth. But if that is not Your will, then help me to have strength to bear it, Father. Strength to face the future without her and to carry on what she has started in all our hearts. Just strength to know Your purpose, whatever it may be. But help me, dear God, help me. *Please give me strength.*"

As Roy turned in the gates of the ranch, his headlights shone on Dale returning from the barn. Jumping from the station wagon, he ran to meet her. And his inevitable question was like a prayer, "How is she?"

Dale shook her head, unable to talk. Then, sobbing, she flung herself into his arms.

When they reached Robin's little house, Lana had risen from the spot on the porch where she had lain for three days. Back and forth the large gray animal was pacing, restlessly back and forth. Then suddenly Lana stopped dead still and began to bark, loudly, mournfully. Dale stopped to quiet Lana but Roy hurried on inside. "And at that moment," Dale says, "I suddenly heard a bird chirping in the eaves of the little house—short, staccato notes like a Morse code. I remembered that day at the city square in San Fancisco, how happy Robin had been when she saw all those birds, how at home she had seemed with them. And it came to me how much love our baby always had for every one of God's helpless creatures. I patted Lana, who loved Robin as much as we did, and I thanked God for letting us know about Robin's kind of love, for His goodness in lending her to us for two whole years."

The door to the little house opened then and Virginia walked out on the porch. "She's gone, Dale," Virginia said simply.

"After a brief storm of weeping," Dale Rogers says, "I suddenly felt a strange peace. I told Roy I couldn't bear to look at my little angel again, I wanted to remember her sunny little smile, and so he went in alone to caress the little girl, so close to his heart. I knew with all my heart that Jesus was in that room. Roy told me later that the pain was gone from Robin's little face, the hurt, the torment she had suffered so long. I felt her release from her earthly limitations and my heart was glad. I realized then that death is a birth, that my baby had lost her clay shell and was safe for always, free from pain."

The last guests were just leaving the party at the Brown Derby when Maxine Garrison was called to the telephone. "It was Roy himself," Maxine says, "and I was simply stunned, for I had no idea their baby was that ill. In fact, I hadn't known anything until Art Rush arrived at the Derby about half past five and told me the Rogerses wouldn't be coming because Robin was sick. I decided not to announce anything, and when Roy surprised us with a brief appearance, I was glad I hadn't. I did notice, however, how he kept retreating from the crowd—trying to leave almost as soon as he got there—and how haggard his face looked between smiles for the photographers."

Roy's voice was quiet and calm when he told Maxine the baby had died. "Please tell Art," he said. And then he paused. "Maxine, God was so good to let me get back home before . . . before. . . ." His voice broke and finally Maxine heard the click of the receiver.

213

Immediately she called Art Rush aside and told him. "We've got to keep all calls away from the ranch," she added. "Shall I phone the city desks and wire services?" Art Rush, however, had already started for the door. "What do you want me to *do,* Art?" Maxine asked, as she followed him.

White-faced, Art Rush struggled for composure. "I'm going to my kids," he managed haltingly. "Do anything you think best."

"I knew our building was locked," Maxine says, "so I quickly looked around the room and went over and asked one of the advertising agency boys still there if he'd take me to his office and let me use his typewriter and telephone for a while."

The next hour was to be a revelation for Maxine Garrison. "I'd been in both the newspaper and public-relations games a long time," she explains, "so I knew what it meant to be on either end of the telephone in cases of disaster. In our business such news gets to be routine and the voices are matter of fact. But this time I was to learn there can be a difference."

"Robin, two-year-old daughter of Roy Rogers and Dale Evans, just died from complications following the mumps," Maxine recited her fixed piece. And when, to the first name on her list, the announcement brought only dead silence, she repeated it. Finally she heard a gasp. "Oh, my goodness! I'm sorry, so sorry," the voice responded with real emotion. "Do you think there's anything, *anything* I can do to help?"

"I just figured that particular reporter was a good friend of the Rogerses," Maxine Garrison says. "But when the same thing happened on my second call and the third and on down the list, I began to see what kind of people I was working for. The next year Roy and Dale were awarded the Golden Apple by the Women's Press Association for being the most cooperative actor and actress in Hollywood. That is a signal honor from a professionally critical audience, is the subject of much controversy, and the awardee list is a very exclusive one. But the hour I spent on the phone the night Robin Rogers died gave me all the evidence I'll ever need to know the es-

214

teem in which her parents are held—even by the so-called hard-hearted press."

When Maxine had completed her last call, she leaned back in her chair and remembered something Al Rackin had told her when he prepared to leave for New York. "Maxine," Al had said, "in our business it is really something to get to work for people you can honestly respect. But because I'm their press agent, you probably wouldn't believe me if I tried to tell you about Roy and Dale, so I've decided to let you find out for yourself." Then he half smiled. "But I'm warning you, honey, you're in for a great experience."

Early next morning the news of Robin's death reached the Rogerses' family minister over his car radio as he drove homeward, returning from a vacation trip. "As I neared Encino," he says, "I felt the need to gather strength in prayer before seeing Roy and Dale, so I went directly to my church."

When the minister entered the church, which always is open, he saw a figure in the dimness. It was Dale Evans Rogers, kneeling at the altar in prayer. He dropped to his knees beside her.

In their small apartment over a store in Santa Monica, Margie and Nancy Hamilton also heard the news by radio. "We were shocked and grief-stricken, of course," Margie says. "And immediately we prayed for Roy and Dale. My impulse then was to go straight to the telephone. But I found myself hesitating. For the first time since I'd met them, I think, I suddenly remembered *who* they were, and it dawned on me that millions of people all over the world would be affected by this tragedy. The thought left me a little awed, I think, and I was reluctant to invade their privacy."

But a short time later Nancy persuaded her mother to call. "Dale has gone to the church and Roy has gone to Forest Lawn with Mr. Rush and Mr. Osborne to make all the necessary arrangements," Emily told Margie Hamilton. "But I imagine they'll be back by the time you could get here."

"Do you really think we should come out today?" Margie insisted.

The gray-haired housekeeper sighed. "Don't hesitate, Mrs. Hamilton," she said, "it will do you good to come and see for yourself. I never knew such courage and faith could exist. They have been able to make every decision easily, they have answered the children's questions beautifully, and it is they who have consoled the relatives. Never before, even in this house, has God been so near."

Dale was sitting in her rocker in the living room when Margie and Nancy Hamilton arrived at the ranch. "Of course, as I stood in the doorway, I remembered that scene the previous Christmas," Margie says, "and my eyes filled with tears. But when Dale saw us, she didn't cry, she smiled. She was more serene than I'd ever seen her. And didn't seem at all on this earth, but with Robin. There was no sorrow in the whole house, really. Telegrams, and long-distance calls, and special-delivery letters, and flowers were all simply flooding in. And still, over everything there hung a strange peace."

When Dale finally spoke, her voice was low. "Thank you for coming, Margie," she said. "The Lord is certainly generous to give us so many wonderful friends." And later Dale told her friend, "Robin was straight from heaven, Margie, just like you said. God was so good to let us keep her for Him for two whole years. And now, forever, we'll have an angel in our house."

August 26, 1952, the day of the funeral, was bright and warm. Roy and Dale Rogers rose early and went together to the kitchen to have a cup of coffee. "We had just sat down and were bowing our heads for grace," Dale says, "when my eyes were caught by the date on a newspaper folded there."

Suddenly Dale jumped from her chair with a sob. "It's our baby's birthday and she's at Forest Lawn!" And weeping wildly, she ran from the kitchen and crumpled to the floor beneath the color etching of Robin that only the night before had been hung to center the family altar.

By the time Roy reached the scene, a woman was helping Dale up, talking softly. Because she was in street clothes, instead of uniform, it was a moment before Roy recognized her as the nurse who had been called in to help Virginia the last few days of Robin's illness.

"Dale," the nurse said, "something happened the night Robin died that I think you should know."

"Yes?" Dale said, staring at the woman as if she were an apparition.

"You remember almost all day Sunday Robin was unconscious, her eyes closed. Well, just a few seconds before she died, she opened her eyes real wide. Then she lifted both her little arms toward the ceiling and smiled radiantly, just as if she knew where she was going and was glad." The nurse hesitated. "I've heard about such things happening, Dale, but in all my years of nursing this is the first time I've ever seen it. And I'm sure your baby met our Lord. *I saw it happen.*"

"At that moment," Roy Rogers comments, "I knew there was no end to God's goodness. That nurse's arrival at that particular time is an example of the kind of help He sent us all during this crucial period—and has continued to send us ever since."

That afternoon of her second birthday a simple funeral service was held for Robin Elizabeth Rogers at Forest Lawn's Church of the Recessional. She was laid to rest wearing her little white christening dress with the wide pink satin sash. Around her neck was a chain with a small gold cross that had been meant for a birthday present.

CHAPTER FIFTEEN

On August 28, 1952, two days after the funeral, Dale Evans Rogers was sitting at her desk reading some of the thousands of sympathy messages that were pouring in from all corners of the world. And she found herself gazing at the color etching of her baby that centers the family altar. "The golden curls looked so like a halo," Dale recounts, "and the blue eyes looked so far away. Then suddenly it dawned on me that they'd always seemed as if they were seeing farther than we. The words from Hebrews flashed to my mind: 'Be not forgetful to entertain strangers; for thereby some have entertained angels unawares.'"

To Dale Rogers the room became heavy with an unseen Presence. "I'll never forget the feeling I had," she says. "From the time Robin was born I'd vaguely sensed she had a mission to perform, that in some way I was to carry it out for her. But I'd been so confused. Now it all came with startling clarity: Robin had been an angel, a muted messenger of God, sent to bless our family, make us better people. She, having strengthened us by showing us there is purpose in pain, by teaching us the real meaning of love and compassion, had concluded her earthly mission, her plan. And I was to carry on for her. I was to go to bat for all little children handicapped like Robin whom people were hiding, often afraid and ashamed even to discuss. I wanted to tell the whole world Robin's story, for it came to me that if people *knew,* they'd *care.* I realized that the blind had Helen Keller, polio victims had had Franklin D. Roosevelt, but that these little children, by the very nature of their ailment, could never develop a leader of their own."

Dale Rogers grabbed a pencil and began writing furiously. Some time later she stopped, drained, her mind bleak and dry. She had tried to write for Robin but evidently she was not a writer. She had hit a dead end. And half the night she was awake, praying. "Oh, dear God, please guide me. . . ."

The next morning Dale dragged herself to a scheduled radio recording session. "While we were rehearsing the script," she tells, "I opened my mouth to read my lines but no words came. My heart began to pound furiously. A light seemed to flood my mind and a voice seemed to say, *'Let Robin write it herself.'* "

The instant the recording was finished, Dale ran to a dressing room and locked the door. "I begged God to lead my hands to put down exactly what Robin wanted to say," she says, "and I started writing then and there on the back of my script. For three weeks I wrote constantly, on envelopes, package wrappings, any paper at hand."

The Rogers organization was readying for the team's appearance at Madison Square Garden the whole time Dale was writing her book. There were costumes to be fitted, acts and songs to be learned. And the heavy schedule of TV films, radio recordings, and other commitments went right on. "But wherever we were, Dale was making notes, writing, always writing," many members of the organization tell. "And later in New York when she prepared her manuscript for submission to publishers, she wouldn't let anybody help even with the typing," Helen Young, Art Rush's secretary, adds. "Somebody else might do a greater job but this is *my* job," Dale explained.

Grimly Roy Rogers watched his wife driving herself by day, writing far into the night, as if possessed. He realized he had to get her away from the pressure of schedules. And finally Dale agreed they should visit her family in Texas.

Before they left home, Roy Rogers fulfilled one last commitment. He appeared at a religious meeting. Before he gave testimony, a woman approached Roy in the crowd and thanked him for a long-distance call he had once made to her ailing child. "Mr. Rogers," she asked, "is it true that all your life you've wanted to be a doctor?"

"Yes," he admitted shyly.

"Well," the woman patted his arm, "maybe our Lord meant for you to heal broken hearts instead of broken bodies. Your songs for my boy did us all a lot of good."

"I'll never forget the humility on Roy's face," the family minister says, "when a few minutes later before ten thousand people he prayed, 'Oh, Father, please help me to be the kind of cowboy the kids think I am.' "

After visiting in Italy, Texas, with Dale's family, Roy and Dale drove to Dallas to take a train for New York. "While we were in Dallas," Roy says, "we felt we wanted to go out to the adoption home and thank the folks there for straightening out our eldest daughter's problem. We'd sent Cheryl to Dallas to talk with them in the early summer, and they'd helped her a lot."

As Dale and Roy Rogers walked up the steps of the home, Dale asked, "Honey, do you suppose by any chance that cute little Indian baby is still here?"

"I doubt it," Roy said. "With agencies always unable to fill requests, it's unlikely that any baby you saw nearly three months ago is still here."

"But in my heart," Roy Rogers adds today, "I suddenly found myself praying that she was. Dale had taken such a shine to her. And it came to me that another baby might help."

There are some people who would feel that a three-quarter Choctaw Indian girl was not a preferred case and that was why she still was at the home. But Dale and Roy Rogers soon were to feel otherwise. When Dale entered the nursery, she spotted the child immediately and the baby smiled broadly. "She held out her fat little arms when I entered the room," Dale recounts, "and she grinned almost knowingly, just as if she were saying, 'Well, at last you've come back.' "

220

Dale Rogers grabbed up the brunet girl and held her close. And with urgency she turned to her husband. "I want this baby, Roy. She's going to need our kind of love and understanding. Perhaps it's part of Robin's plan for her still to be here. Why else would I have seen her before? Why else would I have remembered her so long?"

Before they left the adoption agency, Roy Rogers spoke with officials and they promised to consider his request. "This is a rare and unusual case," the supervisor explained. "All of us will have to give the matter grave thought."

So with Robin's story in her hands and a prayer that they would be given the Indian baby in her heart, Dale Evans Rogers departed for the station with her husband to board a train for New York. "As we walked through the Dallas station," Dale goes on, "my tear-swollen eyes fell on a book at the newsstand. It was Dr. Norman Vincent Peale's *A Guide to Confident Living,* and we bought a copy."

By the time the Rogerses got to New York, they had read Dr. Peale's book. And Dale had made up her mind to see him. "I knew I had to take Robin's story to Dr. Peale," she says, "that he would know if I were doing the right thing, that he was a person who would help me if he could."

The minute the Rogerses reached their New York hotel room, Dale put in a call to Dr. Peale. His secretary told her the minister's schedule was filled for two weeks. "But I must see him at once," Dale insisted. And the urgency in her voice brought Dr. Peale to the telephone. He asked her to come to his office the next morning.

When Dale Rogers talked with Dr. Peale, she revealed every detail that had led her to him. And then she asked him if he would read her manuscript. "She had an assortment of papers—from envelopes to package wrappings—the likes of which I'd never seen," Norman Vincent Peale said, with a twinkle in his eyes, "so I suggested that she read it *to* me."

When Dale had finished reading her pages, she looked up at Dr. Peale and she saw his eyes were misty. "I feel privileged to be a part of Robin's plan," he said quietly. "Would you like me to pray for it?"

Dale Rogers nodded. And Dr. Peale started to bow his head. "But

I noticed that girl getting out of her chair and dropping to her knees," he tells. "And I really knew then I was in the presence of a soul who lived close with God, one who *believed* in prayer."

Norman Vincent Peale rose from his chair and knelt beside Dale Evans Rogers. Together they prayed for divine help and guidance for Dale's book, *Angel Unaware.*

Dale had written her short book in the words of Robin talking with God about her brief sojourn on earth, explaining how her parents had come to feel her visit was a divine plan. A plan to benefit other children handicapped like Robin. One to help their stricken families, and all people, to see them as innocent angels sent with a message from God. And as soon as Dale could type her pages, the manuscript was hurried to a publisher. Word came back promptly: "We are sorry, Mrs. Rogers, but the story is just too sad. We feel people today don't want to cry." Two days later came a second publisher's rejection: "We fear the public would object to such presumptuousness."

Dale Rogers's heart was heavy. She went to Central Park and sat on a bench alone. "I heard a bird chirping just as I'd heard one the night of Robin's death," Dale says. "And my whole being began to cry, 'Oh, God, why, why did you have to do it?' Then I closed my eyes in prayer. When I opened them, my heart broke anew. For there before me stood a Mongoloid child, about twelve, harnessed to an attendant nearby. After a breathless moment, I felt He was again showing me what could go on happening unless people everywhere understood and shared their neighbor's burden. And I knew I must go on with Robin's plan."

Dale Rogers jumped up and began running back to her hotel. "Suddenly a lifetime seemed such a short while for all I wanted to do," she says. "And I made up my mind I'd spend my last penny getting the book published and my last hour giving it away."

But, as Dale puts it, that was not the plan. When she reached the hotel, Roy was holding a message for her from Dr. Frank Mead of Fleming H. Revell Company. When Dale called Dr. Mead, he explained that a reader with another firm had been unable to forget her book and had recommended it to Revell. Dr. Mead was leaving for Chicago and he asked if he might take along the manuscript to read on the train. "I'll send over for the book right away," he said, "and I'll call from Chicago and let you know."

Daily the Rogerses had been contacting the Dallas adoption agency about the Indian baby. The idea that the child was meant to be theirs seemed to have obsessed them. "And the thought that Dusty, our six-year-old son, was suffering for male companionship was nagging me every minute," Roy Rogers says. "I was so worried and confused, I knew nothing to do for any of us, all of us, but just pray."

Through everything, through all their preparations for their appearances at Madison Square Garden, the thought of the Indian baby that they might adopt and their hope for Dale's book dwelt heavily on their minds. It was then that Roy and Dale Rogers made the decision which might easily have endangered their whole future —the decision to add a religious number to their program. They took this step with all the firmness that their new-found faith had brought them and explained their reasons to their gang at a tense meeting at their suite at the Sherry-Netherland, the very afternoon of the day when they were to open at Madison Square Garden.

Then minutes before the show was to begin, Roy and Dale Rogers faced a special committee that had been formed to try for the last time to persuade them to drop the religious number. It was then that Roy spoke the words that committed them beyond any doubt to their plan. "If we can't do our religious number, we won't go on at all. Mama and I have talked it over. We'll pack our trunks this very night and head back for California."

The tension of the meeting was still with Art Rush as he quickened his steps along the tunnel backstage at Madison Square Garden just as the performance was about to begin. Would Roy and Dale's plan be understood? What would the audience's reaction be? This one decision of Roy and Dale's might easily turn out to be the most costly one in their lives.

Art walked on toward the Rogerses' dressing room and met Dale in the corridor. A kerchief, tied jauntily at the neck, matched her sky-blue gabardine cowgirl dress. A full skirt was aglow with silver kidskin stars. The waist was shining with rhinestones. Her white Stetson, smaller than Roy's, its brim rolled almost to the crown, was held on by a narrow chin strap. White boots, with heels lower than street shoes, made her seem tinier than ever. Rush saw with a pang that she had been crying.

"You know, Art," Dale said without preamble, "I've been thinking. If you live to get to the top, you forget somewhere along the way *why* you wanted to get there. Roy and I prayed together after you and that committee left our dressing room and we asked God to let tonight's performance show us the answer. If during the religious number we get booed out of the arena, then that will be that. But we have decided that the only way we can really find ourselves is to lose ourselves in work for others, that the only thing anybody can hold on to on this earth is what he gives away."

"I could only stare at her, wordless," Art says.

Dale stood on tiptoes and kissed him lightly on the cheek. "Don't worry, old sad-eyes," she said, with a half-smile. "As you've always told us, things will work out the *right* way."

Whatever Art Rush might have answered was lost in the sudden explosion that all but rocked the building. "I knew that an ovation like that could mean only one thing," he says. "The grand entry was over and Roy was tearing into the arena on Trigger at breakneck speed!" Dale gasped and flew toward the entrance where Glenn waited with Buttermilk. Art was out of breath by the time he reached his director's post and grabbed the telephone that connected him with the sound monitors and lighting boys. Roy was already getting off Trigger and speaking into the mike that dropped down as from thin air. "Howdy, pardners," the familiar voice brought the familiar greeting. "Welcome to the 1952 World Championship Rodeo." The people went wild. He quieted them. "Now, if you please, I'd like to introduce to you a wonderful little gal from Texas who means a lot to me and our kids and does a fine job of keeping a Christian home for us. My wife, the Queen of the West, Miss Dale Evans."

Dale had made it, Art saw with relief. She and Buttermilk were entering the arena. Art shaded his eyes and scanned the hazy Garden. He spotted Al, Jim, and Larry, each holding down a fort. Mary Jo, Dorothy Kent, and Helen Young were huddled close together in seats near the press box. He knew they still were trying to reassure each other.

"Nobody in the audience at the Garden that night seemed to notice that the smiles on the Rogerses' faces were fixed," says Mary Jo Rush. "And there were only a few, I'm sure, who remembered that they'd buried the only child of their union exactly a month before. None knew the secret about her. And even we didn't realize what its revelation was going to mean. But later, when Roy came out in all-white regalia, I knew the moment had come. And I closed my eyes tight and prayed. When I opened them, I saw that even the excited children were quieting."

"You go to school five days a week to improve your mind and learn how to be a success in the business world," the cowboy king was telling them. "I want you to go to church one day a week to improve your soul and learn how to appreciate it. The most important thing that ever happened to our family was when we started going to church and began practicing what we learned there. The luckiest thing that can ever happen to you is to get to live in a religious home." Then Roy smiled warmly at the children. "Believe me, pardners, it isn't sissy to go to Sunday school. For, don't ever forget, a *real* cowboy needs *real* faith."

Then suddenly the Garden was darkening and spotlights were forming a large cross in the center of the arena. A great hush fell over the crowd as Roy began to sing his hymn-ballad, "Peace in the Valley." Nearby, Trigger knelt in prayer.

At the end of the show, Roy and Dale rode slowly around the arena, shaking as many small outstretched fingers as they could reach. "Although we didn't know then that the press reaction would be favorable," Dale says, "we knew in our bones that the warm response from that first-night audience was our answer from God. And we promised Him that night to spend the rest of our lives shak-

225

ing hands with little children. For we were sure then that He had sent Robin to show us we were successful entertainers because our purpose was to work for Him."

When Roy and Dale Rogers returned to their hotel that evening, they found a telegram from the Dallas adoption agency: THE INDIAN BABY IS YOURS.

Early the next morning Dale Evans Rogers received a long-distance call from Chicago with the good news that Dr. Frank Mead liked Robin's story tremendously and that Fleming H. Revell would publish Dale's book for Easter release.

Before that time would come, after much investigation, Dale would assign her entire author's royalties to the National Association for Retarded Children, then a new and struggling organization made up of local parent-groups. Today, with much help from the Rogerses, the nonsectarian organization is set up nationally. And the thousands of dollars they received from *Angel Unaware*—which soon after publication became a best seller—are helping toward advancement of research and therapy and other integrated programs for the care of mentally retarded children.

"There are nearly four million children in this country alone who are doomed never to grow up," says Dale Rogers, "and a large percentage are capable of rehabilitation almost to the point of self-management. But help in many forms is desperately needed. The divorce and desertion rates are shockingly high among stricken families. And above all, there is a lack of understanding from the public for both child and family."

Today the nearly two hundred organized NARC parent-groups are helping these heartbroken, bewildered people help each other and themselves. On one occasion Dale Evans Rogers told these parents: "I know many of you can't give your children the expensive care you would like to. But you can give love. And in doing that you will find new spiritual strength—which God intends for you to have. And if the neighbors and the nation and the world will give these children the love and understanding God intends, we will all become less selfish and less lonely of heart. That's what we feel Robin wanted."

With Dale's book settled, a new baby waiting to be picked up, and messages pouring in from parents grateful for the religious portion added to their program, Roy Rogers and Dale Evans finished their run at Madison Square Garden with lighter hearts. They planned, after ending their short tour of one-night stands, to pick up their new daughter in Dallas and arrive home on October 28, in time for Dusty's birthday. They told him on the phone they were bringing a "real" present. They meant the little Indian baby. But they were destined to bring more.

Toward the end of their tour at Cincinnati, Roy happened to open a telegram atop a pile of messages. It was from a woman in Covington, Kentucky, asking him if he would see her little girl who suffered from cerebral palsy. These requests flood in daily wherever the Rogerses are, and it has become impossible for Roy and Dale to personally answer them all. Nonetheless, Roy went directly to the phone and called the woman, telling her to bring the child and he would pay all expenses. During the conversation, the woman mentioned that she acted as a foster parent for the state, caring for fourteen children, all unadoptable cases. "You don't happen to have a little boy there, about six, do you?" Roy asked. The woman said she did but that he was slightly handicapped. Roy said, "Well, bring him anyway."

Today Roy Rogers looks back and comments, "This incident, like other important turning points in my life, can have only one answer —God. What other explanation can there be for Guy Baumgartner's arrival at Duck Run at the moment I needed help so desperately? What other explanation can there be for Sol Siegel's appearance at the studio gate the instant the cop was ousting me?"

It was during intermission that the trio from Covington was taken backstage to the Rogerses' dressing room. "The little fellow was a

227

sad sight," says Jack Lacey, who was acting as stage manager for the tour. "He'd suffered rickets and curvature of the spine as a result of malnutrition. Braces had just been removed from his legs and he toddled unsteadily. His nose had been bashed in and his face and body were scarred, evidence of beatings. And he had a very bad cold."

"He was abandoned twice," confided the woman who had brought him. And from beyond her skirt the awed child gazed at Roy Rogers. Finally he managed a crooked smile. "Howdy, pardner," his voice came in true Rogers lingo. Roy reached out and gathered him in his arms.

Roy and Dale finished their show that evening. But they couldn't eat their dinner. They sat up most of the night talking about the little boy. About three o'clock Roy Rogers faced his wife. "Dale, God hates a coward."

"Yes," she said, "anybody can adopt a perfect child."

The Rogerses thought they needed a little boy as a playmate for Dusty. But they had found a little boy who needed them. Roy went to the phone, despite the hour, and called the woman in Covington. And early the next morning they went across the bridge to arrange court approval for the adoption of the little son they promptly named Sandy. Proceedings weren't difficult and didn't take long. Nobody objected. The boy's leaving the foster home would make room for another "unadoptable" case. "The only hesitation came from Sandy himself," Roy remarks. "He was worried about who would carry on his work there—the feeding of an even weaker child who'd suffered meningitis."

Roy and Dale hurriedly bought some jeans and a cowboy shirt for Sandy. But because of his tiny feet and unsteady legs, they couldn't fit him in boots. Roy carried the child in his arms to the bus.

"We had a full troupe with us on the bus," Jack Lacey says, "including a group of musicians from Chicago. And when the Rogerses arrived with the boy, and he opened a paper sack and took out his only belonging—a shabby sweater—there wasn't a dry eye among us."

At lunch that day, his eyes wide over so much food, Sandy ate

228

far too heartily. And a few miles down the road he was sick all over his new parents. Between heaves he lifted his sad little eyes. "Please don't be mad. Please don't take me back. I'll make it up to you, honest. I can hoe corn real good."

At the end of their tour, the Rogerses left their troupe and flew with Sandy to Dallas to pick up the Indian baby they had decided to name Mary Little Doe. "We gave her both a Christian name and a tribal name," Dale explains, "so when she became older she could take her choice. But almost immediately we all started calling her 'Dodie.'"

And so it came about that two months after Robin's death, Roy and Dale Rogers flew from Dallas to Los Angeles, arriving, as promised, on Dusty's birthday. Dusty, Linda, and Cheryl, with Emily and Virginia, Tom and Barbara Fox, with small Mindy, Andy and Mattie Slye, other relatives, friends, business associates, and the usual horde of photographers, newsmen, and fans were gathered at the airport to meet them, expecting two weary, heartbroken parents to emerge from the plane. Tears were in their eyes, but they were smiling too, as proudly they came down the ramp carrying their surprises. First down the steps came Dale, holding Dodie. And then came Roy, holding Sandy. A silence fell over the crowd as Roy and Dale walked over to Dusty, kissing him, and saying, "Happy birthday!" Roy put Sandy down beside Dusty. "Your birthday gift can be shared with all of us, son." Dale went to Cheryl and Linda. "And now we have another baby for our crib."

For once, even the newsmen hesitated to barge in on the family group. Then finally one laughed, breaking the silence. "Including the Foxes, you now have *eight* children!"

"No, we have nine," Dale answered. "Robin is with us now more than she ever was. She has blessed our lives and we'll always love her. And because of Robin we'll always have more love for all children everywhere."

CHAPTER SIXTEEN

Sometimes God says "No," sometimes God says "Yes," sometimes God says "Wait." Knowing their story, it can't be denied that the wait for Roy Rogers and Dale Evans was long and hard. But today they share much happiness with their large family. And surprisingly, to most who get to see for themselves, in an atmosphere of simplicity that belies fame and wealth.

"I'm so glad we've learned not to run away," fifteen-year-old Cheryl comments. "When Mother Arlene died, Daddy moved us out of that house as fast as he could. And we moved into Hollywood. Then when Robin was born, we moved out here to the ranch. But here we've stayed because we know now you can't run away from trouble. It will go along on your insides so you might as well face it."

Spending a lot of time with the Rogerses, one finds little division between their personal and public lives, and it is difficult to understand how they manage to hold up to all they do. "Things haven't always been this way," Tom Fox explains. "But since Robin, Mom and Dad have found peace within themselves, with each other and us children—through God. They never bother to pretend about anything any more. Where there's no pretense, there's no tension. And where there's no tension, there's no fatigue."

At their ranch, the Rogerses raise cattle, chickens, and an ever-changing assortment of pet animals. They have 3 of their 5 acres under cultivation and raise, can, and freeze most of their simple food. Deermeat chili is the children's favorite delicacy. And when asked about it, Linda answered, "We like it best because it's really *ours*. Daddy gets the deer and Mama makes the chili."

The Rogers home, a weather-beaten stucco, its ten rooms bulging and cluttered, has at least one picture of Jesus in every room, a Bible on most tables. The atmosphere is strictly "family," wholly informal. When not in regalia, Roy Rogers usually wears jeans, a T-shirt, and sneakers. Except when performing, Dale's clothes are ordinary ones. The children, extremely well mannered and amazingly unaffected, usually wear stair-step hand-me-downs. "Robin taught us to walk softer, to speak quieter, and to appreciate being well and healthy," Linda comments.

Roy and Dale Rogers manage extra time with their children—when school permits—by taking the boys on location, the girls to indoor sets. In the summer when they tour, they take the children along and include them in the show. "At present Dodie still is too young to be in school," Dale says, "so we can take her in the winter too. Those hotel rooms just seem more like home when we have a child with us."

Roy spends much of his free time with his sons in the woodworking shop he built himself. "I have a lot of fancy gadgets in it," he says, "but I never walk into the shop that I don't think of that one treasured, sorry knife I had for whittling when I was a kid."

Before the children's bedtime prayers, said together at the family altar in their parents' bedroom, what is called "a family session" is often held. Chores and allowances, based on age, are among matters discussed. And the children's prayers that follow sound much like those in millions of other homes. "Dear God, please help me to ride a bicycle without somebody holding me up," asks Dusty. "Please help me to listen better to what my teacher is saying," says Sandy.

There absolutely is no favoritism shown among the children in the Roy Rogers home, and severe discipline comes to anyone who dares stray into the realm of dishonesty, which includes failure to keep a promise. "We believe in love and discipline," says Dale.

231

"We discipline our children when they need it but we let them know we love them all the time."

Determined that their brood shall grow up unspoiled, Roy and Dale ration the toys their youngsters receive. Throughout the year, and especially at Christmas, gifts flood in from their parents' friends and fans all over the world. The majority are sent to hospitals and orphanages. "Too many toys take away a child's sense of appreciation and his imagination as well," Roy says.

But even Roy Rogers himself runs into snags on the problem of rearing children. "Living on a ranch, surrounded by so many animals, and having answered all their questions truthfully," he says, "we thought our kids had grown up understanding the miracle of reproduction." But to Roy's consternation he was to learn otherwise. The incident occurred when Dr. William C. Menninger, the famous psychiatrist, was visiting Los Angeles with his wife and asked to meet Dale so that he could thank her in person for the help he felt her book was bringing to parents of handicapped children. Roy was away when the Menningers arrived at the ranch, and while Mrs. Menninger chatted in the house with Dale, the doctor was taken by the children to see the animal quarters. "I happened to drive in about that time," Roy remarks, "and when I heard a lot of the dogs barking, I didn't know what was up. At the time, for very good reasons, I had Lana, our female Weimaraner, locked up. And I thought sure the kids had forgot my instructions and were letting other dogs in her pen." When breathless Roy reached the kennels, he was relieved to see that all gates were closed, as he'd left them. But Dusty was perplexed over his father's anxiety. "Dad," the small voice said, "you've explained to us all about Lana and little puppies, and I understand why you have her locked *in*. But why do you have all the boy dogs locked *out?*"

The "King of the Cowboys" looked helplessly toward one of our country's most eminent psychiatrists. "Golly, Dr. Menninger," he muttered, "what do I say now?" Dr. Menninger looked equally helpless. "I don't know, Roy." He waved his hands. "I honestly don't know."

232

Even television is rationed at the Rogers home because Roy and Dale want their children to grow up knowing how to make their own fun rather than depending wholly on others for it. But Sunday evening, after an early supper, is the most looked-forward-to time in the week, for that is when the Roy Rogers show is telecast on the West Coast. A typical Sunday evening finds Mattie and Andy Slye filing into the living room with the Rogers family. Two small chairs are set in front of the TV set for Dusty and Sandy, and behind them sit Linda and Cheryl, usually squabbling over who is going to hold baby Dodie. Dale, tired after a full day, reclines on a contour lounge. Emily and Virginia sit on one sofa, Andy and Mattie on the other. Roy finds it difficult to sit anywhere. Although he has overcome a great deal of his shyness, he still can hardly bear to watch himself on the screen.

When the title of the show flashes across the screen, the atmosphere in the room becomes almost electric. And at first sight of their parents, dressed as the "King of the Cowboys" and the "Queen of the West," the children cheer excitedly. Cheryl, hoping madly to be an actress herself, is apt to comment with careful enunciation, "Congrats, Mama. You're certainly sitting Buttermilk well in that scene." But the smaller kiddies are lost in the magic world of Mineral City in Paradise Valley. And when the inevitable time comes that Dale must flee the villain, Sandy can contain himself no longer. "Mama," he says, as he turns to Dale uneasily, "you'll get away, won'tcha, huh?"

"Yes, son," Dale replies, smiling reassuringly, "don't worry, I'll get away."

Then when the villain fails to catch Dale and turns his evil designs toward a helpless widow and her children, Dusty cries, shaking a small fist, "You just wait, you mean old man, you. My daddy is Roy Rogers and he'll get you. He'll get you good."

When at last the thirty-minute show is over, Andy turns to Mattie. "You know, Mammy," he says, with a sigh, "there's only one thing wrong with this program. It's never long enough."

"Yes," she agrees. "But that villain was hitting our boy too hard in the fight scene. Believe me, I'm going to call Jack Lacey the first

233

thing tomorrow morning and tell him to be more careful about that in the future."

Roy and Dale Rogers would the the first to admit that their children are forever presenting new problems. And with little Sandy there have been many to solve. But today his legs—after proper diet, medicine, and therapy—are sturdy. His breathing—after a nose operation—is normal. "Dusty showed great signs of jealousy over his new brother," Dale says, "and the first day he went to school after Sandy's arrival, he took care to hide all his favorite toys. I tried to talk him out of it by explaining that all material things wear out sooner or later but that a brother was something he could love all his life." Nonetheless, Dusty's mind was made up. When he returned from school, however, Dusty found Sandy waiting at the gate where he had stood anxiously most of the day. "And when Dusty realized that Sandy wanted him, not his toys," Roy adds, "a real friendship between them had begun."

When Dusty got his first good look at Dodie, he stared. "Why is she so sun-tanned?" he wanted to know. Dale explained that the child's dark skin was natural, that she was an Indian baby. "An Indian?" Dusty cried in alarm. "Gosh, will she have feathers when she grows up?" Yet it was Dusty who was soon begging to carry Dodie in his arms. And it was he who taught her her first word, "Bi-ba" for Bible.

Perhaps of all the problems that their increasing fame has brought them, the one that worries Roy and Dale Rogers most is the impossibility of personally answering every letter and plea for help that comes in. But each one is carefully handled by their staff and the truly urgent ones do reach the Rogerses' desk. "I read them," Dale says, "and I answer as well as I can. Roy and I simply can't lose sight of the fact that no matter how high the stacks or how far away the postmark, each one bears a human heart." Much of Dale's mail since the publication of *Angel Unaware* comes from parents with a similar heartache. "Thank you for helping us recognize our own angel," write many. "I'll never again look with disinterested eyes at a child who is different," confess those more fortunate.

234

"We are beginning to see real concrete results from our efforts," Roy Rogers says. "At Madison Square Garden we always stage one free performance for handicapped and underprivileged children, and it's always been gratifying. But when we appeared there in 1954, we noticed a great difference. For the first time, retarded children were brought out in droves. The problem is far from solved, of course, but at least it's out in the open now. Parents of these kids are no longer afraid and ashamed because the public, in finally understanding, is growing kinder."

In November, 1954, when the National Association for Retarded Children held its first large-scale money-raising campaign, Roy and Dale Rogers served as national cochairmen. Under their leadership, many school children throughout the country became a Roy Rogers–Dale Evans "Helping Hand Rider" and pledged: "When I see a boy or girl who is mentally handicapped, I will not laugh or jeer. But I will undertstand that God has not given this child the same wonderful gifts He has given me. When I play with a boy or girl who is mentally handicapped, I will be patient and I will try to help the child."

"Many organizations find it difficult to understand that Roy and I never lend merely our 'name,'" Dale says. "If we accept membership on a committee, we do so intending to really work. And with our schedule, it's hard to find the necessary extra hours. On Thanksgiving Day, 1953, a man came to our Philadelphia hotel to discuss that NARC campaign with us. We were on tour, both of us had severe colds, and I was so exhausted at the time I simply felt unable to say 'Yes.' But after he'd gone, I was miserable because I hadn't."

From Philadelphia, the Rogerses went to Detroit. "We visited our radio sponsors, the Dodge people, there," Dale goes on. "And Bill Newburg, the president, asked me to autograph a copy of my book for him." As Dale went to do so, the book fell from her hands. "When I picked it up, I saw that it had opened to the page where Robin was telling God what had happened when we learned she was a Mongoloid baby. I had wept and told her daddy that perhaps it was time *we* did something about a foundation for babies handicapped as she was. And, of course, it hit me like a revealing flash. Again, God had shown me an answer. And I knew that no matter what else we had on the agenda, Roy and I would spearhead that first NARC campaign."

When the Rogers got back to Hollywood, Dale quaked in her boots—as she puts it—when she had to tell Art Rush, Al Rackin, and Maxine Garrison the decision. "I knew we couldn't do it without their help and experience," Dale says, "and, bless their hearts, they stay overloaded all the time." But when Dale proposed the idea, none batted an eye. They agreed the cause was not only worthy but urgent. And they began pitching in, formulating plans that very day.

"When I called the man in Philadelphia soon afterward to discuss the matter," Al Rackin says, "he didn't understand right off."

"The plans are excellent," the man said, hesitatingly, "but I think you've misunderstood, Mr. Rackin. We are in no position to pay for such undertakings. In fact, we are in no position to pay even for the services of a public-relations expert like you."

"I had a hard time making him realize that none of us were to be paid," Al goes on, "that we felt personally privileged to help out, and that our services were being provided by Roy Rogers and Dale Evans."

"We have so many requests for visits backstage to the Rogerses' dressing room," Helen Young says, "that the past year we've had to hold the list down to ill or handicapped children. When we explain that there are only twenty-four hours in a day, and that Roy and Dale are merely human beings, most people understand. But occasionally we hit trouble. Recently in New York, one woman called and asked to bring her son to talk with the Rogerses. I explained the situation and she retorted, 'But my boy *is* ill. He woke up this morning with a sore throat.' I wanted to say, 'Madam, if you saw some of the sights I see, you'd fall on your knees and thank the dear Lord that all your son has is a sore throat.' I didn't, of course. I patiently explained our predicament until finally the woman understood. These incidents make us a bit angry sometimes. But they are definitely in the

236

minority. Most people, when they realize the work Roy and Dale are doing, cooperate beautifully."

The Roy Rogerses have done about three thousand benefit performances. And sometimes the formality of these shows throws Roy into a role he finds uncomfortable. In 1953, when the Rogerses appeared at the Chicago "Harvest Moon Festival" along with Bob Hope, Jimmy Durante, Marge and Gower Champion, and other such topflight performers, they were required to wear evening dress. Roy had a handsome Western tuxedo tailored for the occasion, but he had much trouble getting into it and finally arrived at the Chicago Stadium minus one shirt stud.

In the center of the stadium arena, Roy Rogers looked highly uncomfortable alone—without his guitar, his horse Trigger, or even the support of a musical group. And some of his simple jokes fell almost flat on the ears of the sophisticated audience. As Roy was leaving the arena, a mink-bedecked matron was overheard saying to her husband, "Well, I certainly can't imagine what on earth that cowboy is *here* for." At that moment a pig-tailed moppet emerged from the crowd and toddled unsteadily on braces and crutches toward Roy Rogers. The incident surprised Roy and he stared at the child a moment. Then the uneasiness left his face and he smiled broadly as he bent down to talk with the young fan. "Oh, Roy," the child said, "I've waited so long to meet you." It was then that the woman's husband answered, "Well, I don't know what on earth that cowboy's *here* for but the look on that kid's face can tell you what he's here on *earth* for."

To date, Roy Rogers and Dale Evans have made well over two thousand hospital visits. Wearing full regalia, distributing gifts, they talk and sing with children in at least one hospital in every city they visit. When possible, they take along Trigger, who has done everything from attending Sunday school to joining the Junior Red Cross.

Always paying their own expenses for appearances at charity drives, fraternal orders, and religious groups, the Rogerses annually give away—besides their countless donations and personal gifts—

237

thousands of dollars worth of their branded merchandise, which they must buy from manufacturers, to sick and underprivileged children. A typical gift—163 pairs of personally fitted boots for all the youngsters at Boy's Ranch—cost $7,800.

The Rogerses pay expenses for many stretcher cases brought to their dressing room while on tour, and Roy visits seriously ill children in their homes. He cuts special records to be played for unusual cases during necessary therapy. And he poses for photographs such as the ones made for the little boy who flatly refused to exercise an injured left arm. "Roy Rogers draws with his right," the child argued. "I don't need a left one." After being contacted by the boy's parents, Roy posed for several shots showing he draws with both hands. "A real cowboy needs two good arms," Roy wrote the child. "Now get to work on those exercises and when *you* can draw with both hands, send me a picture and perhaps we'll arrange a little visit together."

"Of all the things we've done together in the past fifteen years," Art Rush says, "the most difficult are our visits to hopelessly ill children. But even then, Roy can often help." Roy once visited a little fellow in Burbank who had cancer. And when the cowboy walked in, with his finest outfit and all the trappings on, the parents were so awed and grateful they became hysterical. Roy went alone to the child's bedroom and the boy was much too weak to smile. He couldn't lift Roy's guns but Roy placed them beside the child, and he patted them as Roy talked. He told the boy that if he'd try hard to eat and in other ways follow the doctor's orders and could become strong enough, he could come to Hollywood and appear in a movie with him. Incredibly, the child improved, did appear in a picture with Roy, and lived for two more years. Another little boy was brought to the Rogerses' dressing room at Detroit. Roy and Dale talked with him and promised that if he were well enough the next year when their rodeo appeared in Detroit, he could ride Trigger with Roy in the parade. The next year the child was there, strong and smiling, and the Rogerses happily fulfilled their promise. One of the saddest cases of all the hundreds they've helped lives in Ohio. She's a little girl whose arms and legs were lost in an explosion. Her parents brought her in a laundry basket to see the Rogerses.

There is one child whose life even doctors credit Roy with saving. The lad is Rusty Rogers (no relation) of Seattle. A few years ago Rusty was in the hospital for the fifth time. The doctors never agreed on a diagnosis. Leukemia was suspected but finally ruled out. At any rate, Rusty was wasting away and seemed to have no will to live. He refused the pleas of his parents to follow the doctors' orders and just lay day after day staring into space. Desperate, the family telephoned Roy Rogers, who had been their well son's hero. After talking with them, Roy called Rusty's doctors. Then he called Rusty. He called him several times. And the last time he told Rusty if he would eat, take his medicines, and get well, he could come to Hollywood as the Rogerses' guest and ride Trigger. Rusty got well. And Rusty came. In 1953, when Ralph Edwards of *This Is Your Life* told Roy Rogers before millions of TV viewers that they had more requests for the portrayal of the cowboy's life than for that of any person in the world, little Rusty was invited to appear on the program.

Roy Rogers has made nearly six thousand long-distance calls to ill children he could not visit. And at youth gatherings he leads the boys and girls in a special prayer for disabled children everywhere. "I have learned you must help the weak to keep yourself strong," he told the 50,000 Boy Scouts at their 1953 jamboree in California. "I want you to help them so you will grow strong too."

The Rogerses went to the jamboree in a bus that very hot summer day. Clad in heavy gabardine and leather trappings, they and the troupe they took along performed in the broiling sun for two hours for the Scouts who were sitting on hills looking down on a makeshift stage erected in a canyon. Although Dale had suffered from motion sickness on the trip, and even Roy urged her not to bother with heavy stage make-up, she emerged from the bus prepared for the Scouts to the best of her ability. And when all the boys could not gather at one spot, the Rogerses put on a second show.

The "King of the Cowboys" and his "Queen of the West" were

wildly besieged for autographs, to pose for pictures. As they were leaving, and the officials were trying to help Dale through the adoring pushing crowd to the bus, she suddenly stood stock-still and the expression on her face froze even the group madly milling around her. At the door of the bus were waiting a father and mother holding a small Mongoloid girl. Dale walked over and without a word took the baby from their arms. Even the Scouts sensed the sanctity of the moment. Nobody made a sound. Somehow it was understood that all the couple had come for—nobody knows how they got in the grounds or found the Rogers bus—was just to see Robin's mother, to know that she was real. Dale finally managed to ask their name and address, and told them she would send them a copy of *Angel Unaware*. She gave them the address of the NARC, explaining they should join one of its parent groups. A scout snapped Dale holding the baby. Shyly, he told the parents he'd like to send them the picture. As he took their address, Dale walked on toward the bus. Soon she was posing again, smiling a last smile for the Scouts' cameras. But she was sick again on the long ride home.

Today Roy and Dale's strong faith plays a part in the actual scripts of their radio and TV shows. And on all tours they include a religious portion in their programs. "A child brought up in church is seldom brought up in court," Roy said in 1954 at Madison Square Garden.

Among those who feel that the faith of Roy and Dale Rogers has played a big part in changing her life is Marjorie Rambeau, a veteran of over fifty years on the stage and screen. "I had been ill for years from the results of an auto accident when I met them one evening at a birthday part for Jack Oakie," Miss Rambeau says. "I fainted at the dinner table and Roy carried me to a bedroom while Dale called a doctor. Later they had a long talk with me and invited me to join the Hollywood Christian Group. That was the beginning of a spiritual happiness I'd never known before. And now I can look back and know that if it took eight years of agony to help me find God, it was worth it. And I'll be eternally grateful to the Rogerses for the part they played in helping me find myself through the Lord."

"It was odd about that evening," Dale adds. "Roy and I seldom are invited to such affairs, and we were very surprised when the Oakies included us. We hesitated about accepting, but Roy said if they were kind enough to want us, we should go—as badly as we both hate parties. Now we can't help but feel that there was divine purpose in our getting an invitation from those people we hardly knew. We know we were sent to help Miss Rambeau, that it was just another one of those incidents that were simply meant to be."

In the summer of 1953, Roy and Dale Rogers took what they term Robin's message to Hawaii. "The shows were sellouts," Art Rush says, "and the response to the religious portion of the programs was heart-warming." In the spring of 1954, the Rogers toured the British Isles. "Actually this trip came about," the family minister says, "because Roy and Dale wanted to appear there with Billy Graham. I had introduced them to Billy and they had been convinced of his sincerity, and being convinced, they wanted to do everything they could to help him. And although the Rogers met with some opposition, they insisted on going."

As is a matter of record, Billy Graham did not at first receive the heartiest of welcomes in London. And even Roy and Dale Rogers, as some of their advisers feared, were included in the criticisms. But sure of their purpose, they went ahead. Then, as also is a matter of record, Graham ended his series of religious meetings triumphant. "And nowhere," says Larry Kent, "have our kids met with more enthusiasm and love from fans. The mobs that were waiting for them everywhere at times were almost frightening."

A few of the more staid drama critics in England, Ireland, and Scotland were dubious about the Rogerses' musical talents and raised their eyebrows at the religious portion of their programs. But even they, it must be noted, never failed to conclude, "No matter what one may question about Roy Rogers and Dale Evans, he cannot question their sincerity."

In the summer of 1954, the Rogerses extended their scope by appearing in Toronto. They broke all attendance records at the

Canadian National Exhibition there. "And then we went straight to Madison Square Garden," Dale tells. "And it was just as if history were repeating itself. I was busy finishing up details for the publication of another book, *My Spiritual Diary*. I've assigned the royalties from this book to a newly opened clinic for retarded children at Los Angeles Children's Hospital, the first such pilot clinic in the country. And Roy and I both were on pins and needles waiting for some official word about Marion, a thirteen-year-old girl we found in an orphanage in Scotland. We thought our family was complete, but when we saw Marion we knew we just had to have her. A British adoption act forbids outright adoption, but we have her here now as an exchange student. And it's been determined that later she will be allowed to make up her own mind about returning to Scotland."

When the Rogerses landed in New York they were met, as usual, by the press. "What would you say is the most important thing you learned about faith in Canada?" one reporter asked Roy.

There is a greatness in simplicity that can never be counterfeited. Roy Rogers moistened his lips, wiped them with his left hand, moistened them again. "Well, I reckon the most important thing I learned about faith in Canada," he drawled shyly, "was the most important thing I learned about faith in Hawaii, the British Isles, and all over the United States—*it works*."

ABOUT THE AUTHOR

Elise Miller Davis was born in Corsicana, Texas, attended the University of Texas, and later took special courses in writing at the University of Oklahoma. She has shown her strong interest in and talent for writing since she was first able to hold a pencil. "But," her father humorously recalls, "she displayed great courage—for she did not publish until she was eight years old!"

Mrs. Davis's work has always displayed her interest in characters with unshakable beliefs. "I abandoned fiction for nonfiction," she says, "because I wanted to tell my readers, 'This *did* happen,' not 'This *could* happen.' And when I was sent to California by *The Reader's Digest* to undertake a story about the Roy Rogers family, I soon realized that theirs was one of the great stories of our time. I felt, however, that it could never be properly told in a short article, that it had to be a book. Because the enormity hit me squarely—whatever happened in the hearts of this home could echo in homes all over the world."

Besides articles for *The Reader's Digest*, Elise Miller Davis has contributed many to other magazines, including *Nation's Business*. She now lives with her husband, Jay A. Davis, and their daughter, Rayna, on Galveston Island—a spot of Texas in the Gulf of Mexico.